To my children

Contents

Foreword

This book is the story of a journey, one that has its origins in research for a doctoral thesis. What was unusual, perhaps unique about the thesis was that the researcher was also the instigator, as well as the maker and the storyteller. They were all the same person. Now published in book form it is a creative act in its own right and in its own writing. I am delighted that as a result it is going to be available to a much wider readership.

The journey it documents is a fraught one in some ways, but it is one that many take. Namely, to assume responsibility for a group of people who want you to direct, coach, cajole and transform them into a creative unit that performs a piece of live theatre.

This book is a record of one such process undertaken with a group of theatre students in England. Theatre making always takes place in a complex set of public or social contexts. But the challenge of the book goes beyond the particular circumstances of its subject, rigorously though that is accounted. What the book demonstrates is that theatre making is not just one process but many; all linked, interwoven, impossible to disentangle. In doing this the book sheds light on a key but neglected area: the private and inner worlds of doubt, reflection, truth seeking and truth denying, not least those of the writer himself. And without these secret and personal worlds of thoughts and feelings no work of theatre would ever be made, or ever be enjoyed by an audience.

Barry Edwards
London
October 2002

Preface

Tracing the Footprints began as an investigation of some of the processes involved in the creation of a performance project. Notwithstanding the fact that the project in question was being 'constructed' by myself, it was my intention that the investigation be largely dispassionate ... that the making would lead to reflection, but that the activity of reflecting would not impact on the ways the work was made. This was the discipline I sought to impose. In practice, the making process proved resistant to the divisiveness of this discipline. It became impossible to achieve. Furthermore, as the project progressed, it was revealed as antithetical to the nature of making work.[1]

   Where writing about performance is often at some remove from the performance it critiques, this investigation is engaged with its subject at an immediate level, and this has emerged as the most telling aspect of this book. Performance is an event as well as an object ... in order to investigate 'process' without resorting to calcification, the writing needs to foreground its own eventness. *Tracing the Footprints* questions the extent to which the documentation of practice can be effective when the documentation and the documented are practised at one and the same time

   The body of this book was written at the same time as the practical project it investigates (*At Last Sight*) was being made. *At Last Sight* was a performance project, which I directed with a group of final year undergraduates over the course of an academic year.

   The immediacy of doing/writing brought with it a specific challenge ... the challenge was not only to question the extent to which one can read one's own work, but to investigate the possibilities of making that reading in a perpetual present. The claim to originality of this book rests on the rigour and detail of the documentation of a performance construction. No similar studies exist. The book, therefore, is an investigation of a particular type of documentation. Crucially, it is not about the theory of documentation. It is about a method of documentation, which is part of the practice of making performance. What follows stands as an exploration of *this* way of investigating process. It is not writing *about* experimental practice, it is writing *as* experimental practice. In this way, what will emerge is an attempt at investigative writing as both research activity and as research. Whilst the idea of practice as research has become relatively well established, the writing up of this is not conceptually agreed at present.[2] The example to follow makes a contribution to this field.

Other than under exceptional circumstances, the present is a given of live performance. Whatever we see is happening in the here and now, regardless of any fictional 'period' within which the work may be set.[3] This concentration on the present can be the benchmark by which the quality of any given performer is generally determined.[4] For the purposes of analysis, however, the present is often delayed. Analysis is generally thought of as comprising reflection, re-evaluation and consideration. In this way an idea can be tested and contextualised within a framework of ongoing research. This book sets out to question this implicit methodology. It asks: 'What happens if I do not work in this way?' 'What happens if the investigation I make is not tempered by time?' As such, this book is the exploration of a different method of selection.

The work repositions the temporal relationship between reflection, revision and practice. What is central to this is that the book would comprise as concurrent a documentation of the practice as was possible. The writing took place at the same time as the practical work was being made. The book is not being presented as the creation of a prototype for future practitioners ... as though a practitioner in the years to come would seek to recreate *At Last Sight* (or something like it) from this record. That is not the intention. The book is a prototype for the documentation of one's own practice: as an example of a way of reading practice from within, rather than as an exemplar of a particular way of making work. It is not about abstracting documentation to something universal, although my own personal practice shares a number of approaches, which might be regarded, as 'common'.

It is important that *Tracing the Footprints* is recognised as an exploration of *a* process of making performance work, not *the* process.

The making of performance is a process plagued with doubt. The work that this book is concerned with was made at the beginning of a century and a millennium, at a time of change, both natural and forced. The writing is at times something of an argument against itself, inasmuch as it is seeking to articulate that which remains steadfastly inarticulate in any form other than the performative. This creates a contradiction within the subject that this book will wrestle with throughout.

As a strategy for dealing with this, I have attempted to acknowledge the implication of my own writing in the processes that I recount,[5] and also to draw the attention of the reader to the overt incompatibility of the ephemeral and the fixed. That the documentation of the processes of performance making is as vexed an area as it currently is gives testament to the difficulty of recording time-based work in a space-based medium. It is for this reason that the writing was made subject to many of the durational demands and limitations as was the making. What emerges is a written work that recognises the linear limitations of writing as something at odds with the experience of performance, at the same time as it seeks to utilise this very linearity through a merging of making and writing. The book is concerned with a way of documenting and with that which is being documented. It is questioning the possibilities, through its chapters, of reflecting on reflection.

During the period in which this book was written my preoccupations were with the challenges of making work, alongside an attendant and in-depth articulation.[6] That these preoccupations speak at once of self and of self-awareness creates an alliance with the self-reflectivity of postmodernism.[7] I can identify certain elements of postmodern practice that have been integral to my own making processes. These are articulated as and when they occur. Without pre-empting the book's narrative I can describe them as

1: a foregrounding of intertextuality
2: an interest in shifting performative identities
3: experimentation with the narcissism of autobiography
4: the revelation rather than concealment of process
5: an absence of closure
6: the exposure of artifice
7: an investigation of spectator/performer relationships.

Tracing the Footprints is primarily concerned with a new model for writing about performance making, rather than ways of making new performance. The inclusion here of these 'making'

elements should not dissuade the reader from a concentration on the investigation of a means of *documentation*.

At all times the research is investigating what happens when the reflective act of writing occurs at as close a time as possible to the performance making.[8] Where this results in sudden shifts in emphases and/or approach the reader is asked to consider these as records of a process that was always as creative as it was analytical. The footprints that lead to performance seldom move in straight lines, and the traces they leave are indistinct.

In most cases it is not practical to look at every object or question, and this case has been no different. The investigator has to work with samples and the usefulness of the findings will depend largely on the extent to which that sample is held to be representative. The process of making performance is not formulaic and events that may be of importance with the value of hindsight may not have been investigated fully at source. Where these omissions occur (and readers will draw their own conclusions) they stand as proof of the representative nature of the study. What was written about was regarded as significant *at the time*, and time was always the most pressing agent of determination. Fieldwork involves observing and asking questions. With this project, those questions have been asked of the self. The writing then stands as an aspect of self-presentation. After Goffman, we can say that this consists of the self's effort to convey a particular image of itself, or information about itself, to other people.[9] If the self-presentation developed in this book seems to be based as much on the self-presenter's own standards as on those of the readers then it is in keeping with Schlenker's belief that self-presentation is the result of a trade-off between favourability and plausibility.[10]

Thinking about the self is not universally regarded as a plausible activity. A blow to self-knowledge came from Nisbett and Wilson (1977), who contended that people are not able to know and report on much that happens inside their own minds. People, they argue, may know their attitudes and opinions, but they are incapable of knowing how they arrived at these. Furthermore, if they think about their attitudes for too long, especially in endeavouring to assess the reasons for these to have occurred, they can end up in nowhere but confusion.[11] The following study seeks to challenge this idea.

A research report tells the story of how a researcher investigated a particular area. Thus, a research report has a linear, narrative structure with a beginning, middle and an end. When joined together in this way information becomes easier to comprehend and recall ... in this way a research report tells a story.[12] Describing this report as a story is not just a convenient metaphor. *Tracing the Footprints* is a story. It is a story that consists of two components: a telling of what happened, and an explanation as to why it happened in the ways that it did.[13] It begins with the construction of a written text for performance, and it explains the reasoning behind key decisions and the impact they had on that construction. Subsequent chapters document the process of making, leading to a 'final' performance. Because, for the bulk of the time, the investigation was carried out between *post* and *pre* rehearsal the thoughts are a blend of reflection and projection. The book asks what happens when one tries to write about performance making in this type of 'present'. A present that makes the writing a part of the performance.

If *At Last Sight* was an act of mimesis, inasmuch as it consisted of actions seen in performance, then this book is an act of diegesis, telling the reader things they did not – indeed, *could not* - see for themselves. In one way *At Last Sight* was not a culturally significant production.[14] The work was never reviewed. No dramatic text has been published. This book is not an attempt to give permanence to an otherwise ephemeral (and almost invisible) event. This is a consequence of the study, not an objective.

Just as 'a successful piece of research doesn't conclusively settle an issue',[15] so this work does not attempt to provide answers for all researcher/practitioners for all time. The findings serve an archival function, documenting a particular type of research. The text also hopes to serve as a stimulus, exciting other researchers to join the investigation of a particular issue, to apply new methods to the study of performance making.

The reader will note that the personal pronoun 'I' is used throughout the book, and that, rather than emphasising the subject above the investigator, I am locating the investigator's developing understanding of the subject as a central aspect. This is not entered into through any ignorance of the (usual) fact that 'the writer's style should convey the impression of impartiality and detachment rather than personal involvement',[16] so much as it is through a recognition that *within this book* the writer's personal involvement is at the core of the study. This is a research decision. It is a means of asking whether the 'I' provides a useful perspective on the making process. The use of 'I' carries with it a certain authority. As though the writer's own words and beliefs create a kind of truth. And the idea of 'truth', with its obverse 'lies', permeates much of the work. Joanna Frueh (1996) has written in *Erotic Faculties* of 'followers who have turned the fascinating and useful writings of father figures of speech into cant and canon.'[17] Frueh goes further to say that 'Cant demeans the reality of personal experience.'[18] My own approach reveals a developing drift towards a faith in this 'reality', even at those times when the vocabulary of choice seems set most firmly against it. Whilst I am aware of the dangers of being seen to disregard that which I also embrace, I am obliged to record *that which happened* ... even when its occurrence ran counter to my expectations. Truth is a contingent category, with no reliability and no absolutes, and yet the truth of my experience appears to deny relativism on my own part. This means that whilst any claim to offer a definite interpretation of events that were *witnessed* is doomed to failure, an event that was experienced *internally* can be held to be true, if only to s/he who experiences. This work addresses whether it is appropriate to ask questions about 'truth' in an investigation of performance.

Where the performance of *At Last Sight* was a masquerade of sorts, this writing is an attempt to deal with the truth *as I saw it*.

Sometimes this is prosaic: I will not, for example, be saying that five people were at a rehearsal when four were present.[19]

At other times, during the reading of events, my engagement will be more complex. For the most part, we can substitute the word 'truth' for 'significance', inasmuch as imbuing an occurrence with significance is less problematic than regarding that same occurrence as 'true' and incontestable.

Truth and reality are subject to certain plasticity, and postmodern practice strives to reveal something of this ambiguity in presentation. Truths, like theories, do not always stand the test of time. It is within this spirit of temporary reliability that the reader is asked to engage with this report.

In this way these words are the record of 'a' truth and not 'the' truth. As *At Last Sight* was open to a series of interpretations so too is this book. It is a characteristic of language that webs of meaning are generated and that any and all texts are necessarily self-contradictory. This work is no different. It is, in Wittgenstein's terms,[20] a language game, inasmuch as it is a work, which, in seeking to capture the language of the performance-making process, is handicapped 'because the attempt to do so itself constitutes a (further) language game.'[21] The writing thus deals in the persuasive, the provisional and the contingent, and it does so as a means of stating a position. The position remains as *mine* and it is tempered throughout by its own deliberate self-referentiality.

To paraphrase Keats' distrust of literature with a palpable design on us, I can say that I am not seeking to convert or influence the views of the reader. It is an investigation, presented as the documentation of my experience as a maker of performance. It explores the extent to which the divide between the observer and the observed dissolves. In this, it is a troublesome work, for when an artwork is also an object of theoretical discourse the worlds of rational objectivity collapse in on those of the subjective and the intuitional.

What follows then is at once a reflection on process and process itself. It became evident during the writing that distinctions between making the work and writing about it were dissolving to the point where one bled into the other without deliberation. In this way, the book has emerged as being as much a part of *At Last Sight* as were any of its performances. *At Last Sight* does not exist *through* this writing so much as it exists *in* the writing. Similarly, the writing/making does not *record* an experience ... it was an experience in itself. As writer/maker I have not been involved in the book so much as being *inside* it ... and it is the analysis of this 'insidedness' that gives the work both its immediacy and its wider relevance.

Giannachi and Luckhurst (1999) begin *On Directing* with a recognition that a reason for 'the scarcity of material on directors and directing practices in Britain must be the absence here of both oral and written traditions in the articulation of process.'[22] Their introduction continues with the statement that 'It is extremely difficult for anyone to theorize the creative processes pertaining to a particular performance.'[23] The following chapters can be read as a response to its authors' opening remarks.

What are the implications of calling a book a performative act: a record of process and also process *per se* ... the documentation of performance making and also performance making as documentation? Is it the case that the importance of this book lies not in its relationship to the referent that was 'the process observed' as in the duality of its existence? What happens when the book is not akin to Plato's shadows on the cave wall, anymore than *At Last Sight* might be regarded as the object/event that threw them there? When report and performance, the investigation and the investigated, are offered as parts of the same process?

Tracing the Footprints forms an address to these questions.

Notes

[1] My findings here are not dissimilar to Judith Butler's experiences of research towards the publication of *Bodies that Matter* (Butler, J. Routledge, 1993).

Butler attempted to 'consider the materiality of the body only to find that the thought of materiality invariably moved (her) into other domains'. p. ix

[2] For distinctions between performance practice-as-research and practice-based research in performance see Kershaw, B 'Performance, Memory, Heritage, History, Spectacle – *The Iron Ship*' in *Studies in Theatre and Performance* Vol. 21, No 3 2001

[3] This is also the case with cinema. However, the distinction with live performance is that the 'here and now' is shared by spectators and performers.

[4] Elizabeth LeCompte regards presence as the area of her work with the Wooster Group that is of prime importance. In an interview with Nick Kaye, she states that 'the constant battle for me as a director is find ways that an actor can be always present, always alive, always thinking this is the first and last moment that she's there'. In *The Twentieth Century Performance Reader*. Huxley, M & Witts, N (eds). Routledge, London & New York, 1996. p.232

[5] I borrow here from the terminology Nick Kaye uses to describe Salman Rushdie's writing in *Shame*. Kaye, N. *Postmodernism and Performance*. Macmillan, London, 1994. p.10

[6] This book was 'written' over a three-year period, which breaks down into three relatively even sections. The period 1997-98 involves a study of the processes of creating a written text for performance; 1998-99 deals with how that text is worked through in rehearsal through to performance; 1999-2000 was a period of reflecting on the process.

[7] It is important at this point to articulate my understanding of the term 'postmodern', as it relates to *At Last Sight* and also to the practice of this book. In part, I am using the term postmodernism because of its very ubiquity: as there is no single 'postmodernism', so there exists no one emanating theory. What we are able to say is that a feature of postmodernism is a desire to reveal the ideological bias contained in the production of knowledge, and that this act of exposure seeks to focus attention on the perspectives from which work is created. This will be a feature of both the creation of *At Last Sight* and this book. In this way any and all notions of neutrality will be called into question. *Tracing the Footprints* forms an invitation to the reader to consider those perspectives embodied in the creation of performance that would under normal circumstances remain hidden, perhaps even from the creating self. In attempting this articulation of the ways in which *this* performance will be created from and through 'self', it is appropriate to acknowledge the stance which is motivating my own research ... to expose my own authorial bias. The approach, which allows for such a declaration of bias owes its allegiance to no single disciplinary stance. It is, therefore, more able to accommodate the complexity of such a self-reflective and postmodern concept as the performance maker reading 'his' own work.

[8] 'Same time' here refers to 'Same time scale', inasmuch as the writing about rehearsals occurred in the midst of that rehearsal period. As a project that took place over the course of an academic year,

there were periods when the writing happened several days after the rehearsal it describes, during vacation periods, for example, when the student-group was unavailable.
[9] Goffman, E *the Presentation of Self in Everyday Life*. Anchor Books, New York, 1959
[10] Schlenker, B.R. *Impression Management: The self-concept, social identity, and interpersonal relations*. Brooks/Cole, Monterey, CA, 1980. P. 41
[11] Nisbett, R., & Wilson, T.D. "Telling More Than We Can Know: Verbal Reports on Mental Processes" *Psychological Review, 84*, 1977. pp. 231-259
[12] Parsons, C. J. *Theses and Project Work*, Heinneman, London, 1978. pp.21-27
[13] In regarding this book as a story we would do well to consider Norbert Grob's opinion that "In real life, stories happen, just like that. Only those who experience it also know about it. But it only becomes graspable when it has reached its end. Only then can it be told as a story. The neding defines the intimate binding of the events." Grob, N *Wim Wenders*. Edition Filme, Berlin, 1991 p.162
[14] Cultural significance is difficult to determine, and I use it here in the sense of the work's low cultural visibility. *At Last Sight* was never performed at a non-university venue ... the festivals it played at were university festivals, making the spaces 'university venues' at the times they were performed in. Few people beyond the performance venues visited would have heard about the work. However, Chris Roberts, a performer in *At Last Sight*, is now pursuing research to PhD, and I have no doubts that his interest in resistant performance (his topic) was fuelled in part by his participation in *At Last Sight*. Liz Hague is now a full-time performer with an established company and Sarah Robertson is a professional drama animateur. The overall cultural significance of *At Last Sight* is impossible to predict with accuracy.
[15] Cohen, J. "A Review of Research and Theory" *Psychological Bulletin, 88*. pp.82-108
[16] Parsons, C. J. 1978. p.56
[17] Frueh, J *Erotic Faculties*. University of California Press, Los Angeles and London, 1996. p.44
[18] *ibid* p.45
[19] I refer here to 'truth' in the terms suggested by Lee Nichol in *On Creativity* (Bohm, D. Routledge, London & New York, 1998). Nichol suggests that "A critical question arises: How can we know if our ... views are true or false? Given that it is folly to presume that the content of any worldview ... is "the truth" ... truth in content relies on observable correspondence: (such as) "It is true that the sun has arisen every day for the past week." (p. xix).
I am asserting certain truths in content, and will not be inventing data.
[20] Lechte, J *Fifty Key Contemporary Thinkers*. Routledge, 1994. p. 247
[21] *ibid*
[22] Giannachi, G and Luckhurst, M *On Directing: Interviews with Directors*. Faber & Faber Ltd, London, 1999. p.xv
[23] *ibid* pp. xv-xvi

Acknowledgments

This book could not have been written without the full participation of the following. Their commitment turned the process of research into a pleasure:

Liz Hague
Andrew Proudfoot
Chris Roberts
Glenn Robertson
Sarah Robertson
Laurent Ruggeri
Anke Sauthof
Sarah Skelton

Their contribution runs through every page.

Thanks to Oliver Fisk, Amy Jackman, Susan Broadhurst, Mike Pearson and, particularly, Barry Edwards. Any qualities in this book stem from Barry's long-term influence and support ... any failings that remain are my own.

Thanks also to those colleagues who – in too many ways to list - helped shape the approach to reflective analysis undertaken here: Val Kosh, John Stephens and Allan Owens.

And to Helen, who was always there.

Introduction:
Preparing the Ground

As an introduction to *Tracing the Footprints* I will declare three areas of address. The first of these is a synopsis of the area to be investigated, the *what* of the study. The second comprises the *how*, the ways in which the subject will be treated, the methods of analysis to be undertaken. The third element is the *why*. Why *this* researcher at *this* time and in *this* way is seeking to explore *this* unknown. The 'unknown' in this case is the creation of a new work of performance. The introduction functions as a pre-text to this, and also as a 'text' in itself, as an integral element of the work. As such, the space given over to these opening remarks will be as great as that which is afforded to later chapters. It is hoped that this is read, as it is intended, as a positive and necessary means of preparing the ground for the argument(s) that will develop over subsequent pages.

The introduction is not designed to create an inflexible pattern for either the writing or the reading of the work, so much as to alert the reader to the complexities of the problem to be addressed, as well as to those of the writer in tackling the task. To provoke an opening up of possibilities rather than to prescribe the course the book will follow. Accordingly, *Tracing the Footprints* is not intended as the articulation of categorisation, of the labeling of work as either 'realist' or 'real', 'modern' or 'postmodern' ... although these terms, the stuff of seemingly endless critical debate, will feature large and often as the book unfolds. The words to come will not demonstrate a concern, in the final analysis, with arriving at any resolution as to what performance work *is*, so much as *how* work (a specific performance-project made alongside this writing) is constructed. The area of investigation is thus broadly defined as a tracing of the creative process.

Contemporary thought, both philosophical and scientific, has come to regard human behaviour as being implicitly subject to the impact of a number of factors: behaviour is determined and, theoretically, a causal rationale, an explanation, can be posited for any and all activity entered into by human beings.[1] It follows then that artistic creation can be subject to a similar process of thorough investigation, locating the 'creator' within an appropriate structure defined by an alliance (always present) of the personal, the public and the private. This is not to deny entirely the romantic-sounding notion of intuition so much as to recognise that creative activity is no less a product of a series of determinants than of that which one might describe as 'everyday behaviour'.[2]

An argument could be made that certain actions, such as reflexes, are not the result of choice and, thus, are not subject to the same level of determination. However, even in those instances where artists deliberately locate themselves in positions of indeterminacy their own reliance on chance is indicative of choice. John Cage's early work on the *I Ching* is an example,[3] as is Stelarc's internet 'performance', wherein his electronically agitated body was choreographed, quite literally, by any interested parties who made the decision to key in the relevant co-ordinates on their own computers.[4] Marina Abramovic's performance project where she was kept 'safe' from snakes by a wall of rapidly melting ice is another noted example.[5] Performances where fatigue is part of the fabric of the presentation, seen in the 1980's work of British companies Station House Opera and Impact Theatre Co-operative, are no less dependent on the training and the intention of the artists involved as any form of practice.[6] Reflexive responses are honed, determined in a multiplicity of ways that separate the performer, or the performative state, from the differently determined spectator. Guy Claxton (1998), Professor of Psychology at the University of Bristol, speaks of reflexivity as something akin to intuition

> We say we responded 'intuitively' when a response occurred faster than thought ... there is some evidence that such lightning reactions draw on ... subliminal sources of information.[7]

Artists are 'free' to make work, therefore, not as a result of being divorced from the structures that determine human behaviour, but precisely because they choose to enter into a world where they are able to make performative that choice given to each of us through biography and society.[8] As such, performance practice emerges as the outcome (a much less problematic term than 'product') of an always specific and individual response to a great body of determinants. The artist operates through choice, and the choices available are no more or less determined than the impetus and ability to work through the choices made.

Caveats abound. It does not negate the claims made only four paragraphs ago to state that the problem is always the *what is* as much as the *how made*. For there is a genuine need to define the potential area of work, not least in a piece of research, a research-outcome, which might realistically expect to be of certain interest to the non (theatre) specialist. To those whose interest is 'creation' rather than that which remains from the process itself. Indeed, whether a clear end to the creative 'process' emerges is something which the process of study, a process borne out through these traces of ink, will wrestle with throughout. I am attempting to engage with the *what* of performance as a necessary set of rules or conventions for the *what* of the book.

The following paragraphs are offered here as a cartography of views, in order that a shared understanding exists between the 'I' of the writer and the eye of the reader. As such, and despite the intrinsic contention of late twentieth century positions on the constituent elements of performance,[9] these views are submitted as preparation of the ground rather than as a persuasive tract; as an indication of this author's intent rather than a statement of authoritative 'fact'. Providing, it is hoped, both a sense of history - unashamedly, a subjectively manufactured history of this writer's own performative determinants - and a point of departure.

This is not an apology. The personally experienced might be regarded as the micro to the macro of more generic phenomena. This book is not concerned with discovering rules for all performance, so much as providing a case study of one performance, and of charting key decisions in its development.

It needs to be said at this early stage that the terms Theatre' and 'Performance', no less than 'Theatre' and 'Installation' are at times regarded as factions that are competing each one against the other. The mainstream in denial of the marginal, the time-reliance of a directed series of events against the seeming elasticity of images located in space.[10] The predictability of the 'Old Guard' set against the progressive spontaneity and irreverence of the 'New'. In setting out the argument thus, my own prejudices are exposed by a choice of words that immediately prioritise newness over age ... whether this prejudice is sustained, compromised or eroded by the following research is one which, at the time of writing, remains distant and unknown. What is known is that this 'introduction' is possessed of a comparable complexity to that which might be seen to exist in the researched area itself. The introduction also needs to establish what it is that constitutes the 'I' of the researcher.

Is the 'I' specific: specifically male, married (twice), with children (two), occidental, of my age? Or does the 'I' strive for the 'one' of assumed objectivity? If the 'I' is to be recognised and prioritised, does this validity deny that which might be valuable to the 'other' reader: female, single, no children, oriental, older? What is the researcher's agenda? If that which is subject to study has already formed part of the researcher's own experiences, to what extent does the past prejudice the present examination? To this end, we need to know whether this prejudice (for prejudice there surely is) is accidental and inevitable or deliberate and contrived. As the facilitator of a practical project as part of this process, am I regarding myself as a researcher/practitioner or as a practitioner whose work is then made subject to a written evaluation? In making a piece of work which, at least in part, is being *created* for the process of its own analysis, to what extent is the (my) inclination towards the theoretically interesting rather than in the direction of the theatrically efficacious?

With such an overtly stated example of practice-as-research as is offered here, the informed reader will generally expect theoretical positionings to emerge from the practice. Indeed, one could say that this is the aim of the book *per se*, and, to a large extent, that will be the pattern here. However, as a full-time lecturer in Performance, the world of theory could also be seen (and not least by myself) to be driving the practice itself.[11] The past is a pre-text for the present, in much the same way as the present is a pre-text for the yet-to-be.

The fact that this book is concerned with the theoretical explanation of a practical activity might suggest that theory follows practice. The relationship is not this straightforward. The two cannot be isolated in a way that locates one before the other. The performance is practical, this book theoretical; but the project and the book are being made at the same time. This means that theoretical positionings entered into on the page will inevitably impact on the ways that the practical work is made. Theory is not *post* practice and the research entered into for this book will not be following behind as some sort of adjunct to the performance it seeks to explain. The practical work is being constructed in the here and now, and it is being constructed by the same person who is constructing the book. At its most interesting and/or complex moments the writing and the practice might be constructed *in the same way*.

Every researcher, regardless of the field, has to work with the knowledge of personal bias; some of this is genuinely unconscious, whilst the remainder is constructively self-imposed. I am confident that a reading of *Tracing the Footprints* will reveal evidence of both types. The art of scholastic research - or the researcher's scholarly art – is not so much an attempt to factor out the biases, for this would effectively remove the passionately inquisitive 'I' of the research. Rather, the most potentially useful strategy, and one I intend to adopt, is the development of a stance which, whilst solid enough to last the distance, is not so rigid as to resist the push of clearly oppositional fact.

As a piece of work intended to articulate the processes through which any findings are arrived at, as work which is concerned with a continuing process of scholarly investigation, the writer (*this* writer) has a duty to the reader to include all relevant material. To expose the footprints that lead to performance. So, the writing details the investigative process. But what is being investigated? How open and uncluttered is the contract between your eye and mine?

The form of this book becomes inseparable from its content. The words used are embedded in the processes (both practical and theoretical) that are producing them. As much as the book is about the ways of making a particular piece of work it is as concerned with the ways of recording in words that process of making. All writing can be regarded as autobiographical, inasmuch as all writers will bring something of an autobiographical self to their work.[12]

This phenomenon will differ in degree from one writer to another, but authorial presence, shaped by personal history and intent, will remain. To the same extent that the autobiography of *At Last Sight* will be made explicit in subsequent chapters, the book itself will foreground the identity of the writer.[13] In this way the writing is a document of the discoursal self. It is a representation of (my) self through discourse.

What will emerge will be a concentration on the writer as well as on the writing. This will not create a denial of academicism. I still feel that scholarly writing is predominantly about thinking something, seeing what other people think about the thing you are thinking, thinking about their thoughts in relation to your own, and then writing what it is that you think. However, this does not mean that this book will develop according to a sequence that is either 'logical' or 'linear'. To write sequentially according to an approved outline undermines the idea of writing as a thinking process, as something responsive, personal and intuitive. Linearity and sequential logic amount to a belief that the words on the page are (no more than) the traces of thoughts already gone. The fact that I am choosing in this introduction to make use of the pronoun 'I' can be read therefore as a statement of intent. The fact that I am choosing through the writing to record thoughts (almost) as and when they happen is another.

The employment of the personal, evidenced in this work, is not intended to function at the expense of a wider, more generic publication of knowledge. The relationship is one of collusion rather than collision, with the necessary critical discourse being at once contained *within* and exercised *through* the product itself. The art-product, the art-event, made as an integral component of this study is unlikely to be so made as to demonstrate its origins to a wider readership than that which might be assumed from a theatre-specific group. In much the same way, conceptual practice *per se* is unlikely, on its own, to disseminate the specifics of any advancements made. Research which leads in intended ways towards advanced understanding(s) is given credence by its inclusion into new, or newly articulated, ways of working: the process is thus intrinsically developmental and progressive. As art influences art, rather than being hermetically sealed and untouchable, so research influences research. This work is determined by readings, writings, thoughts and actions, which were in their own part determined by their creators' histories and influences.

This remains the case even when these same thoughts and actions are not 'published'. Influence is pervasive, and it does not follow that it is the permanently enshrined that affects us most strongly. Snatches of half-remembered conversations may sow the seeds for a lifetime of work, long after heavyweight texts are gone and forgotten.

The ways of making the specific performance in this research-process are individual and at times perhaps idiosyncratic, but this is not to deny the fact (we know that it is as certain as that) that a number of works previously seen, and at times participated in, have had a major influence in the creation of the very 'ways' that make this art my own. That art influenced this art. To those practitioners responsible I offer my appreciation in both the permanence of print and the ephemerality of performance.

Works of performance seen and drawn upon will not feature in the bibliography included at the close of this book. The influence is more subliminal than that which might occur when a published text offers those moments of clarity and insight familiar to students of all disciplines. Separating the purposive from the incidental is always a vexed issue in terms of one's attitudes and reactions to art; images that take root in the darkness of the theatre space might not bear fruit until long after the initial image is 'forgotten'. In this way, resonance outlasts reference and the citation of sources becomes either all encompassing or selectively exclusive.

In order for academically oriented ideas to be considered as either insightful or significant, certain criteria will usually apply. A framework exists through which peer-assessment is able to operate according to its own established patterns of procedure. In this way, thoughts about performance, for example, are exposed to critical reflection from experts within the field. During this process of review by one's peers findings will be tested and an assessment of their critical value will be established. Central to this review is the notion of building on the past; of locating the new within a context of the currently accepted. Theoretical positionings, which do not satisfy this criterion, will encounter inevitable difficulties in terms of acceptance. The footprints are traced to their starting point, a place where overlaps are recognised as a type of *a priori* qualification, as a probing into the future from the knowledge of the past.

Directors direct: it is a statement of fact. Shakespeare (mentioned once now and henceforth lain to rest) offered us text in the guise of two hours' traffic of the stage. And yet text is no more traffic, in the sense we understand it, than a director of performance is a white-gloved and be-whistled police officer, a keeper of order and shape, a guardian against the rough and the unruly, against the errant and the untoward. Text is not traffic. Text is texture, feeling, tone and colour.

The Greeks had a word for it, *lexis*, or diction; the language of the play. The blueprint for performance. One of the seeming cores of this book is located at those points where language, the text for *At Last Sight*, is created. At the site where imagination and cognitive thought combine in the formulation of material for presentation, for performance. Where the measurable and quantifiable world of 'reality' and the cavernous potential of the conscious and still subconscious imaginings are coalesced into a third 'created' world of manipulated art. Where aesthetic perception is married to an informed (though as yet, and of definition, unformed) state of creative thought.

Some words may be required here on the making of text. Or at least on the making of *this* text. The creation of performative and performable text is an act of metaphor. Emotional connections are sought through the selection and ordering of words in such ways that 'information' (in the broadest possible use of the term and including mood, for example, as much as meaning) has the potential to be transmitted to spectators in ways which are recognisable and resonant beyond the sum of their constituent and purely linguistic parts. For the purposes of this study, and also as a general principle, text is considered to be at its most 'valuable' at those times when it functions, or when it can be *made to function*, as a thing much greater than the representational and descriptive arrangement of 'meaningful' words in a coherent and accessible way. What this allows, or *suggests*, to the director of the given text (and this applies no less when the 'director' is also the 'writer') is a variety of ideas that are not comfortably or effectively communicated through other, less imagistically provocative, means.

A radical, postmodern or in any way deconstructionist approach to the analysis and direction of text (for such, again, exists at or very near to the dual core of this report) is most often associated with practitioners who work against the reductive and insulating methods of naturalism. This is not to say that no attention is paid to psychology ... psychology might be most adequately described, in these introductory paragraphs, as that which drives the 'play': the part-hidden, part-revealed rationale for why things happen. It is important that we recognise this at an early stage and that we do not allow psychology to be appropriated and subsequently 'owned' by naturalism.

Reinterpreting or deconstructing the writer's view (if such a thing could ever be identified) is in and of itself more likely to lead to an opening up of the world of the play to a series of reinterpretations by the audience than to closing it down to one shared (?) world view.

Indeed, subsequent pages of this introduction will explicitly challenge the very notion of a universally coherent world-view. In so doing, a context for the specific project upon which much of the evidence for this book hangs will be provided and made clear.

When directors question rather than prioritise and publicise the playwright's choices, they are not attempting to uncover and articulate the 'truth' that in its own turn would lead to the 'correct' production, making of directing a search for the Holy Grail of authorial significance. The Russian word *zamissel* refers to 'the sense of the whole', the thought or central premise that, in the case of theatre, binds together all elements of a play. Some, perhaps even *most*, directors seek to discover the *zamissel* in the writer's words and in the social history of the play, others seek to find it in their own approaches. For some, like Peter Brook, the director's job is to find the meaning and make it meaningful; for others, like Robert Wilson, 'meaning' is always open, left for the individual members of the audience to discover. One approach works towards and embraces mono-interpretation, one works against it.

Science has taught us that perception is not absolute; it is always relative to the perceiver's notions; with naturalism, the director's perception is fixed and offered to us in that state. Quantum Theory, with its argument that reality is not fixed and logical but disjointed and in a state of perpetual change, takes us one step further away from naturalism and realism than this.[14] Quantum theory suggests that when we move into the realm of *unconscious thought*, we are, in fact, participating in the creation of reality, we make a leap (a 'quantum jump') from the known into the unknown. When directors engage in processes akin to quantum jumping, they are no longer recreating the playwrights' worlds, they are actively creating new worlds. The 'fixing' of reality (the once only?) into realism (the repeatable!) is perhaps theatre's truest absurdity and the furthest away from that very 'truth' it seeks to portray.

If the methodology of science can offer only the most approximate description of reality, alongside a generally held understanding that 'reality', such as we understand the term at all, is created by our own personal, prejudicial and learned observations, then how can realism lay claim to the 'real' within its name? If our senses are not to be trusted to give a total and authoritative view of reality, then how can directors of naturalism maintain such a faith in their own, overtly unchallengable views of the world? If that which we comprehend as the 'real' is only ever in the here and now of the perceiver; if that which has been experienced ceases to be *real* and becomes *memory*, whilst that which is to come (the word, the sentence, the breath after this) is no less ephemeral than *imagination*, then the *unreal* world must always be greater in substance than the real.[15] The fact of theatre's intrinsic *incompleteness* augurs against any directorially imposed fixity. Furthermore, the false attempts to complete, or square, the circle of art (of any art, but for our purposes, performance) can only ever (ultimately) serve to exclude the viewer from the equally intrinsic participation in the elusive and idiosyncratic creation of meaning.

Within the permanent, perpetual present performance offers itself to us as a motif of the referential past and the resonant future: of the 'as was' *via* the 'as if' towards the always elusive 'to be'. An endless present, which, in its time-basedness, keeps pace with the viewer, moving from moment to moment with a shared synchronicity. Theatre convention, regardless of any shockingly unconventional origins it may possess, deals with the past and the future more strongly

than the present. In this fashion, that which we know by experience
fuels a capacity to imagine that which will probably follow, living
through performance in a semi-comatose state of nostalgia and
prediction, fused into a knowing sense of departure and arrival. Even
the rather peremptorily disabused notion of text as traffic serves here
only to take the members of its audience down routes so familiar as to
pass in a blur. In opting for the text to take us somewhere, to deliver us
unto some climactic *grand finale*, we have to miss the moments, more
swift than numbed perception, wherein the text, like the bodies, like the
light and shade of all we see, is always already and always only forever
in the here and in the now.

Even within the immediacy of performance the words used are
generally rooted in either the past or the present. In a performance text
one is more likely to say 'I am going for a walk' or 'I went for a walk'
than 'I am walking'. It may be the case that to speak of an action whilst
it is being carried out is to engage in no more than tautology or
contradiction. The speaker is either walking, in which case the words
only describe what the spectator is already seeing, or the speaker is not
walking, in which case the words are a type of blind. The text of *At
Last Sight*, both in terms of language and action, will attempt to locate
itself in the present of performance even as its referent is the part-
remembered past.

Criticisms of progressive performance, and this term is used
here to describe those practices which attempt, in a variety of ways, to
subvert and/or constructively re-deploy the traditions of the Euro-
American playhouse,[16] might be said to stem from an articulated
tension between cultural conservation and popular culture. Between the
'high' art of the permanent text and the 'low' here and now-ness of the
performance activity. Cultural conservationists will feel, instinctively,
that there are clear and hierarchical demarcations between the 'well-
made play' and those traces of text left over from performance. This is
in much the same way that theatre itself will generally be afforded a
higher and more worthy place than work which comes under the
umbrella-heading of 'performance'. That there is some sort of naturally
arrived at league table of aesthetic experience and activity.

Rather than offering a celebration of the diverse range of
aesthetic approaches found in contemporary performance, (mainstream)
critics seek to actively discourage the inclusion, in any recognised
locus, of any form of practice which contradicts the(ir) traditional
notion of 'theatre'. Willis (1990) argues eloquently and persuasively as
to the dangers of such an exclusive and endemic view, writing that

calcification occurs as a consequence of ... the complete dissociation of
art from living contexts.

> This is where the merely formal features of art can become the
> guarantee of its 'aesthetic', rather than its relevance and relation to real
> life processes and concerns: installed in the antiseptic stillness of the
> museum.[17]

Post-structuralism has taken us some stages nearer to an
understanding of the workings of mainstream sensibilities, if not quite
providing society (and art) with a key towards its emphatic taking
apart. Post-structuralism grew from a formalised empathy with the
series of alternative and/or minority groups that emerged during the
1960s. The 'progressive' ethos of this period provided a platform
(albeit a fragmented and fleeting one) for these groups' voices; voices
which still, despite the impact of post-structuralism, continue to be
marginalised in terms of politics and power. What post-structuralist
approaches have allowed is the at least quasi-legitimisation and
acceptability of a challenge to the white, middle class, heterosexist
cultural politics, a politics that implicitly and explicitly enforces the
strong and further disenfranchises the weak.[18] Versions of the world
from lesbians, gays, diverse cultural and ethnic groupings, alongside a
number of increasingly post-colonialist perspectives, have combined to
transform 'traditional' ideas as to that which has hitherto been
presented as either 'natural' or 'normal' within our society. This
transformation has been wrought through a foregrounding of the
ideologies at the core of specific representations (and of ideology itself
at the core of representation). This has been aligned to an
understanding that the notion that all people(s) wish to belong to a
'perfect' western (Euro-American) society of phallocentric
heterocentricism is a constructed and destructive myth of Dead White
Males, kept in a state of simmering potency by the live white ones.

Notwithstanding the impact of post-structuralism, critics
continue to (feel able to) speak as if notions of commonly held views
of performance, and of the values there found, are possessed of a
currency which exists without any attendant reference as to precisely
who the(se) 'values' relate to, of who those who sit, not in judgement
so much as approval, happen to be.[19] When we speak, for example, of
aesthetics, of whose aesthetic 'standards' do we speak? Is it the case
that 'definitions' (even the word seems sloppy, full of leakage and
loopholes) which seek to exclude the plethora of performance-based
activities from the world of 'theatre' are in any way 'natural', or is

theatre beginning to broaden its scope in the light of postmodernism's literal post-modernism?

As a method of analysing culture, post-structuralism attempts a destabilisation of our notions of natural, as opposed to 'non-natural', behaviour; to jolt the receiver with a clear reminder that one's view of the world is only ever one's own. For some this is less a reminder than an unheeded (rather than unheard) wake-up call. Our perception of events is determined by a myriad of conscious and unconscious experiences, expectations, moods, gender, age, education, politics, desires, fantasies *et al* as well as, at its most immediately obvious, the location from which we perceive. As such, notions of 'audience', as if such were a single entity of like-minded, like-experiencing and like-responding automatons, have lost much if not all of their critical appeal.[20]

The spectator is always an active participant in the art's construction, which is not to suggest that the consumption of art emerges organically alongside its creation, but that the subsequent reception by a viewer complements, if not quite completes the process. This recognition of the spectator's constructive role has emerged from a variety of sources, being as central to certain key ideas of post-modernity as it was to Marx, who wrote that

> Consumption produces production ... because a product becomes a real product only by being consumed. For example, a garment becomes a real garment only in the act of being worn; a house where no-one lives is in fact not a real house; thus the product, unlike a mere
> natural object, proves itself to be, *becomes*, a product only through consumption. Only by decomposing the product does consumption give the product the finishing touch.[21]

Marx was arguing from his own historically recognisable perspective, a perspective wherein one might say that 'existence' is being used as a metaphor for 'usefulness'. In this way, the garment achieves its purpose rather than its identity through the act of being worn. Many well-documented examples of performance contradict Marx's views on consumption at the same time as, in the very act of their publication, they achieve something of their own usefulness through dissemination.

In 1988 Ulay and Abramovic walked along the length of The Great Wall of China, Abramovic departing from the eastern end at Shan Hai Guan and Ulay walking from the west at Jai Yu Guan. The walk was witnessed and filmed for a fraction of the way but was nevertheless primarily 'unseen' by all but the walker's own perception of her or his walking self. Undoubtedly, the public 'knowledge' of that activity, whether by personal information from the artists themselves or *via* subsequent reportage in video, photograph, essayed analysis or anecdote, can be said to complement the activity, for such was at least part of the purpose of the walk.

However, to take the line proposed by Marx that the walk only 'became' a walk by dint of its consumption is to take us back to the schoolchild's favoured debate about the existence or otherwise of the unheard tree crashing to the forest floor. Performance is performance without an additional witness (despite the protestations of much-cited luminaries such as Augusto Boal)[22] because the performance is always witnessed already by the self.[23]

To a large extent, we are allowed the luxury of locating the spectatorial within the performative because of the work of Grotowski. Grotowski moved from a strong insistence in his early work on the relationship between spectator and performer towards an acknowledgement that the performer/spectator is now internalised within the single body of the performer. Grotowski's trials have provided a significant encouragement to those currently engaged in thinking about this central aspect of theatre and his legacy needs to be noted here.[24]

Spectatorship can never be taken for granted and even relatively recent generalisations, such as those put forward by the influential writer, director and founder of the 7:84 Theatre Company, John McGrath, have been exposed as anachronistic, intrinsically patronising and even pernicious mistruths. His chapter on 'Mediating Contemporary Reality' in *A Good Night Out* (1981), itself the transcript of lectures given at Cambridge University, goes as far as suggesting the 'tastes ... of working class audiences'. According to McGrath "Working -class audiences like laughs"; "Working-class audiences like music in shows, live and lively, popular, tuneful and well-played"; "working-class audiences can also love sentimentality ...they like clear, worked-for results".[25]

This desire for an homogeneous audience, twitching in conditioned response like Stelarc's electronically manipulated body, flies in the face of any and all notions of individuality, offering in its stead a vision of a Big Brother art of formulaic matter. Audiences are sophisticated because we live in a sophisticated time and the idea (the ideology) of an absorbent mass (re) constructing messages transmitted in the fashion of hypodermic art is a fundamentally incorrect reading of what actually occurs.[26] This could be regarded as anomalous to my own argument, in as much as the denying of one perspective (the other) in favour of another (my own) seems to be restrictive. But what is meant

to be communicated here is that positions that favour homogeneity are
closing work down whereas the ones that deny it are not.

Cultural codes are not only more complex than at any time in
the past, they are also much more eclectic. The working-class audience
of McGrath's thesis do not read the same literature, eat the same food
or watch the same television as each other any more than 'they' think,
feel or behave in a uniform way. The members of an audience are not
one mass, a like-minded and slavish whole, and the fact that each of
them (each of us) is of the genus homo-sapien does not mean that we
are not also intrinsically *sui generis*.

If we accept that any reading of any culturally manufactured
product, of any art, is an act of interpretation, then we are also
recognising that the 'meaning' of the work is interpreted, and, as such,
that all meaning is interpretative and personal.[27] Every art product can
be consumed in a multiplicity of ways and the ways in which this art is
interpreted is subject to innumerable variations of perspective. Meaning
can no longer be discussed without referring to the question of *who*
reads the work, of *where*, of *when*, of *how*. In this sense, notions of
cultural reception, of aesthetics that are inseparable from the vagaries
of reading are central to all aspects of this book.

We are led here to the question of whether a 'correct' reading
of a text (written, visual or performative) can ever be said to exist. The
sentiments expressed in earlier paragraphs would suggest that the
notion of 'right' or 'wrong' readings is one that has been exposed as
false by the rigors of hermeneutic study. This has not always been, and
is not always, the case. Gadamer (1976) argues a position of moderate
relativism, wherein understanding is always one's own. In this way,
interpretation is neither 'good' nor 'bad', it simply 'is'. Prejudice
becomes a positive force, to the point where Gadamer can claim that

> Prejudices are not necessarily unjustified and erroneous, so that they
> invariably distort the truth. In fact, the historicity of our existence
> entails that prejudices, in the literal sense of the word, constitute the
> initial directedness of our whole ability to experience.[28]

Prejudices, or 'preconceptions', shape the way we start to
view, and any subsequent rationalisation is conditioned by this first
response. The circle is thus interactive and anticipatory in nature, with
the viewer, the spectator, approaching the object, the performance, with
the inevitability of projecting certain meanings onto and into the work.
This happens in a variety of ways: the theatre space (or the space(s)
designated for the theatre) attended; the price of admission; the dress-
code required; the previous work of either the creative personnel

involved or the 'theatre' itself; any reviews encountered; one's previous and/or abiding predilection towards certain types of work.[29] Gadamer uses the term 'satisfactory understanding' to describe the end-result of this relationship between that which is seen and the one who sees; referring to a mediation between the author and the reader which nevertheless stops some way short of licensing an infinity of meanings. To Gadamer's mind, the intention of the author plays a considerable part in this construction of the satisfactory response, and it is expected that a similar philosophical approach will permeate the creation of the 'text' (written, visual and performative) of *At Last Sight.*

Gadamer has his adversaries, notably E. D. Hirsch Jr., who prefers to speak of 'valid' and 'invalid' interpretations. For Hirsch, the job of scholarship is to somehow arrive at the author's own intended meaning.[30] In this way, the 'correct' meaning of, for example, Shaw's *Major Barbara* or Robert Wilson's *Einstein on the Beach* would always lie within their own 'authorial' intention, rather than relating to it, in the Gadamerian sense. Where Gadamer embraces subjectivity, Hirsch favours the assumed objectivity of meaning arrived at through archival evidence and literary, rather than dramatic, excavation.[31] The text is thus a puzzle for the scholar to solve, with, presumably, the prize of meaning as the ultimate goal ... a goal which is only ever attainable by the scholar. Both Gadamer's and Hirsch's positions are exposed and subsequently attacked by the theorist and lexicologist Roland Barthes (1977).[32] For Barthes the author's voice is banished entirely from the equation of meaning, thus

> We know now that a text is not a line of words releasing a single 'theological' meaning (the 'message' of the Author-God) but a multi-dimensional space in which a variety of writings, none of them original, blend and clash. The text is a tissue of quotations drawn from innumerable centres of culture .... Once the Author is removed, the claim to decipher a text becomes quite futile. To give a text an Author is to impose a limit on that text, to furnish it with a final signified, to close the writing. Such a conception suits criticism very well, the latter then allotting itself the important task of discovering the Author beneath the work: when the Author has been found, the text is 'explained' - victory to the critic.[33]

Barthes' approach is not being followed in the creation of the performed work that will be (that already is?) *At Last Sight.* This is not because *At Last Sight* will tread too radical a line for Barthes. It is because I am aware that in the creation of material for an audience, and as a result of my own determinants, I will undoubtedly make choices, which have as their intention a preferred response. Tonal and spatial decisions in the directing of the work will endeavour, however obliquely, to result in certain moods and feelings in those who spectate. An appraisal of how this specific text is (being) constructed will follow this introduction. It is salient at this point to relate my own approaches to certain philosophical structures under discussion. It follows that the performance will still exist for any spectator who interprets the work in a different manner to that which this author intends and that her or his response is, by my own liberal definition, a valid one. The ideology of the creator cannot be expressed in the work of art; instead, a process of mediation occurs which amounts to a dialogue between the reader and the read.[34]

It is at this point that the critic comes face to face with the artist: the maker of the work, which is to be simultaneously exposed to analysis from that same maker. The relationship is Janusian, inasmuch as artistic decisions are not made in the same way that critical responses are formed. Critically, I am with Barthes, creatively, I am with Gadamer, albeit with decidedly Barthean leanings. The result is a seeing two ways, with perhaps too little visibility in either direction: the critic is taking the work apart before it is made, in much the same way as the creator is inordinately conscious of the criticism to which the work will inevitably be exposed. Indeed, the work is being created *for* critical analysis and, to a large extent, it is being created *through* analysis itself.

This is no mere exercise in linguistic chicanery: the problem is real and pervasive. As a scholar, my role is to go beyond the satisfaction of interpretation. It goes with the territory of teaching at a university that I am expected to take my own responses, and the responses of my students, more deeply than a surface reading would allow. To move into an explanation, an analysis, as to why we interpret work in the ways that we do. To articulate the theoretical positionings which result in our 'feelings'. Whereas the practice I create may be able to exist, and to do so comfortably, within a situation which allows the aesthetic ideas contained therein to remain unexplained, my twin role as a lecturer and researcher leads me into a seeking out of identifiable traits, alongside the subsequent dissection, of that which might be termed the nature of contemporary performance.

There is more at stake here than a surface understanding of semiotics, an ability to rationalise, both in a directorial and analytical fashion the signification of signs. The realisation that interpretation is always already an act of re-creation stems from the polysemic nature of performance itself. The codes on which performances are built are complex and, semiotics notwithstanding, the ways in which these codes are deciphered are never absolute.[35] That which Esslin (1992) chooses to regard as the exemplification of an 'incorrect' reading is embraced by other 'schools' of practice as an exemplar of a post-semiotic world of polysemia. Italian art critics coined the term *inesspressionismo* to describe that art which, through the creation of moments of loaded ambiguity, aspires to a state whereby it means whatever the viewer chooses it to mean. For those of us who regard the Derridaen idea that things may not mean what their creator intended as an eminently acceptable philosophical positioning, *inesspressionismo*, or inexpressionism, can still seem like a leap into an excess of liberality. In reality, inexpressionism differs very little from the negotiated readings inherent in all forms of communication, with the perceiver incorporating 'intended' and 'accidental' responses to any given subject. As indeterminate works, performances cannot but leave spaces that the spectator will fill in in the process of spectating; the spectator, therefore, fixes *that* meaning in the process of spectatorship. That the work means something else to other spectators, as it will to the creator and any participants is to be embraced.

Inexpressionism fails as a philosophical as well as a critical phenomenon, ultimately, because of the impossibility of creating an entirely 'open' text: indications always exist, whether they are recognised as such or not. If the text is never open then it follows that subjectivity is always compromised by indications. Performance work draws on the preconceptions of a spectator (and it is important here that we do not fall into the trap of losing the individuality contained in 'a' to the neutrality of 'the'). There is no ideal or idealised watcher and the work must not be made to fit into the lowest common denominator of seeking to be all things to all people. A spectator is guided by the structure of the performance, which suggests that the range of interpretations, although infinite in the subtlety of their variations, is chiefly situated within the artist's version of events.[36] Meanings are suggested, although not demanded, by the rigidity or otherwise of the codes in operation and these codes will, for the most part, be manipulated by the artist, by the creator of the work.

When writing text, for performance or otherwise, there is an awareness that what one is doing is on one level controlled and on another surprising, almost accidental.[37] Writing, therefore, involves a sensitivity to correspondences and resonance even when words have been arrived at without conscious thought. This is not the same thing as automatic writing, made famous by the surrealists and also by Freud.[38] Whereas automatic writing denies the possibility of editorial interference, creative writing *per se* involves a recognition that the act of writing is itself in part a process of discovery, and that new ideas may stem from writing as much as writing functions as the articulation of ideas. There is no fixed sequence in the process of writing, and all that is written is not planned. Indeed, one can write in order to find out what it is that one thinks.

At the time, in the very action, of its being constructed the text will combine a number of potentially contradictory indications, or signifiers, and these will inevitably result in an equally diverse set of responses. My own intentions as writer of this text are still important to the intended meaning, or overall tone, of *At Last Sight*. Notwithstanding the fact that I am writing the words with an awareness of the impossibility of conveying all, and only all, that I intend. In this sense, the work is intended to function with rather than against the ideas of polyphony and polysemia, inasmuch as it is my intention that the text that emerges will contain within it a recognition of the ambiguity of word, voice, gesture, pace and duration.

On one level, this would appear to be the proving of an already accepted point: if all text is intrinsically polysemic there might be little point in making polysemia itself a stated aim. However, in my role here as both documenter of practice and practitioner it seems illogical to attempt to make practice which is dispossessed of a theoretical grounding. Indeed, the practice is predetermined to be invested with an underpinning of theory by dint of the conditions of its being made. To try to divorce the 'why' of analysis from the 'how' of creation is impossible to me, at this time, in these circumstances. So, I have located myself in a situation wherein I am aware (of my own belief) that the notion of an author as a free creator of direct and incontestable communication has ceased to operate with any validity. The concept of authorial dominance, of a literal authority, has been subject to searching examination by contemporary critical approaches, to the extent where, perhaps, the most an author is able to do is to make the first suggestions as to the ways in which the work will be perceived.[39] As director as well as creator of the text that will constitute *At Last Sight*, this 'authority' is doubled in proportion to the difficulties inherent in an avowed avoidance of an attempt to 'persuade'. The ways in which this balance will be sought (if not always achieved) will form the basis of Chapter Two. Chapter Two will constitute an analysis of the practical decisions involved in the crafting of performance with a group of students. This is a feature of the approach I will be bringing to the research. Whereas the pace at which I write Chapter One, as with this introduction, is relatively measured, the pace of Chapter Two's construction will be determined by the development of rehearsals. This is an intentional feature of the research methodology being developed.

A feature of writing *about* making at one and the same time that the making is taking place, is that linearity or progression is sacrificed to the immediacy of rehearsals occurring in the midst of reflection. Whether this means that the words of this book will be playing 'Catch Up' with the activities of practical creation, or *vice versa*, is something that only experience will reveal. Even now, it is easy to foresee situations where I will be struggling for the words to describe and explain an element of rehearsal that has already been removed and replaced by another. The reader will observe from this that it is not my intention to attempt a separation of 'theory' from 'practice'. That they are indivisible is one of the beliefs that provide fuel for this project. If this results in a not quite coherent experience for subsequent readers, all I can say is that the experience of reading this book may be more reflective of the experience of making *At Last Sight* than a more compartmentalised approach could have achieved.

The process of writing this book, like the process of creating *At Last Sight*, will draw more heavily on divergent approaches to thinking than to the convergent. This will not be a work where the conclusion is the more knowing twin to the introduction. It is not an attempt to find out if a particular theory holds true, so much as it is an attempt at recording and making sense of what it is that takes place, *as it is taking place*. In order to be consistent any processes of revision will be visible and transparent. If this book were to be written by hand rather than typed then the reader would encounter a series of crossings out, each of which would leave the displaced words legible. Mistakes and blind alleys are the stuff of rehearsal: the stuff of creating practical performance. Just as mistakes are valuable stages of that process, so are they valuable stages of this. To this end, I will not be deleting sections if and when those sections no longer 'ring true'. If something happens in rehearsal that seems important at the time then it will be included and commented upon.

Processes vary from person to person. So do practices. The term 'practice' as it appears in this book will refer to more than the practice of a physical act. It will be used to describe the choices made in the putting together of this project. In recognising that a practice is also always a choice I am identifying my own approach as one among a myriad of possibilities. One practice selected from immeasurable practices. We can say that in the context of originality the word 'practice' relates to the idea of protypicality ... where one engages in a practice that will subsequently serve as a model for others. But practice

also relates to employment of existing practices. Ways of making work
are shaped by work seen, just as one's own practice is informed by the
practices of others. Practice *happens*, and because it does it cannot stay
fixed. Practice then becomes process and *vice versa*. The terms will
overlap and fold in each other as the book develops ... in the same way
that the documentation and the construction of *At Last Sight* will come
together to form one project.

As with 'practice' and the increasingly unstable concept of
'the audience', ideas of 'the natural' have been exposed as a series of
constructions. The sense and meaning of words such as 'aesthetics',
'art' and 'theatre' have been recognised as culturally and ideologically
manufactured. Accordingly, there are no definitions of theatre that
exists without an ideological baggage.[40] Recognising theatre criticism
in this sense gives us more information as to the ideology of the
individual critic than it does the provision of an objective (*sic*)
perspective on performance. Ideology is always prevented, excluded,
from the notion of 'outside' and nothing experienced can ever be
'new'. Attempts at removing ideology from any given equation are
futile in the extreme ... all that can be done is to recognise the prejudice
that comes with experience and to acknowledge the exclusivity and
bias of one's view. In fact, if we choose to examine closely that which
we 'recognise' as theatre, we will see that there are few if any common
properties in the form; those which appear to be common are only
strands of similarity. Theories of what it is that defines 'Theatre' are
generally made up of doomed attempts to conceive of as quantifiable
and closed that which, in essence, is demanding, always, of an
openness of approach.

In 1956, at the same time as John Osborne and The Royal
Court were initiating 'redefinitions' of British notions of theatre,
Morris Weitz was arguing a persuasive case against closure

> Aesthetic theory - all of it - is wrong in principle in thinking that a
> correct theory and definition of art is possible ..... What I am arguing
> then, is that the very expansive, adventurous character of art, its ever-
> present changes and novel creations, make it logically impossible to
> ensure any set of defining properties.[41]

Attempts to shift notions of Euro-American performance away
from the vainglorious belief that this state somehow sanctifies the
premise of an essential 'known' have been posited by Grotowski,
Mnouchkine, LeCompte, Schechner, Barba, Wilson and even, in his
post-Jungian days, Peter Brook. Each of these practitioners (and they
are representative of a much larger group) have moved towards forms

of performance and performance-related research which have denied both the omnipotence of the literary text and the seeming supremacy of the white males' gaze. Schechner (1988) writes that we should

> ... situate theatre where it belongs; among performance genres, not literature. The text, where it exists, is understood as a key to action, not its replacement. Where there is no text, action is treated directly.[42]

Experimentation in performance, or even deviation from 'normal procedure', has led to a less than complimentary press, from within as well as beyond academe, as Susan Bennett (1992), describing the origins of performance theory, points out

> Performance theorists responded to mainstream North American theorists who berated the devaluation or even total rejection of text by performance artists. Traditional theorists saw this as the final straw in the alienation of audiences, sending them to the 'culturally inferior' entertainments of cinema and television.[43]

Dramatic literature has an in-built potential for permanence, which is denied by the ephemerality of performance; this makes the study and analysis of work which is 'performative' rather than 'literary' in origin and impulse an uneasy academic discipline.[44] As we have already seen, cultural conservationism continues to uphold the tenet that there is an indisputable line that divides the 'High Art' of (their) classical, scripted theatre from the 'Low Art' practices of the seemingly undisciplined and, sacrilegiously, 'unskilled' matter of (our) contemporary performance.[45] I am aware here that the use of the inclusive 'our' seeks to inculcate in the reader a certain shared perspective, shared, at least, with the perspective of the writer. I am aware also that in acting thus I am contradicting the ideas of *sui generis* mentioned earlier. Ultimately, the safety of simply deleting the word is sacrificed here in the hope that the reader's eye will recognise it as a desire towards an openness, both of location and response. We know, after all, that the "terms of high art are currently categories of exclusion more than inclusion".[46] Terms which, rather than celebrating the rich aesthetic diversity that is a feature of our age, encourage us towards an exclusion of any forms of performance which do not conform to these conceptions. Faced with this recent history, the makers of progressive performance, alongside their band of articulate apologists, have begun to develop theoretical positions ... partly as an inevitable consequence of current developments and partly as a defence, as a shoring-up against attack.

My own predilections, in terms of practice and analysis are (for better or worse) towards postmodernism.[47]

It is important to remember that other forms of progression exist, and that the postmodern approach posited here is only one of a number of ways in to current work. The non-mimetic performance traditions of African, Asian and Oriental forms, for example, have had a radical impact on the ways work is made in the West.[48] The exposure to the alternative philosophies aligned to these traditions has resulted in an increased questioning of the dominance of European and North American beliefs, from Aristotle through to Stanislavski. More and more, we are seeing an inclination within performance theory towards the hybridity of anthropological and aesthetic interests. With a desire to cross over from the borders of theatre (which, as we have seen are untenable inventions) into other genres of performance: into ritual, ceremony and play. Brooks McNamara (1992) makes the point, albeit less forcefully than Weitz, that

> Performance is no longer easy to define or locate: the concept and structure has spread all over the place. It is ethnic and inter cultural, historical and ahistorical, aesthetic and ritual, sociological and political. Performance is a mode of behaviour, an approach to experience; it is play, sports, aesthetics, popular entertainment, experimental theatre and more.

The key question in theatre is not 'what is happening on stage?' so much as 'what is happening to me?' Not 'what the butler saw' or even 'what the butler is seeing or might see next' but 'what can I see?' For the 'I' of the reader is inseparable from the 'eye' of the viewer and, just as the eye is never fully fixed, but always flickers, always shifts, so the reading 'I' is in motion from moment to moment, moving at pace with, but never fully in line with, the writing performed and made 'real' as we watch. In this way, art no more imitates life than life could be said to imitate art ... apparent, and even artfully designed similarities are at once both more and less than they may seem

Directors who engage their imaginations towards the creation of new forms and approaches are not so much decrying the real as denying the false. Usually, the production's theatrical images are the result of the director's researched and relativistic perceptions about the play. About a concern with the nature of the play's narrative, characters, ideas and atmosphere; at other times the production tells us more about the director than the directed, more, perhaps, about performance than that which is being performed. The first is primarily interpretative, the second creative. In all cases, whether the production serves the text or the text serves the production, what is necessary is an ability to select and creatively manipulate the diverse elements of performance: (usually) movement, duration, speech, pace, rhythms and design (all of which are contained in a working understanding of semiotics). An aesthetic literacy aids the director in her/his choice of images and/or motifs that have the greatest potential for communicating *at the requisite level* that which the director deems fruitful. To this end, the creation of moments of loaded ambiguity might be more taxing to the director (and ultimately more satisfying to the audience) than the directing-by-numbers of Chekhovian *mythos* after the style (the *school*) of Stanislavski, or Brechtian *dianoia* according to the principles laid down in the *Short Organum*.

Heiner Muller (1990) claimed, famously, that to 'use' Brecht without challenging him was to betray him.[49] Brecht himself argued against the very canonisation of technique that has been used to calcify his own once-innovatory practice. It is worth quoting Brecht at some length on this point. His essay of 1938, entitled *The Popular and the Realistic*, contains the following still timely warnings

> The concept of realism ... is an old concept which has been much used by many men and for many purposes, and before it can be applied we must spring-clean it too .... For time flows on ... methods wear out, stimuli fail. New problems loom up and demand new techniques. Reality alters; to represent it the means of representation must alter too .... What was popular yesterday is no longer so today, for the people of yesterday were not the people as it is today. Anybody who is not bound by formal prejudices knows that there are many ways of suppressing truth and many ways of stating it ... great experiments in the theatre ... involved the exploding of conventional forms .... One cannot decide if a work is realist or not by finding out whether it resembles existing, reputedly realist works .... The intelligibility of a work is not ensured exclusively by its being written in exactly the same way as other works which people have understood. these other works were not invariably written just like the works before them.[50]

We are dealing now, as ever, with duration and space, with location, with image, sound and form ... with *people*. These are the givens of performance and it is to the creation of performance that this book now moves. If this chapter-length introduction has served its purpose, it has prepared the ground for a study of one way of making work; a 'way' which is personal, but which is also attempting to locate itself within a recognisably theoretical and aesthetic frame of reference. In the final analysis, perhaps, the most effective way of discussing the making of performance is to focus, as *Tracing the Footprints* intends to

do, on a performance which is being constructed at the same time as its
construction is being made subject to study. For to do otherwise would
result in the alteration of that investigation to an examination of the
previously 'made', to a view of performance as a thing already done
and complete ... to an object, rather than the event we know it to be.

Whether the relationship in one body of the creator and the
critic will prove more fruitful than frustrating remains to be seen,
making the analytical aspects of the book as much of a genuine leap
into the darkness of the yet-to-be as those elements that will remain
indubitably performative.

Notes

¹ Cage, J *Silence*. Western University Press, Middletown, Conn., 1967. pp.46-
47

² At the time of writing, something of a furore has erupted over the work of the
late British artist Francis Bacon. Bacon was insistent, throughout his life, that
his paintings were entirely intuitive; that he never drew. A consequence of this
was that his art was seen as stemming from an almost mystical and, centrally,
an immediate relationship between the artist, the paint and the canvas. The
recent 'discovery' (the provenance of which has been challenged in some
quarters) by the artist's friend and companion Barry Joule of a vast array of
sketched-over and otherwise manipulated photographs, (known as the 'Joule
Archive') alongside a series of associated and developmental drawings, gives
lie to (t)his claim, suggesting as it does that Bacon was both a dissembler of
truth and a systematic assembler of ideas. The scope of this book is not wide
enough to accommodate any in-depth analysis of the work of non-performance-
based artists; however, Bacon's desire for his art, and the 'creation' of that art,
to be seen as somehow less 'determined' than that of his peers is worthy of
note; it suggests something of the tendency of artists' disinclination to engage
in, or even admit to, an analytical engagement with the mechanics of their
work.

³ See *Conversing with Cage*, compiled by Richard Kostelanestz and published
by Omnibus Press, 1989. Cage speaks at some length about chance; on page 17
we read the following: "Most people who believe that I'm interested in chance
don't realize that I use chance as a discipline. They think I use it --- I don't
know --- as a way of giving up making choices. But my choices consist in
choosing what questions to ask."

⁴ Stelarc's performance of 'Split Bodies: Voltage In/Voltage Out' is discussed
in *Total Theatre*, Volume 8, Number 2, 1996 in an article by John Daniel
entitled 'Invaded Bodies'.

⁵ Information on the work of Marina Abramovic can be found in *Performance
Research*, Volume 1, Number 2, 1996 in articles and interviews by Chrissie Iles
and Lynn MacRitchie; in *Performance Art Into the 90s*, Art & Design, Volume

9/10, 1994, London; and in *Ulay/Abramovic: Performances 1976-1988*, Stedelijk Van Abbemuseum, Eindhoven, 1997.

[6] The work of both Station House Opera and Impact Theatre Co-operative is chronicled in the journal, *Performance*, London. This journal has ceased publication; however, back-issues can be obtained by contacting David Hughes at *Live Art Magazine*, PO Box 501, Nottingham, NG3 5LT, England.

[7] Claxton, G. *Investigating Human Intuition: Knowing Without Knowing Why*, in 'The Psychologist'. Volume 11, Number 5, May, 1998. p. 219.

[8] Bohm, D *Causality and Chance in Modern Physics*. Harper & Row, New York, 1958. p.96

[9] Carlson, M *Performance*. Routledge, London & New York, 1996. On page 5 of his introduction, Carlson states that 'performance is an essentially contested concept'.

[10] See Carlson (1996) and Counsell, C *Signs of Performance*, Routledge, London & New York, 1996 for discussions of varying theatre forms and their terminologies.

[11] Since 1985, I have lectured in Drama, Theatre and Performance at Crewe + Alsager College, Edge Hill, Liverpool Polytechnic and University College Chester, as well as running workshops, giving conference papers and creating performances at a number of institutions outside Britain.

[12] See Clark, R and Ivanic, R *The Politics of Writing*. Routledge, London & New York, 1997 for a discussion of the ways in which the self is always made present in one's writing.

[13] Foreman, R *Plays and Manifestos*. (ed. Kate Davy) New York University Press, New York, 1976. p.192: 'All creative work should be about the author trying to CREATE his subject and structure in a way that is necessarily about the person who represents that subject matter .... If the artist is involved in the artwork not only as maker but also its subject, it becomes the study of one who sees himself seeing himself.'

[14] Stapp, H *The Tao of Physics*. Boulder Press, Colorado, 1975. p.136

[15] Bridgman, P *Reflections of a Physicist*. Philosophical Library, New York, 1950. p.108

[16] Progressive performance might be further defined in its adversarial relationship to cultural conservationist notions wherein practice is rooted firmly in those traditions of preservation rather than challenge; where the literary text is always more central, more important, than the act of performance itself.

[17] Willis, P. *Common Culture*. O.U. Press, Milton Keynes, UK. p.3

[18] *Voices for Change* (1993) ed. Lawrence; specifically, Neelands, J. 'The Starry Messenger', which contains a thorough analysis of post-structuralism within a context of drama pedagogy.

[19] I am referring here to theatre critics such as Michael Billington and Benedict Nightingale in mainstream newspapers such as *The Guardian* and *the Times*, whose reviews of performances are dominant in British culture.

[20] Freeman, J 'The Location and Theory of Looking' in *Journal of Dramatic Theory and Criticism*. Spring, 1998.

[21] Marx, K and Engels, Frederick, *On Literature and Art*, Moscow: Progress. Published in translation, 1976.

[22] Boal, A, in *The Rainbow of Desire: The Boal Method of Theatre and Therapy*. London, Routledge, 1995, argues that theatre demands two people, a passion and a platform.

[23] My argument here is that performance is an innately spectatorial act. We watch ourselves performing, inasmuch as we (almost) always have an awareness of certain activities as more performative than others. In this way all performance is witnessed, if only by the performer.

[24] See particularly Kumiega, J. *the Theatre of Grotowski*. Methuen, London, 1985.

[25] McGrath, J. *A Good Night Out: Popular Theatre: Audience, Class and Form*. Methuen, London, 1981. pp. 36-60.

[26] See Bennett, S *Theatre Audiences*. Routledge, London & New York, 1992.

[27] 'By interpretation I mean here a conscious act of the mind which illustrates a certain code, certain 'rules' of interpretation.' Sontag, S *Against Interpretation*. Anchor, New York, 1988. p.5

[28] Gadamer, H. G. *Philosophical Hermeneutics* (1976). Los Angeles, University of California Press. p. 9.

[29] See Beckerman, B *Theatre Audiences*. Routledge, London & New York, 1993.

[30] See the section on Hirsch in Bateman, A *Philosophy of Art*. Routledge, London & New York, 1997.

[31] Hirsch's views on interpretation can be found in *Validity in Interpretation*, 1967. London: Yale University Press; and *The Aims of Interpretation*, 1976. London: University of Chicago Press.

[32] See *Image, Music, Text*. Roland Barthes. Fontana press, London, 1977, particularly the chapter entitled *The Death of the Author*, pp. 142-148.

[33] *ibid.* pp. 46-147.

[34] See Bauman, Z *Intimations of Postmodernity*. Routledge, London, 1992.

[35] See Esslin, M *Fields of Drama*. Methuen, London, 1992 and Eco, U 'Between Author and Text' in *Interpretation and Overinterpretation*. Collini, S (ed.) Cambridge University Press, Cambridge, 1992.

[36] Bennett, S (1992)

[37] Clark & Ivanic (1997) pp. 165-173

[38] Notwithstanding its legacy of visual art, surrealism began with experiments in writing as a means of pursuing 'pure psychic automatism' in its art. See Breton, A. *Manifestos of Surrealism*. (Huntington, J trans.) Penguin Press, London, 1987

[39] See Barthes,

[40] See Carlson, M (1996) pp. 8-16

[41] Weitz, M, in *Philosophy Looks at the Arts: Contemporary Readings in Aesthetics*, ed. Joseph Margolis, revised edition. Philadelphia: Temple University Press, 1978. p. 122.

[42] Schechner, R. *Performance Theory* London, Routledge 1988. p. 28.

[43] Bennett, S (1992) p. 28.

[44] See Clark & Ivanic (1997) for a discussion of the ways in which the permanence of printed words brings with it the implication of authority, and

how this, in its own turn, is celebrated in conventional approaches to academic study.

[45] See David Hornbrook, notably *Education in Drama*, Falmer Press, Brighton, England, 1991, and 'Can we do ours Miss?' in *Drama and Theatre Teacher*. Volume 4, Number 3, 1992.

[46] *Common Culture*, Paul Willis. Open University Press, Milton Keynes, England, 1990. p. 173.

[47] Whilst Philip Auslander is able to cite Andy Grundberg's declaration that 'postmodernism is dead' in his introduction to *Presence and Resistance* (University of Michigan Press, Michigan, 1994. p. 1) I am not yet ready to throw in the towel on postmodern performance as the still-vital performance mode of our time. A number of texts are contained in the bibliography that will provide the reader with an overview of postmodern performance. Of these Birringer (1991), Kaye (1994), Wheale (1995) and Auslander (1994) are perhaps the most informative.

[48] See Schechner, Turner and Barba.

[49] Muller, H *Germania*. Rathbone, London, 1990. p. 37

[50] Brecht, B, from *The Popular and the Realistic* (1938, reprinted in *Brecht on Theatre* ed. and trans. John Willet, New York: Hill and Wang, and London: Eyre Methuen, 1964), pp. 108-110, 111, 112.

Chapter 1:
The Construction of Script

To the Reader

It is here a book of good faith, reader. It warns you, right from the outset, that I here envisaged no end other than a domestic and private one. Here I in no way considered your interests, nor did I look to my own glory. Such a project lies beyond my powers. I have destined my book to serve as a certain comfort to my parents and friends: having lost me (which, indeed, they soon will) they will find here not a trace of my condition or humors, and thus will cherish more wholeheartedly and vividly the knowledge that they have had of me. Had it been a matter of seeking the world's favor, I would have adorned myself better, just as I would have presented myself in a more studied manner. I wish to be seen here in all of my simplicity, quite natural and ordinary, without effort nor artifice: for it is myself that I paint. Insofar as respect for the public will allow, my flaws will be readily legible here as will be my artless shape. For had I found myself amidst those nations that are said yet to live under the gentle freedom of the first laws of nature, I assure you that I would more than gladly have painted myself here in my entirety, and completely naked at that. Thus, dear reader, I am myself the subject of my book.[1]

This chapter will analyse the creation of a written script, *At Last Sight*. This script is being constructed in advance of meeting and commencing collaborative practical work with a group of undergraduates on a course of Theatre Studies. And yet this is only part of the story. The script is also being created as a means of suggesting something of both content and form in order to channel my own processes of thought into the project at an advanced date; of providing a focus for creative planning. Whether this will make the rehearsal period more of an experience of interpretation rather than devising is something which, I suspect, will develop into a more vague and elastic process than this polarisation would suggest. Why *At Last Sight*? The title itself provides a play on words that interests me, being suggestive, as it is, of a final act of seeing and also of the processes of vision arriving after some delay. Both aspects seem to be in accord with my intention to create a piece of work, which is, broadly speaking, nostalgic in content and visual in form. I want the work, or let me say at this stage that I *feel* the work, to be elegiac in tone; to deal with loss.

There are reasons, which are becoming increasingly apparent to me, as to why this should be so.

I am not entirely unaware of in how bizarre a fashion these opening paragraphs may read, particularly in the context of a scholarly probing towards a transferable advancement of knowledge. Ominous hints of a confessional tone, of a desperate striving for an unqualifiedly cathartic experience for the artist, may, if you will pardon the bastardised metaphor, set alarm bells ringing in the ears of the reader, and rightly so perhaps. But I would not wish the simplicity of the language used here to detract from the contribution these sentiments can offer to the sense of the overall work. A feature of *Tracing the Footprints* will be the way in which notions of participatory performance research will be developed. Because the researcher is, in this case, also the researched it is important that the reader is made aware of this factor.

The importance of this relationship cannot be overstated. It provides a key to the ways in which research methodologies will be implemented and it creates a context within which subsequent conclusions can be located.

There is an issue of catharsis at work here, and it is, at least in part, made up of a concern for my own notions, flawed and imprecise though they be, of a sense of (or a hoping for) a form of redemption through art. As a teacher of and also a maker of performance, it follows that this is the *type* of art through which I will pursue this aim. Although the specificities of performance, in terms of its relationship to other' forms, make performance an often less than ideal platform for the working out of one's own personal interests (or demons).[2]

The material of drama is mediated in ways that other arts do not have to contend with. Music can be played and preserved according to its composer's wishes ... s/he may even play the instruments required; an artist can leave marks on a canvas that remain *as those marks* regardless of the shifting perspective of the viewer. With performance, however - and this is one reason why so much of that which has come to be known as live art is non-collaborative to the point of self-obsession - the work is mediated *through* the performer. The 'creator' or the instigator of that work is rarely seen within the performative frame. There are a number of noted examples that challenge this general principle. Of these, the late Polish theatre director, artist and designer Tadeusz Kantor is one of the most highly regarded. Kantor 'controlled' the performances of his work by the simple and engagingly effective device of positioning himself on stage for the duration of the work, haranguing the audience as well as the actors whenever he felt so inclined.[3]

Without anticipating at this stage any similar methods of locating myself within the presentation of the performed product, I am attempting to locate the work as 'my own' (my own sense of 'truth'?) rather than as something which might be seen to 'belong' to the group of performers. This remains the case despite the fact that these same students will doubtless play a large part in the offering of suggestions and the making of decisions, which are themselves a recognisable part of the fabric of even the most dictatorial of rehearsal processes.[4]

At Last Sight is a project that will attempt to deal with the aestheticisation of memory. This memory (or these memories) will be either 'real' (at least in origin) on the part of the writer/performers/creators involved in the initial stages, and/or with the memories of those who will eventually assume their own actively interpretative role as spectators of the work. The script will demonstrate an interest with the issues of narratology, with evidence of both narrative and narration. It might be useful to refer here to the script, inasmuch as it has been constructed up to this point, as being informed by a process of meta-narratology, of narrative, which functions within an active and visible state of change.[5] The way that narrative is treated within the script is therefore a complex one, and the relationship between that which can be recognised as contributing more or less directly to the narrative *per se* and the disembodied extracts of material that exist elsewhere in the work is consistently shifting. *At Last Sight* does contain an allusion to meaning, and yet the structures through which stories are told are subverted too often for a through-line to emerge with any clarity. 'Real' time and 'acted' time are as likely to be alternated without expressed intention in much the same way that the script itself will drop in and out of different European languages. In a similar fashion, memory and fiction, experience and invention vie for the position of prime potency.

There is a distinction to be made here, which relates to the process of memory itself and also to its twin, 'remembering'; it is a distinction, suggested initially by Freud, between remembrance, *memoire involontaire*, to use Freud's term, and memory, or *memoire volontaire*.[6] Whilst memory serves to put the past into some semblance of chronological order, absorbing that which is being remembered into a deliberate continuum, which locates the distant past at one end and the present at the other, remembrance destroys the separation of past and present. In other words, at those moments when images from the past are set off or triggered by sensations that are being experienced in the present, remembrance manages to fuse the past *with* the present. In this way the linear continuity that is generally seen, *via* memory, to exist between past and present is taken apart, deconstructed. Linear time is no longer then accepted as a given of tradition, so much as its destruction becomes an accepted fact. Time that was lost may in this way no longer seem to be so, for through remembrance that past is not made subject to an act of revival but one of renewal. A consequence of this is that the notion of theatrical tradition is exposed to scrutiny.

That which is commonly known as 'breaking with tradition', however, is not really what is happening here. Performance consists of a series of broadly recognisable conventions, and conventions are the stuff of tradition. Inasmuch as progressive practitioners seek to free themselves and their work from the shackles of tradition - as convention as the dread conventional - those practitioners do so by locating their own approaches within the world of other similarly minded artists. Thus, one set of traditions is exchanged for another. What this means is that radical developments, original productions, are rare.[7] The progressive practitioner is engaged in a dialogue not with the past so much as with her or his own interpretations of the past, alongside that of a host of other practitioners. What happens is that the 'fixed' sequence of the past is challenged. Indeed, the very idea that the glories of the past can be preserved in new work by the inculcation in any one member of an audience of memory as reverence is attacked by progressive performance practice.

Talk of the past leads to talk of linearity, of a narrativised understanding of time, which, in its own turn, and despite best intentions to the contrary, threatens to translate the fleeting present into a point of stability, of closure. If a type of contradiction is beginning to emerge in the idea of *At Last Sight* between that which might be regarded as an interrogation of performative form and a romanticised and quasi-factual use of content, then so be it. Subsequent paragraphs will seek to explore the reasons behind the script's seeming obsession with time and with loss. For the moment all that can be said is that the content and the form are not so easily separated out as may at first have appeared. The *doing* is inextricably bound up with the *to be done* and that which appears as antithetical is an inevitable consequence of making work to exist initially in a literary form, which will then be presented as part of a live performance.

Ideas of the past, in whatever ways that 'past' is treated, are only ever accessible through acts of detailed and deliberate excavation; it has become a feature of our time and of our art that narration itself has been replaced to a large extent by quotation.[8] Within this spirit, extracts of other writers' published words are freely integrated into the script of *At Last Sight*, creating a work, which I have no hesitation in regarding as my own.[9] Recent performance practices, let us say recent *postmodern performance practices* in particular, have been characterised by their inclusion of quotations from the past;[10] furthermore, this 'past' has tended to be treated with a relative dispassion, with a sense of a curious and always (oh so) cool detachment. Accordingly, the past seems to be taken further away from the present through the form of its revisitation than the sometimes scant years between the particular past and our specific present would suggest. Stripped of its authenticating powers, of its authority, the past has become the stuff of fragmentation, quotation and collage. We know this as the very stuff of postmodernism, of a blatant end to the foundations of history; what it also heralds is a potential end to the notion of story itself. The new tradition is therefore an intensely self-conscious one, relating to the shifting present rather than the fixed past. Stripped of its role as an agent of authenticity, narrative has emerged as a system of coerced delusion. It reads to us now as a system which, in favouring the bogus *there and then* above the actual *here and now* seeks to submerge the truth of experience beneath the intrinsic falsity of empathetic absorption.

This does not mean that *At Last Sight*, any more than the flimsiest postmodern performance itself, is simply a question of citation as art. For unless the past is brought into the present through a process of metaphorical imagination, through imaginings that remove both past and present from within notions of linearity, allowing their common or salient features to emerge, then there can be no sense of renewal. This is the central challenge to *At Last Sight*, both in terms of written script and performance text. The postmodern 'values' to which I am drawn seek less to 'renew' the past than to parody it. In so doing, a mockery is made of the idea that the act of quotation is more of an 'honest and truthful' process, by dint of its status as a presumably untampered with reality, than that which is being presented in a narrativised and hence fictional way. At a time when the past can no longer be fully believed in, perhaps the only authenticity available to postmodernism is that fragments of that past are able to speak to the present in the form of quotation, of inverted commas around everything. The resultant degree zero flattens everything out to the level of art as ironic disenchantment, which is neither the tone nor the tenor required for *At Last Sight*. In fact, we know that nothing that is framed by art can ever speak for itself, and that an absence of mediation is impossible within the intrinsically and knowingly mediated form that is public performance.

Art that seeks to renew the past needs to somehow put that past into a type of order: to engage in an act of discrimination. The act of citation, almost by its very nature, denies that activity of discriminatory ordering, replacing an ordering of the past with an uncritical acceptance of the present as a framework within which any number of interest-arousing soundbites from our cultural past can be chaotically placed. Thus, music from the cartoon characters *Tom and Jerry* is as likely to be utilised as snippets of dialogue from *Gone with the Wind* and Adolf Hitler's speeches. All can be relocated alongside each other in the name of a polysemia which is (all too) often no more than a blasphemous reincarnation of Duchamp's notion of 'found objects'. This cannot really fail to mislead us into a belief that the past is an easy state for performance to acquire. Furthermore, in making the selections from this endless back-catalogue on the basis of immediate interest rather than any potential for metaphorical value, selective eclecticism is sacrificed to pluralism, to the new lowest denominator of a performative 'anything goes'.

It is for this reason that the script of *At Last Sight* is being constructed within a framework that includes realism as well as postmodernism. This seems, at face value, to present the work with an insurmountable contradiction. For realism is postmodernism's fiercest opponent and *vice versa*. However, it is my intention in this project to use a type of realism in order to expand on the structures and the composition of earlier, more traditional notions of realism, in the same way that postmodernism feeds off itself with a voracious appetite.

Whether this 'appetite' is self-defining or self-defeating is a moot point; what matters is that *At Last Sight*, like all work, will look backwards and forwards at one and the same time. In seeking to escape the recent past of modernism, contemporary performance tends to utilise a self-conscious method of playing off its past inheritance, its golden traditions, against its current desire for the topical. Indeed, within the extended framework of the knowing work and the knowing audience, the play of past and present actually *creates* the topicality. This does not amount to a value judgement on the work of others, for judgements based on categorisation have no real place in the pages of this book. Ironic postmodernism is as capable of creating an efficacious theatrical form as any other working practice. All that is being attempted in these paragraphs is a bringing to the reader's attention of some of the reasons why postmodernism will inform *At Last Sight*, without that same script conforming to any fixed notions of postmodernism.

There is a point to bear in mind here about issues of innovation - about Brecht's 'exploding of conventional forms' - because a contradiction exists between the modernists' commitment to finding new ways of articulating new ideas and the postmodernists' comfortable and incessant pillaging of the innovations of the past. Even at their most highly subversive, postmodernists feel able to draw upon past forms and past traditions, using a process of re-framing rather than re-invention.[11]

What this means is that a view exists within the elasticity of postmodern approaches to performance that the subversion of theatre form cannot be entered into without utilising in some ways the very forms which are being placed under attack. In this fashion, it follows, inasmuch as an interest in postmodernism is informing the work, that *At Last Sight* will be no less concerned with form than a more overtly modernist piece might be. The script will, however, reveal its concern with form in a slightly different way. A characteristic of the written script and of the subsequent performance will be a quasi-theoretical type of self-consciousness relating to the particularities of the modernist practice it is seeking to displace.

The danger (or at least one of the dangers) in this approach is that what has come to be regarded as crucial to postmodernism is an ironic distancing. A sophisticated and elitist understanding, which, in its refusal to engage fully with the form, may result in a corresponding lack of engagement from a spectator. How to *engage* spectators, without providing those elements of *denouement*, characterisation and climax that have become the staples of drama is a challenge that *At Last Sight* will have to rise to. Failure to do so will (within my own sense of what the piece will be) amount to an inadequacy. Theory may be driving the project, at least to a degree, but it is performance that the project is being driven towards. The responsibility of providing the students involved with the work with at least something of the presentational satisfactions they are seeking is as real as the responsibility to make the work demanding of their faculties of intellect, creativity and emotion. As such, issues of sharing are central to *At Last Sight*. This is not about a dilution of my own creative and intellectual ownership of the work. It is a recognition that the nature of performance is collaborative and that the imperative to create a positive situation for the participants is strong. My own role here as a teacher is no less complex than my role as maker of the work and reader of that which is made. The situation is of my choosing. It is not a question of compromise, nor is it a matter of reneging on my directorial responsibilities. I am working within a set of circumstances, each of which I was aware of before commencing work on this project.

There are dangers, and the one that threatens me most directly, is that of academicism, of a gnawing sense of sterility. This can occur when forms which have been stripped of the commitments and beliefs that fostered them continue to be used. Postmodern performance is naturally responsive to the availability and accessibility of the past of modernism, and, in the way that it attempts to divide that past from this present it runs the risk of indicating little more than a particular type of adherence to a moribund form. In this way, postmodern tendencies are repeated rather than developed and the work wallows in its sense of a partially concealed homage to other work seen.

This is linked in some ways to the issue of sentimentality. By 'sentimentality' I refer here to the prompting of familiar responses to equally familiar stimuli; to the risk of evoking responses which are less about the creation of fresh challenges than they are, or become, a series of nostalgic references to previously experienced and only slightly re-packaged sensations. This can be seen as one of the defining features of reactionary art, which is not the intention of the work made as part of this investigation into the documentation of a particular practice. What needs to be avoided is a surrendering of the impulse to make new work to the familiarity of received notions of 'acceptable' or 'appropriate' performance.

The irony here is that the desire to create new work which stands outside of and at a distance to any invidious comparisons with mainstream theatre, and which aims instead to be measured in accordance with its own 'situatedness' within a localised and transient sense of that own newness, can only ever fail. It does so because, ultimately, all performance, like all art, is judged on the same scale. It competes for our interest and for our approval and in so doing the theatre past to which the bulk of those who make and see new work in the West are all conditioned by and to, sets standards that performance art can subvert but never fully escape. A difference between 'new' work and 'old' then may not be so much a question of those formal qualities of style which we all have come to recognise as 'postmodern', so much as a feature which resides in the ways in which memory is treated. As a feature rather than a rule, progressive performance indicates a refusal to rely on memory, and in so doing it identifies itself as being in vigorous opposition to the repetition of comfortably established forms. When quotation is offered *as* remembrance we are simply substituting repetition for parody. That which memory is unable to renew, quotation cannot fully revive, the act(ivity) of remembrance is more reliant on metaphor than the installation of quotation within performance (to the point where we are now becoming accustomed to seeing subsequent quotation marks placed *around* the first quotation marks) will generally allow.

If the past is/was a lie then the present can be regarded in some ways as a cure - as the antidote of honesty or the therapy of recognition - and this 'cure' is made manifest in the fashion of self-narration. This leaves us with two ways of dealing with that narration. We can either collapse away the distinctions between narrative and meta-narrative, writing ourselves into the wider world and exposing the act of writing as we do so. Or we can elevate the fragmented and partial narratives of our own lives to a point whereby those lives are presented as things of considerable importance.[12] Whichever option we choose, it is clear that the idea of narrative itself has not disappeared. The script of *At Last Sight* is comprised of a blending of the first option with the second. It is a feature of our age that lives are being increasingly lived in ways which seek to make the present little more than an endless number of narratives to be told in the future of the past. Derrida has identified this feature as 'archive fever',[13] as a sense of writing a future story out of current deeds. What this results in is a type of *mimesis* in reverse, a condition wherein our lives begin to imitate the stories we read and see rather than the *vice versa* of stories which attempt to relate to our lives.[14]

We can take this further and suggest that this leads us into a new definition of interpolation. One that not merely engages with the process of locating the viewer into and within the narrative being played out on the stage, through a type of identification based on the specificities of cultural targeting rather than the 'mankind-inducing' empathy, but which eliminates the need for identification *per se*. The spectator is propelled into the spectacle precisely because the spectator *is* the spectacle. If our own lives are being lived increasingly as stories, then we might well ask what need we have of additional, performatised narrative forms. And yet the opposite is the case: in essence, we have reached the stage where we do not really believe things to be 'true' until such time as they have been narratologised and archived, re-packaged into news bites and dramatisations.[15]

At Last Sight will tread an uneasy way through all of this, as neither declared fictionality nor ironic imitation, as neither realism nor postmodernism, an attitude to the authority of representation is not simply 'out there' waiting for the taking. The attitude has to be created alongside and as part of the process of making the work. There is a curious type of mimetic referentiality going on here, because in highlighting the nature of narrativity the work itself becomes intrinsically intertextual. Without relating directly to 'other texts' it nevertheless invites a contemplation of the fact that the past is not being shown *as it was* so much as *how it is being represented*. This demands an interest in the procedures of performative representation, an interest, in fact, in a view of performance as a state wherein ideology and representation are inseparable elements. It is worth reiterating the fact that ways of making performance are inextricably linked to that which is being made performative. The form *is* the content and the content *is* the form, and we are unable, or unwilling, to separate out the teller from the tale.

In writing the lines that I am, my mind is being drawn away from an analysis of *what* the work will seek to do and towards an appraisal of *how* the work under discussion will be used, of how it might 'fit'. It seems in many ways as though the script is beginning to explore the paradox of my own history. It is at once both 'real' and 'fictional', both discursive and intuitive (some sections of the script are ostensibly 'crafted', whilst others are written as a sort of stream-of-consciousness). The script is subjective, inasmuch as it draws attention to its own (to my own) narrative voice in a variety of ways. It is possessed of a form of self-reflexivity that will seek to break with the illusion of narrative at the same time as it hopes to absorb viewers into its own created world. It locates something of my own history as an exercise in creative writing and much that was experienced first-hand is deliberately offered up in the guise of fiction.

We can recognise here certain sites of something we can call a doubling of enunciation. This refers to those elements within the script of *At Last Sight* which are characterised by instances of *deixis*, a use of language that refers to the writing agent ... to the writer. The sites of enunciation create a linguistic pattern, or a network, that attempts to articulate the concerns of *making* which exist both on and beneath the surface of the work. If the instances of narrative and the constants (?) of mood create a consistency within the script, then so does the self-reflexivity of the writing itself. As a result of this, a reasonable expectation can exist that a spectator will be able to adopt a manner of viewing, a mode of receptivity that recognises and accommodates the particularities inherent in the presentation of this type of script. The writing is seeking to provide a series of words which are a *part* of the very performance text that they provide comment on. In a sense then, the content of the script will be intrinsically embroiled in the enunciative fabric of the performance, at the same time as it also exists as a cohesive appendix to it. A consequence of this is that the words contained in the script will offer to the spectators both content and context. Creating an early indication of the performance's intention to reflect on an absence of artifice alongside the overtly artificial, to display the process of making (the *then* and the *now*) within the immediacy of the made.

If the making is part of the made, so too is the self an integral element of the subject. What then is involved in the process of writing the self into performance? Am I writing *about* myself or am I writing the (a) self? These questions are being played off against each other just as they are also working in close accord. What is of interest, to me, initially at least, is the relationship for a spectator between that which is encountered as script - 'I am myself the subject of my (work)', to paraphrase the Montaigne of this chapter's introduction - and that which is subsequently or simultaneously offered as performance. To what extent that which is seen will contradict that which is heard is, at present, unknown, perhaps even unknowable. What is 'known' is that it is in this exchange between these two quite separate semiotic elements that a defining tension within the overall work is expected to exist.

I have no clear rationale as to why I am drawn at this point towards an exploration of my self; neither do I have any real sense of whether the self I offer is a 'true' one. As Luis Bunuel told us

> Our imagination, and our dreams, are forever invading our memories; and since we are all apt to believe in the reality of our fantasies, we end up transforming our lies into truths. Of course fantasy and reality are equally personal, and equally felt, so their confusion is a matter of only relative importance.[16]

What does it mean to show oneself, to make oneself visible, to seek the offering up of oneself so as to be read as 'subject'? Montaigne's 'To the Reader' reveals an introduction to a number of key issues here, issues for which his text also provides explicit illustration. This occurs because that which Montaigne describes is more than (just) an introduction to the idea of the self-reflexivity of his and our time; it also speaks to us of the ego of the artist. The signature of the artist, we might say, is not placed, as is usual in visual art practices, at the bottom right hand corner of the work, at the last point at which the eye, conditioned to the reading of a page from top to bottom and from left to right, will reach. The last 'word' in every sense. Neither is the author's name on the front cover, spine and title page of the work, eminently visible yet always a part of the frame rather than the work. With Montaigne's 'I am myself the subject of my book' the signature, the author's name, is at once enunciator and enunciated. The subject of the artist takes for itself the position of the subject-proper, both a part of the frame and also that which is being framed.

As Oscar Wilde informed us, life imitates art to a much greater degree than art imitates life.[17] Artists invent 'types', which are then assimilated into human behavioural patterns. Writing at the close of the nineteenth century, Wilde's epigrammatical style may have lost much of its flavour, and yet his comments on the relationship between truth and art remain pertinent to late twentieth century performance. When Wilde chastised the artists of his day for presenting for public consumption their "tedious *document humaine(s)*"[18] he sent a timely warning to all of those (all of us) who attempt to offer up the barely repackaged self as subject. "The justification for a character", Wilde tells us "is not that other persons are what they are, but that the author is what he is."[19] In this sense, *At Last Sight* might reasonably be regarded as my own attempt to articulate who and what it is that I am. And yet, if a part of who I am is a liar, then the integrity of anything I produce can never be taken at face value. If, as a liar, I say that the work is truthful my claims cannot be believed; by the same token, any claim I may make that certain sections of the work are false is suspect.

It is no Wildean wordplay to state that art is as concerned with the creation of aestheticised lies as it is with the articulation of truth. If it is 'myself that I paint', then the subject of 'myself' is defined by the I of the artist; what is shown, revealed to the spectator, is always already mediated, selected and made false by the maker's judgement (as are the word written here). In this way, it is not the subject of 'myself' that is being offered to the spectator, so much as the artist's, *this* artist's, sense of self.

In his book, *Working with Emotional Intelligence*, Daniel Goleman cites an example of this phenomenon with reference to the former American president Ronald Reagan

There was a downside to Reagan's emotional intelligence capabilities, as he displayed a certain lack of self-awareness, if not outright self-deception. At times he seems not to have known the difference between films he had seen or stories he had heard and the actual facts. Reagan once brought tears to the eyes of Yitzhak Shamir, then prime minister of Israel, with a story about his days with the U.S. Signal Corps recording the atrocities of the German death camps at the end of World War II. The problem: Reagan spent the entire war in Hollywood recruiting for the army's film units. He had, however, seen

footage from the liberated camps and, apparently, convinced himself
he's been there.[20]

Whether Reagan's comments indicated delusion or a
conscious attempt to delude can never now be known. All that we can
say is that fantasy and reality were blurred to the extent that an
identity was made subject to a process of fictionalisation. Reagan's
assertions were such that the 'lie' could not survive for long without
being discovered. For those of us whose assertions are smaller and
whose lives are lived beyond the scrutiny of biographers, the 'truth' of
any given claim is harder to determine. Reagan aside, and
notwithstanding John Cage's advice that the self should only ever
rarely be the subject of art,[21] we can recognise self-portraiture as a
form with strong historical precedents. Further, we can see - certainly
no less in performance terms than in visual art - that it is generally
reliant on four elements for its existence.

These elements are the artist as subject (as model, as theme);
the performance event that accommodates or provides a platform for
the expression; the image of the self, the 'myself', within the artist's
own notion of that self; and, finally, the spectator's reading of the
work. A fifth element exists in *At Last Sight* inasmuch as the 'self' of
the subject is presented *via* the selves of the performers. *My Self*
mediated through *Their Selves*. The script alone can stand outside this
equation, and the importance of the ways in which this script, or
aspects of it, are to be presented and made public is becoming
increasingly apparent.[22]

The mediation of my own work through the contribution of
others creates issues of creative and intellectual ownership. With
issues of performance *per se* collaboration is contained within the very
fabric of its being: in all but the rarest of cases performance *is* an
intrinsically collaborative act. As part of an investigation of practice as
research, however, the relationship takes on a different slant. The
question of who 'owns' the work moves beyond its usual realm of
philosophical enquiry into the no less pertinent field of accreditation.
This is an issue inasmuch as it creates something of a paradox, at least
potentially. For that which stands as common practice in both
direction and writing for performance is a type of 'giving away' of the
work. To the creation of a climate wherein the suggestions contained
within the script, alongside any directorial preconceptions, are not
generally allowed to blind the director to contributions from
participants, be they performers, designers or technicians.

In those instances where work is being made with students, as part of a wider programme of study, the compulsion to provide space for the creative and intellectual engagement of those student-participants is, if not necessarily stronger than in any other sphere, then certainly more overt. This is evidenced not least in increasingly prescriptive learning outcomes, which, as well as threatening to imbue all creative work with banal and unworkable notions of 'equivalence', seek to dictate the terms of closure to that which has not yet been made.

Not all of these academically imposed 'requirements' have a negative aspect. Creative involvement, in the sense of decision-making, for instance, alongside a marked degree of personal engagement with the subject matter, is a feature, if not always a prerequisite of First Class work in practical modules. Certainly, in terms of *At Last Sight*, I am hoping to gather around me a group of creatively fertile and intellectually astute individuals who are in no way content to be moved through the period of rehearsal like so many sheep.[23] But how much of the process of making the work can be 'given away' to the *participants* without the work itself ceasing to stand as my own? The fact that there are no satisfactory answers to this does not mean that the question itself should not be addressed. Notwithstanding the fact that the issue is more central to the work as part of a book than it is to the creation of work for public presentation.

The issue of creating an example of practice as research, in which the participating students are also being assessed is complicated. There are a variety of reasons as to why this is the case. Many of these reasons are subject to ongoing debate between the Standing Conference of University Drama Departments (SCUDD) and those British Government bodies which, act in response to the submissions received from respective departments as part of their particular Research Assessment Exercise (RAE).[24] These responses determine the level of funding afforded as an increasingly necessary top-up to the departmental subsidy received from students' tuition fees. The need for this additional income means that departments are becoming more inclined to include in their curricular a preponderance of modules which are designed to satisfy these exercises in staff-research evaluation rather than the more traditional requirement of learning outcomes which relate to the student. A consequence of this is that whilst *At Last Sight* has its genesis as a research project, and that it seeks the continuance of that status, the project must also, and firstly, be seen to satisfy the learning outcomes for the students involved. This means that an exploratory project is being entered into which will have to satisfy certain outcomes ... a state which is almost entirely antithetical to progressive performance practice.

Whatever this means it must not mean that the piece becomes all things to all people, a safety net through which nothing, be it a learning outcome, an advance in theoretical understanding or some development in new performance can ever be allowed to slip. The fact that different people involved with the work will have different agendas for that involvement will not be allowed to hinder the project's intent. The students involved will thus be given something of the task of research assistants inasmuch as they will, in their role as performers, form a considerable element of the material of that which is to be presented. They add to the creation of a research framework within which their own selves are being researched.

If the processes involved in *At Last Sight* are being offered here as a case-study of the making of work for performance then the work itself must not be made in a climate of fear connected to a crossing over of the line between *my* work and *theirs*. The work is being made in the here and now and it is being made to satisfy various and not always overtly compatible criteria. It is thus both *mine* and *theirs*. It is at one and the same time a student-project for *these* students and a student-project for *this* student. It is what it is, and it cannot, with any sense of legitimacy, disguise itself as anything else. If one paradox of the performance is that it will be seeking to deal with the (unattainable?) idea of truth through the artifice of theatrical presentation, then another is that it is at once both mine and not mine.

The intention, therefore, must be to articulate with as much integrity and accuracy as is possible those points when new directions and possibilities are put forward by members of the group. In this way, the participants become collaborators in the widest sense, rather than mere communicators of my words and thoughts. The ways in which this happens - and we know already that happen it surely will - will form one line that will run through Chapter Two. Up until that point, I am afforded the luxury of an unhindered megalomania ... a megalomania which (if the truth be told) is as much about a putting off of the moment of collaborative enquiry as it is a preparation for it.

There is a link in this work with the nature of performance itself, inasmuch as the work is concerned with a making visible, with a showing, of that very basis on which the notion of *mimesis* stands.

With the image of a man which is being produced and articulated (enunciated) by the very means of the artefact of reflexivity ... of the mirror image. All performances are self-portraits to a large extent: the selves of the director, designer, writer, performer *et al*. Of these, it is the performer, usually but not always, who is the most highly visible and yet the least powerful. The performer performs other people's stories and the name, above the title or at the bottom right hand corner of the canvas, is rarely the name of the artist (of the subject) who is seen. *At Last Sight* is not a subversion of that 'rule' so much as it is an exploration as to how far and to what extent the performer can present no intentionally fictional sense of self and yet still act as a signifier for another self. The 'myself' of the 'I' of the unseen other.

There is an arrogance at work here. It is a type of arrogance, furthermore, that locates itself at the centre rather than the fringes of the work. It is the arrogance of a presence, which, notwithstanding an act of representation and realisation through others, sees itself as able to permeate each and every aspect of the work. An arrogance which seeks the public identification of the 'self' as a subject worthy of spectators' and performers' time and efforts. There is, however, a fear that exists as part of the arrogance: it is the fear of an absence of something essential to the man of the artist which can only be dealt with, put right (?) through the presence of performance. *At Last Sight* is thus as much about that absence as this presence, as much about the painfulness of experience as the pleasures of aestheticisation; as much about loathing as much as serving the self.

If the self is not known. And if what little is guessed at is not particularly liked by that same self, then the self-portraiture or autobiography of certain types of art may well stand as a flawed but otherwise respectable attempt at locating, through the instability of performance, some sense of redemption through enunciation. Of catharsis.

The material being dealt with here is about composing a life, and about composing a text for performance: that much, at least, is known. The challenge, is how, working with the self as subject, that subject can at once contain much of the at all times subjective and fragmentary complexities of existence and also maintain the legitimacy of a performance text which communicates something relatively coherent to the spectator. Generally speaking, autobiography exists in order to provide an insight into the lives of important, influential and historically significant individuals ... in those instances, one's own pre-knowledge of the subject creates a veneer, or an illusion, of objectivity. With the subject of *At Last Sight* being this writer's unknown self - an 'ordinary life' - then no such objectivity can be argued for. Performance provides platforms from which to speak in voices which are authentic at the same time as they will always be heard as 'art' by dint of their qualities of presentation in front of an audience.

For some time now, performance has functioned as a form for the presentation of self as much as the representation of other. In this, a distinction, or schism, has developed between theatre and performance. With the illusory nature of theatre acting standing apart from the more overtly personal tone of performance. This has happened to the degree that we can now say that when a spectator attends a performance art event, s/he does so with a fair assumption that that which will be presented will bear some considerable relation to the concerns of those who are doing the performing. The performer here is in the role of the performer, rather than in any character.

Writing from a gender-specific perspective, Catherine Elwes has described performance as "the real life presence of the artist (who) takes no role but her own. She is author, subject, activator, director and designer. When a woman speaks within the performance tradition, she's understood to be conveying her own perceptions, her own fantasies, her own analyses."[25] By putting her own or his own body and experience forward within a live (arts) space, the artist becomes both object and subject within the frame of the work, and, as a consequence, this situation allows the artist to interrogate and articulate that relationship. The reference to the 'real life' persona of the artist is the stuff of performance art. The context of performance provides the performing artist with the opportunity for a live address which is markedly dissimilar to the Brechtian *verfremdungseffekt* that comes with the breaking through of the imaginary fourth wall between spectator and spectacle. Within performance art, it is far more likely that the notion of there being any fourth wall to subvert would be regarded with a great deal of cynicism and a healthy mistrust. We can say, therefore, that the performing of oneself is a feature of performance, even something central to it, whereas the submergence of self into character is a defining trait of acting.[26]

If the mode of performance deals with the unmasking of self, of the act or event of performance as self-revelation, then where does this leave *At Last Sight*? It is interesting to note that we refer to the one who is present in front of the spectators as the 'performance artist', suggesting an identification between the watcher and the watched which, at least on the part of the watcher, seeks out an 'honest' communication. This may mean that the performers in *At Last Sight* will be functioning as actors in a performance of self, rather than performers who are offering their own fantasies and analyses for perusal. This is a serious distinction, because the ways in which the spectators view the work will have a considerable bearing on that which they actually see. The role of the artist as performer is one which allows for the assuming of a series of transitory identities at the same time as the artist's own live presence is being signalled. No less complex, though in rather different ways, is the role of the performer as 'self' and representer of an unseen, writerly and directorial (and, let us not forget, *teacherly*) 'other'. When the performer speaks of 'I', within the context of *At Last Sight*, which 'I' is being referred to? To which artist does the 'I' refer?

Spalding Gray's 'I' is clearly his own,[27] just as the actorly Uncle Vanya's 'I' is Chekhov's. The device of 'I' is generally held to be an attempt at the expression of self, a self that is particular and irreducible, and yet the 'I' is available to any individual spectator - just as it is to each and every performer. It can therefore be regarded as the least particular of all words.[28] Accordingly, the 'I' of *At Last Sight* has an unsettled nature, and this is made manifest in a writing which is demanding of multiple readings. The 'self' in *At Last Sight* functions as a site wherein the meaning of identity is contested rather than confirmed. Where, through the self-revelatory act of performance, the artist (at this stage still and only the writer) is able to fix and unfix the relationship between representation and presentation and between the writerly and the performative selves.

In seeking to bring the real self, or selves - the Duchampian idealisation of the everyday - into the domain of art, and an attendant breaking down of the boundaries between art and artist, performance has been brought even closer to the realisation that whilst life and art may at times be one and the same thing, they are also always different. The difference is in context rather than content, but the two are the same inasmuch as *life*, like *art*, is always mediated, and the space occupied by the everyday is every bit as much a product of construction as that for performance. According to Kwame Anthony Appiah

> Every human identity is constructed, historical; every one has its share of false presuppositions ... invented histories, invented biologies,

invented cultural affinities come with every identity; each is a kind of
role that has to be scripted, structured by conventions of narrative to
which the world never quite conforms."[29]

The textual strategy of *At Last Sight* is not to assume a false,
collective identity, preferring instead to speak of slippage and
fragmentation. To this end, no lines of script are attributed to specific
speakers, either by gender or any other distinction. The script is
written out as a series of sections, which, at this stage, may be
addressed by one or any number of voices. The fact that these extracts
of script, neither monologue nor dialogue, cross constantly between
fiction and truth, lies and artifice, will, ultimately, be regarded in
significant ways as much by who speaks the words and in what ways
as by any key qualities in the script's construction.

If all of the voices contained within the script are my own,
either as a result of experience or invention, then the question of
whose mouth utters the words would seem to be a matter of singular
unimportance. In fact, because any descriptions in the script, such as
they exist at all and being of either person or place, are emphatically
not descriptions of the potential performers and/or the theatre spaces
to be played in, then the gender of the speaker is, by definition, largely
inconsequential. And yet this is to deny almost all of our experiences
of performance, experiences which tell us that what we see is at least
as important as the words which are heard. Linguistic distinctions
certainly exist between television viewers, with a concentration on the
view, and theatre audiences, with their concentration on the audible,
and these are no doubt rooted in good sense, but such distinctions have
been eroded by a collapsing of the once-vital differences between the
forms.[30] Consequently, the visual elements of *At Last Sight* will inform
the individual spectator's responses to the overall work in ways which
are considerable.

The semiotics of performance bring with them a complexity
which is every bit as demanding of the visual attentiveness of a
spectator as it is of that spectator's aural sensibilities, and the ways in
which work is presented go beyond issues of form, becoming essential
elements of the content itself. The different performers attracted to the
project will each bring with them different qualities and
characteristics. These will, hopefully, be deployed to a positive effect.
Prior to meeting with the project's participants, there is considerable
effort involved in the writing of words which are not so much neutral
as loaded with potential for a variety of voices.

If my expectations of the performers have to remain at times frustratingly open, am I able to determine what it is that is expected of the spectator? What is it that I 'want' from the spectators? For I am surely making the work with an intention that it will achieve certain things. *At Last Sight* is not being offered up as a copy of the world, either my own small occupied space or the spectators' obviously wider one, and, accordingly, I would not wish to see a spectator impressed overmuch by any aspects of mimetic realism which might appear in the work. Philostratus warned viewers not to fall into this trap, arguing that to do so is to

> praise an insignificant feature ... one that has solely to do with imitation; but we should not be praising its intelligence or the sense of decorum it shows, though these, I believe, are the most important elements of art."[31]

Philostratus is talking here of visual art, but the comparison with performance holds true. By the same token, and despite the feel of this chapter, which is offering an articulation of the reasons 'leading to' *At Last Sight* rather than taking the script apart line-by-line and providing an analysis as to where the words 'came from', theory may prove to be an anathema. Not to the book itself, which demands a theoretical approach as its natural right, but the performance, which I have no wish to develop into the thin theatricalisation of theory. Theory provides us with an invaluable means of reading the activities of ourselves and others, of reflecting and communicating much of that which is done, rather than merely accepting things as 'happening'. At the same time, we need to recognise the fact that theory will sometimes amount to no more than a self-satisfying endeavour to justify the narrowness of the world in which much of those same activities take place. At its worst, the seeming clarity of sight made possible through theoretically sustainable argument might actually reduce the potency of activity to little more than the legitimisation of tired techniques under the veneer of academic respectability and a dubious advancement of knowledge.

These sentiments are not intended to suggest that an interest in theory will always work against activity. Or that talking about art in some way augurs against the making of it. The words are offered as recognition that theory *is* capable of determining activity in advance. That it can allow and even encourage the continuance of certain forms of practice simply by dint of the fact that those practices are grounded in a shared and critically established methodology. Used in this way, theory permits activities which deny the specificity of particular investigations; it creates, in fact, the absurdity of experimentation as genre, of new work which is made to conform to the shape of the old.

The line between a theory which drives work forwards and a theory which holds work back is a fine one, and difficult to trace. What occurs in the making of work for performance is that it is the specificity of *this* encounter, at *this* time and determined by *these* variants which determines the theoretical approach to be taken. That the work, and the attendant theorising, may lead those involved in its study beyond the usual Catch-22 of its enclosure, taking them towards a new topography of terms, is germane to the ways in which new work is made. As such, *At Last Sight* is not being deliberately constructed as a paradigm of a particular *type* of work. Considerable efforts are being taken to ensure that the writing of *these* words is not allowed to pre-empt the writing of *those* words of script, in much the same way that directorial and performative decisions, articulated in Chapter Two, will be the subject of analysis rather than that, which takes analysis as its subject.

The writing of *At Last Sight* is poetic, or poeticised, at least to the degree that none of the sentences reads like 'natural' dialogue. Although there are some quite brief sections of the script which are designed to be indicative of two people engaged in conversation, these 'conversations' do not attempt to mirror those patterns of speech encountered in that which is regarded as 'real life'. There are a number of distinctions between poetry and prose, the chief, perhaps, being the idea that prose represents reality, whilst poetry, ultimately, refers only to itself. This distinction results in the act of prose being illustrative of an effort to translate an intention into an appropriate *result*, whereas poetry is more of a gratuitous discipline, one that is neither consequential nor motivated. As such, and sometimes perversely, poetry is both self-contained and open to a multitude of interpretations. *Feelings* are thus suited to poetic treatment in much the same way that *facts* are themselves the very stuff of prose. Lacking the documentary drive of prose, a poetic approach seems appropriate for the material of *At Last Sight*. If it is the case that the act of specific remembrance itself is fundamentally inarticulate, in that any of the words of prose we might possess and use are incapable of communicating much more than the factual details of the phenomenon. Then the script of *At Last Sight*, written in the way that it is, is intended to function as an inculcation of a spectator's personal emotional experiences. It does so through the elegising of my own partly disguised responses to a difficult (and difficult to deal with) time.

It may be true to say that postmodernism's predilection towards self-reflexivity has resulted in a situation wherein autobiographical material has become commonplace, where that which is, on the one hand, specific, is also representative of a rapidly tiring theme. In contemporary visual art we have seen enlarged endoscopic photographs of Mona Hatoum's internal organs projected onto gallery walls. We have walked around and into Tracey Emin's tent-installation, made art by the inscription on the canvas of the names of each of her overnight bedfellows, as we have gazed at her unmade bed. We have looked at Piero Manzoni's canned faeces, *Merda d'artista*, '100% Pure Artist's Shit' in its absolutely literal sense. We have recognised Marc Quinn's heat-reduced *Shit Head* and deep-frozen *Blood Head*. We have gazed at Cindy Sherman's relentlessly imaged face, whether in its guise of 1940s film-still, pathologist's photograph or Renaissance painting. In performance we have seen Carolee Schneemann's *Interior Scrolls* produced from her vagina; Karen Finley's down-stage-pointing, yam-juiced anus and Annie Sprinkle's 'Public Cervix Announcement', a torch-lit invitation for her audience to peer inside her.[32] At perhaps its most extreme, we see the performance artist Stelarc suspended by hooks through his non-anaesthetised body as he hovers over New York streets. As we have seen Orlan subjecting herself to a series of surgical re-configurations - to plastic surgery - as art-event. The residuum which is left over from Orlan's operations have become objects of art in themselves, with Madonna, amongst others, owning a section of flesh which was removed by scalpel from Orlan's thigh.[33] Orlan is anaesthetised, but only locally, in order that she can speak to her specators for the duration of the procedure. It is possible to make out a considerable list of self-reflexive practitioners, but to do so would serve only to labour an already-realised point. To the extent that the *self* has become the *subject*, so the subject of self has become an accepted and acceptable theme of contemporary art and performance.

Along the growing continuum of body and performance artists, of those who project rather than use their own life histories, psychologies and obsessions, my own approach to making work might seem quite tame. It is unlikely, for example, that *At Last Sight* will involve any elements of physical risk on the part of either the performers or spectators. The notion of taking risks in performance may provide for those artists, and perhaps also for some spectators, some form of liberation, a making-sense of the difficulties of existence. The less ostensibly emblematic risk-taking involved in the construction of the script for *At Last Sight* is in its encounter (in my encounter) with that which is most feared. With the personal perceptions and daily pain of past actions. The script 'for' is also the text 'of' *At Last Sight*, but the use of the word 'of' carries with it the suggestion that the script *is* the work. The work of the script and the work of the whole process is thus redemptive - it already is, in part - inasmuch as it is built upon a desire to come to greater terms with the ramifications of my own behaviour.

The art is being made with a multiple purpose. There is no one 'authorial intention', because that which the author intends is precisely that which is intended to remain hidden from view. The work is aiming for a form of redemption, and yet that which is being redeemed is not about to be made manifest to the spectators. What potential for *truth* there is in the work is thus made *false* by its very act of presentation. The fact that the presentational aspects of *At Last Sight* function through metaphor does not add to the falsity. The work is always already false in that there are no good reasons to support the idea that redemption achieves a greater value by dint of its being theatricalised and made public. We can say that the concealed nature of the rationale behind the project serves a purpose in that it prevents any notions of martyrdom from fuelling the performance. But this only serves to make the endeavour even further removed from any claim it might make to be regarded in some way as an 'honest' piece of work. The desire to tell in this way invalidates much of that which is told ... subsequently, we can no more trust the teller than the tale.

"No art could ever be truth", Richard Foreman informs us "the truth of art is in the audience's, the individual's awakened perceptions. It is not in the work of art."[34] If this is so, and I believe that it is, I have to question my own reasons for making work in the way that I am. Just as naturalism is theatre's truest absurdity, so honesty is the greatest myth of performance. Does this mean that I am making a crafted lie (the stuff of theatre) at the same time as I am basking in the self-gratifying illusion of truth (the fiercely guarded territory of performance art)? Certainly I am. Of that I have no doubt. I want to make work that succeeds as theatre *and* performance; to make art that works within and without artifice. This reveals a desire on my part to synthesise live art and lived experience. To synthesise without also arriving at an unknowing state of confusion.

We know enough to know that the attempt to *be* oneself within a performance frame will always fail and become a (re)presentation of self, inasmuch as the frame of performance precludes authentic presentation ... as Mrozek states in his article *Reality versus Theatre*, " trying to work out how to look genuine will never achieve life's authentic spontaneity."[35] The event of *At Last Sight* will be purposively mediated by the spectators, who will translate the experience *via* the individual processes of perception which they apply to the work. In effect, they will act as mediators between themselves and the stimulus, in much the same way that the participant members of the group will mediate between my intentions for the project and their own.

It might well be the case that to increase the stages of removal from whatever *realness* existed at the outset of the piece is to also increase the spectator's experience of a type of isolation. That the greater the mediation, the less potent is the sense of connection between the watcher and the watched. Exe Christoffersen, like Wilde, warns us against the pursuance of the real, telling us that

> authentic and original behaviour is an illusion. When the thought is first thought it is no longer something unspoiled, a change has taken place: a cultural change."[36]

Irrespective of location, frame or context it is the spectator who culturally and subjectively creates a meaning and a 'place' for the work. The spectator may be passive in an auditorium seat but is nevertheless active in a role of formulating a response to that which is seen.

> The see-er does not appropriate the world she sees, but in looking opens herself to it, lives in it from the inside, and becomes immersed in it."[37]

If we combine this with Michael Kirby's well-documented 'Symbolised Matrix of Acting'[38] then the intention of *At Last Sight* can be seen as an affording to the spectator of a central point of "identification of self-hood".[39] As Marvin Carlson puts it, "The audience is invited and expected to operate as a co-creator of whatever meanings and experience the event generates."[40]

It is to be hoped that the heavily end-noted nature of these concluding paragraphs does not result in a structure which decelerates the thrust of this report, even as it inevitably slows this chapter to a halt. The references are intended as a preparation for the impetus of Chapter Two. A chapter which will attempt, within the context of subjecting a creative and collaborative rehearsal process to analytical documentation, to pick its way through a postmodern preoccupation, which is also my own. To grapple with the uneasy and shifting relationship between the signifier and that which is signified; to map a route through semiotics, poststructuralism and phenomenology which takes the reader through the making process and on to performance.

From the 'My Self' of this chapter's introduction, the drift has taken us towards the Baudrillardian concept of reality as that which is not only capable of being produced, but "which is always already reproduced."[41] Towards Kantor's declaration that "in art truth is elsewhere."[42] It seems a relevant point of closure to this section. One which is also an introduction, and an invitation, to Chapter Two.

Notes

[1] Introduction to the Pierre Villey edition of *Essays*, Montaigne. Michel de Montaigne, Presse Universitaires de France, 1580.
Montaigne wrote an autobiography, published in 1580, which contained within it a justification for devoting a book to the 'trivial topic' of himself. Whilst admitting that his topic was relatively unimportantm he argued that this was offset by the fact that he knew his subject so much better than any other author could hope to know his. Montaigne's implication was that knowledge of one's self was the most complete and perfect form of understanding.
[2] By this I mean the following: That the public nature of performance amounts to a type of secret-telling to a room of strangers ... which seems antithetical to the subject matter. That channelling (something of) my own experiences through other performers and thence to spectators might amount to a form of dilution. That the activity of crafting something performative out of truth will take the presented form away from its origins and on towards something no less 'fake' than a well-rehearsed lie. That, as Philip Auslander points out when he refers to Andy Kaufman in *Presence and Resistance* (1994) 'any "Andy Kaufman" that appears on television cannot be real simply by virtue of having been constructed by the medium.' (p.151). In the same way, the fact

that *At Last Sight* is being constructed for performance augurs against the sense of 'real' I am pursuing. That performance might not be the most appropriate form to work through. The fact that performance is my 'area' does not mean that the concerns of *At Last Sight* might not be more effectively worked through in another medium. I am not sure, for example, how much will be constructively added to the script of *At Last Sight* by its being performed. Perhaps the work would be 'better' were it to be 'only' a written script, or a sculpting, or an abstract design. A part of this is not about a lack of confidence in my own abilities to make work of a certain quality so much as it signifies a lack of faith in performance itself.

[3] See Kantor, T 'The Theatre of Death (1975)' *The Drama Review* 30.3, 1986.

[4] For a detailed examination of a number of devising processes see Oddey, A *Devising Theatre*. Routledge, London & New York, 1997.

[5] See *Metafiction: The Theory and Practice of Self-Conscious Fiction*. Waugh, P. Routledge, London, 1984.

[6] Freud, S. *Art and Literature*. Penguin, London, 1985. pp. 66-68.

[7] For some of the occasions when this has not been the case see Bentley, E (ed.) *The Theory of the Modern Stage*. Penguin, Middlesex & New York, 1982

[8] See Onega, S and Landa *Narratology*. Longman, London & New York, 1996. Particularly Part Three, No. 9 'Authors, Speakers, Readers, and Mock Readers (F. K. Stanzel). pp 161-171

[9] By 'my own', I mean that my organisational and selecting participation in the *At Last Sight* project is likely to make my own sense of where the work should go the most dominant factor in the group. This is not to deny participation on the part of group members. I am expecting the project to draw heavily on the creative input of its personnel. However, the group will be made up of students, and the performance module this project will be a part of carries with it an insistence on staff-direction rather than devising in a non-hierarchical spirit.

[10] See Kaye, N (1994) Particularly the chapter 'Theatricality and the Corruption of the Modernist Work'. Pp. 24-45

[11] *ibid*

[12] See Macdonald, C. 'Assumed Identities: Feminism, Autobiography and Performance Art' in *The Uses of Autobiography*. J. Swindells (ed.), Taylor & Francis, London, 1995. pp. 187- 195.

[13] Derrida, J. 'Psyche: Inventions of the Other'. *Reading de Man Reading*. Ed. L. Waters and W. Godzich. Minneapolis: University of Minnesota Press, 1989. p. 194.

[14] See Hutcheon, L *Narcissistic Narrative: The Metafictional Paradox*, Methuen, New York, 1984. pp. 17-35

[15] *ibid*

[16] Bunuel, L. in *The Surrealist Connection: An Approach to a Surrealist Aesthetic of Theatre*. David G. Zinder. UMI Research Press, Michigan, 1976. p. 40.

[17] See *The Decay of Lying* (1891). Wilde, O. Penguin, London, 1995.

[18] *ibid.* p. 9.

[19] *ibid.* p. 16.

[20] Goleman, D. *Working with Emotional Intelligence*. Bloomsbury, London, 1998. p. 355.

[21] Cage, J. *Silence*. Marion Boyars, London, 1995. Cage states "I have come to be interested in anything but myself as art material." p. 70.

[22] It is evident by this point that, notwithstanding Barthes' assertions that 'text is a tissue of quotations drawn from the innumerable centers of culture' (Barthes, R 'The Death of the Author', *Image/Music/Text*, trans. Stephen Heath, Hill and Wang, 1977, p.146) I am regarding the text of *At Last Sight* as 'mine'.

[23] The students involved in *At Last Sight* selected the project. The directors or leaders of projects are expected to leave the students to reach their own conclusions as to which proposal to opt for, and canvassing by tutors is actively discouraged. Certainly, as far as *At Last Sight* is concerned, I approached no students in advance.

[24] For the relevant documentation regarding research assessment exercises visit the SCUDD web-site.

[25] Elwes, C. 'Floating Femininity' in Catherine Elwes & Rose Garrard (Eds.) *About Time*, London, ICA, 1980. p. 42

[26] Auslander describes this as 'The blending of real and fabricated personae and situations that occur when performance personae assume the same functions as "real".' Auslander (1994) p.78

[27] Spalding Gray was a member of The Wooster Group for several years, developing ideas of his own self through the work, to the point where he now describes himself as a 'monologist', teller of the tales of his own life. The impetus for this work began with his mother's death, which became a central aspect of The Wooster Group's performance of *Rumstick Road* (1976). The confessional tone of the work upset many critics, and a thorough description of both the work and the subsequent response can be found in David Savran's *Breaking the Rules*, TCG, New York, 1988. pp. 74-101. The development of Gray's work, away from 'character-acting' is chronicled in his own book *Swimming to Cambodia*, Picador, London, 1986.

[28] See James, W. 'Sameness in the Self as Known' in *Psychology*. World Press, New York, 1948.

[29] Appiah, A. K. *In my Father's House: Africa in the Philosophy of Culture*. Oxford University Press, 1992. p. 96.

[30] See Goodwin, A. *Dancing in the Distraction Factory: Music, Television and Popular Culture*. Routledge, London and New York, 1993, for a

discussion on the ways in which live performance and video are collapsing in on and simultaneously feeding off each other.

[31] From the Loeb edition of *Imagines*, ed. T.E. page, E. Capps and W.H.D. Rouse. William Heinemann, London and New York, 1931. p. 34.

[32] Work of this description is documented in Rebecca Schneider's *The Explicit Body in Performance*. Routledge, London and New York, 1997. Writing from a strongly feminist perspective, Schneider interrogates and contextualises culturally framed depictions of the explicit body in performance.

[33] A detailed analysis of Stelarc's performance activities can be found in Stelarc and Paffrath, James D. (eds.) *Obsolete Body/Suspensions/Stelarc*, Davis, CA: JP Publications, 1984. Orlan's work is discussed in the final chapter of Zarrilli, Phillip B. (ed.) *From Acting to Performance*, Routledge, London and New York, 1997.

[34] Richard Foreman, cited Drain, R. *Twentieth Century Theatre*. Routledge, London and New York, 1995. p. 68.

[35] Mrozek, S. *Theatre versus Reality*, 'New Theatre Quarterly', Vol. VIII, No. 32, Nov. 1992. p. 301.

[36] Christoffersen, E. *The Actor's Way*. Routledge, London and New York, 1992. p. 158.

[37] Merlau-Ponty, cited Klaver, E. *Spectatorial Theory in the Age of Media Culture*, 'New Theatre Quarterly', Vol. XI, No. 44, Nov. 1995. p. 312.

[38] See Michael Kirby, cited Zarrilli, P. *Acting (Re)Considered*. Routledge, London and New York, 1995. p. 44.

[39] Klaver. p. 313.

[40] Carlson, M. *Performance*. Routledge, London and New York, 1996. p. 197.

[41] Baudrillard, J. *Simulations*. Semiotext(e), New York, 1983. p. 146.

[42] Tadeusz Kantor cited in Drain, R. *Twentieth Century Theatre*. Routledge, London and New York, 1995. p. 67.

Chapter 2:
Script into Text

The group of students participating in the *At Last Sight* project has been determined. Now begins the process of developing a written script into text for performance.

I offered what little explanation I had at that time as to how we might commence the work. I had copies of the script for *At Last Sight*, which I passed out to the group. I emphasised the fact that no sections of the script had been written for either a male or female voice, but that I hoped the group would somehow draw on certain elements of that which was written, discarding others. I went to some lengths to explain that the script was to be regarded as one potentially influential ingredient in the creation of *At Last Sight*, but that we were not to regard it as an imposition. That it suggested a place to start rather than investing the project with a premature form of textual closure.

The students asked me to read the script aloud. When I did this two things became apparent. The first was that script, written as an elegiac, mournful exercise in what might be regarded at best as a striving for some sort of catharsis, at worst as a wallowing in aestheticised misery, *sounded* like an aggressive interrogation. The second, equally alarming aspect was that those sections which were originally *intended* to be confessional in an overtly romantic sense were now coming across as the words of an obsessive, of someone (let me throw caution to the wind here and say a *character*). A character, furthermore, who seemed to be confessing to a killing.

Reading the script to the students felt like reading someone else's words, except that I was aware at all times that this was not the case. What I know is that I have had no inkling of this *interpretation* (another caution to another wind) prior to the forty-five minutes that it took to speak the script.

On one level, this was and is pleasing. It suggests a way into the work that has been absent up until this time. It suggests something of mood, at the same time as it provides an in-built opportunity for pace. My own history of making work is that whenever I am at a loss for ideas I opt to slow the performers and the subsequent performance down, leading to moments of *longueur*, which I consistently struggle with.[1] The idea of an interrogative and aggressive feel to the piece creates a relatively new challenge to my own experiences, which is to the good. The problem, at this stage, is that I am concerned that the shift in direction pushes me away from the thoughts contained in both the introduction and first chapter of this book.

Without mentioning these new thoughts to the group, although with the suspicion that the manner of my own reading of the script, as my ideas of it developed, betrayed at least something of my thoughts, I asked the students for their first impressions. All said they felt, without prompting from me, that *At Last Sight* was a 'question and answer' script: a script for multiple voices and that it possessed a strong narrative drive, which related to the confessions of a man and the disappearance, reappearance and possible death of a woman. One student felt that the 'male' voices were precisely that, that they were plural, creating a 'narrative' made up of several confessions.

Reading the script now, as I interrupt the writing of this chapter, I cannot easily see how I could spend so many months without the slightest hint of these aspects, which now seem to permeate and drive the script, and also, inevitably, the production to come, quite so emphatically. I had become aware, in the days leading up to the establishment of a performance-group, that the script was 'dark'. That it might lend itself somehow to a certain *film noir* look and feel, but these thoughts did not serve as any real preparation for a directional, and directorial approach to emerge. I worry now that this may seem like the setting up of some false and deliberately fabricated dichotomy. That I might appear to the reader to be manufacturing an opportunity to say that whilst *then* I was thinking like a writer, *now* I am functioning as a director, with all of the intentional ramifications which that particular shift in role and responsibility carries with it. The only way I can answer those potential misgivings is to state that these are doubts which I myself do not feel. For me, this is a case of re-visiting one's own work with a fresh perspective.

One point, which needed to be stressed early on with the students, was that the work itself was going to be approached in a manner that embraced notions of heuristic research methodologies. Heuristics stems from *heuriskein*, a word that comes from the Greek and means 'to find'. It is more broadly associated with the idea of a search for information and knowledge which is as closely linked to internal and personal development as it is to the principles of fact-finding most commonly associated with research. I referred the students to a key text, 'Heuristic Research', in *Challenges of Humanistic Psychology*,[2] and explained that heuristics allows, and indeed demands, that the opinions, feelings, moods and intuitions of the researcher are present throughout the period of research. And that in addition to an increased understanding of the area being studied, the researcher will also chronicle the specific phenomena of increased self-knowledge and awareness.

The students were interested in these notions and seemed positive about the opportunity to legitimise their own feelings within a research programme. Heuristics can sometimes be regarded as 'soft' research, as a liberal inclination towards a reading of mood, rather than the offering up of hard, scientific data. I was pleased and impressed with the students' immediate grasp of heuristics as an addition to conventional approaches and not as a substitute for 'hard' analysis. Research through practice such as is being undertaken here involves people. To approach the work as though that human material were to function as something inanimate would be to disregard the very thing that makes performance what it is. Live work is lived, and the lived experiences of the participating students need to inform the book. How could they not? To separate the two out and say that the students will influence the practice but not the accompanying theoretical writing is to miss the point. *At Last Sight* is a written script. In one capacity it will always remain so. More importantly, however, it is now a project. People are involved.

As was outlined in the introduction to this book, we can say that heuristic processes offer an embrace of notions of self-discovery. As such, these processes are aligned to the type of creative rehearsal

which this project seeks to employ. The very act of discovery leads the discovering researcher to new points of knowledge and new directions to take, just as the irregularities of rehearsal, the all too familiar stop/start of thwarted ideas and precious days 'lost', leads the director into new areas of practice. As surely as the practical project which I am calling *At Last Sight* is being commenced with no real sense of how the finished work will appear to an audience, so the writing, these words appearing now on the screen as I write them and on the page as you read, provide mute evidence of a heuristically driven journey towards an unknown and unknowable point.

There is an immersion process with heuristics, which necessitates an openness and receptivity to the fluctuating (and frustrating) rhythms of research and rehearsal. In many ways, heuristics does not merely share a number of common features with the putting together of a creative project; it *is* a creative project. This means that heuristics functions as much more than a peg to hang the work on – as, in effect, a neat legitimising agent – it articulates a way of thinking, and a way of thinking *about* thinking, which has always formed the spine of the work.

Because heuristics is concerned primarily with the nature of knowing, whatever thoughts and attitudes exist in the mind of the researcher/maker, however temporary and disconnected they may appear to be, are imbued with the capacity to shift the process of investigation on into new fields of thought. Accordingly, research into the ways in which a practical performance project is being made is this at the same time as it is also other. The process provides space for the extension and development of a knowledge which is subject-specific at the same time as the self of the researcher is enhanced.

The thrust of this chapter is to be a report on practical creative and rehearsal work undertaken with the group of seven students. In this way, it is expected that a pattern will emerge, apparent in the documentation, which the quite different pressures of rehearsal will not always reveal. In some ways, therefore, I am predicting that a more clinical and critical observation of the processes of making this production will be arrived at through the greater distance provided by *writing* than *doing*. I believe this to be the case, not because in the mode of writer I am any less 'involved' in the project than when I am functioning as a staff-director, but because, by definition, a great number of directorial decisions are suggested without necessarily having formed an *a priori* understanding of the reasons behind the choices. The relationship between director and cast is a responsive one. Ideas move back and forth and a series of adjustments, compromises and re-negotiations are undertaken.

It is difficult within the context of such intense collaboration to keep track of whatever justifications might lie behind words offered and direction given. The process of documentation does not automatically lead to clarity, but it does provide a period, albeit brief, of reflection.

My primary motivation in documenting the creative process as it relates to *At Last Sight* is to create a certain type of structure. A structure wherein I am able to recognise more fully the routes by which practical performance work is arrived at and to make that recognition public in a coherent manner. This calls for an equal measure of reflective and communicative skills ... for without the former the book is devoid of purpose whereas an absence of the latter would deny the successful dissemination which publication demands. In the documentary and analytical process, I will face, as I have already, a series of recurring doubts as to my ability to make the work *work*, alongside a gnawing concern for issues of structure within the self-avowed liberality of my chosen approach. For example, if what I *feel* about the nature of heuristic research (and heuristic rehearsal) is that my own ongoing and *immediate* observations and intuitions are both authentic and *ipso facto* valid, then I am unable, in advance, to know much, if anything at all, of the territory through which the book and the performance project will move.

The way forward is to let go of structure. To recognise that the data, which this book will contain, resides already in me as much as it does in the nature of that which is being examined. To realise that the structure taken is the structure that is. The challenge is to extrapolate and articulate the salient elements of the process. This might appear to carry with it the implication of an editing process, of an after-the-event manipulation of material in a way which would then suggest a hidden structure (discernible to the informed reader) of a recognisably linear path through the process. This will not be the case here. Other than for the purposes of proof reading, this book will not be modified in any way *via* the knowledge afforded through hindsight.

In place of a pre-ordained structure, the heuristic approach undertaken here will evidence a direct and personal relationship between 'my self' the researcher and 'my work' the researched. This relationship ties in with the autobiographical thrust of the

performative written material that is, at present, *At Last Sight*. It
foregrounds the very ideas of self-directed search, immersion and
experience which have already categorised both 'Tracing the
Footprints' and the performance project thus far.

The 'new' feelings about the ways in which *At Last Sight*
appear to be developing will be conveyed within and through the
differing manners of documentation. It may be the case that theoretical
perspectives leading to analysis are integrated cleanly into some
sections of the documentation, whilst at other times the 'description'
of activities might be written with little or no attendant critique of the
work itself. The activity of writing this section as an integral part of
the process of creating a performance event means that, at certain
points, the distance between the *doing* and the *writing* may well be too
brief to allow thoughts to develop to an informative degree. If this
should happen, creating a chapter of variable worth to respective
readers, then it is hoped that those same readers will not lose too much
faith with the book itself. Whilst it will seem to some readers
inevitable that a chapter (*this* chapter) written during the process of
rehearsal is essentially a draft, subject to suggestion, criticism and
revision. It is the very linking in time of this chapter with the period of
developing the script of *At Last Sight* into a performance text that
makes the work what it is. Accordingly, and heuristically, this chapter
is commenced with no real idea as to where it might lead or by what it
might be led, or even whether it will emerge as one chapter or more.
It is thus as lacking in any projected sense of closure as the production
itself. The fact that this is being entered into without reservation is
central to the work and to the ways in which the work is subsequently
understood by future spectator/readers.

Because of the nature of this simultaneous doing and
recording, it is necessary here to lay some theoretical foundations.
Again, however, I am uncertain as to the extent to which I am creating
and installing foundations as opposed to exposing those already extant
positionings, which underpin the work being made. In many ways the
work cannot be made other than from the theoretical positions I
already occupy. The determinants mentioned in this book's
introduction have not disappeared and they still govern even the most
seemingly intuitive approaches. The following paragraphs then are
offered as an attempt at articulating those theoretically discernible
phenomena, which are fuelling the practical decisions and suggestions
being made to the cast of *At Last Sight*. Accordingly, that which I am

now writing is not dissimilar to the words I have spoken to the performers.

As an exercise in *teaching* as much as *directing*, I am duty-bound to discuss the rationale behind ideas, to foster a climate of developing confidence and collaboration amongst what amounts to an *ad hoc* and self-selecting group of students. A group, furthermore, of varying abilities and experiences. The students, all of them, wanted to know something about the 'structure' of the work, about how it might 'look', about the type of performative 'attitudes' they might be asked to adopt. None of the members of the group, for example, have any experience of entering into a production where they are not playing 'characters'. Although each member of the group has encountered a variety of methods of making work, they would, by almost any definition of the terms, be regarded as 'unskilled' and 'inexperienced' performers. They are less than comfortable with the idea of an absence of fixity, which means that I may be tempted to give them more clues at this stage as to where the work might lead than I would by choice.[3]

One of the first questions asked by the group about *At Last Sight* was about narrative. As this was the group's first concern, I shall begin there, although as the reader will note, the word is only used at this stage as a means of opening and broadening the area of discussion. I explained to the students that notions of narrative - much stronger to me now than they were just one week ago - alongside notions of character (vague but nevertheless apparent) were leading to questions of semiotics. Of what is intended to be significant in this work: of how I wish, or am imagining the audience to enter into the world of the performance. Ideas as to reality and artifice, which seemed to be driving me towards the project, are being joined as I write by issues of narratology and theme. As though that which once was concerned primarily with performative and non-performative states, with 'acted truth' and 'presented lies' is now being made to attend to issues of what might almost amount to plot-conveyance. This does not mean that the production-work will be allowed to drift too far away from my original intent. Indeed, the postmodern preoccupation with discerning signs from reality and also the phenomenologists' approach of a direct contact between an observer and an object or event which is classified as 'art' are still relevant to the ways the work might now develop. As also are those 'might have beens' of the way that it was shaping up to be before *people*, that sometimes-frustrating given of performance, altered my own insidious form of closure in the guise of freedom.

My 'ideas' for the first stages of rehearsal are being influenced by my interest in *Joiners*, a photomontage by the artist, David Hockney. *Joiners* has been utilised by Rienelt and Roach in an introductory explanation to the fields of structuralism and deconstruction.[4] It was through their incisive relocation of a purely visual form into the realms of performance that my own long-standing interest in Hockney's work, and particularly of *Joiners*, was both accelerated and enhanced. Approached as a paradigm for the ways in which work is read, *Joiners* provides an interesting way into performance, a way which is not suggested by Reinelt and Roach, and which is demonstrative of the processes through which the viewing of aestheticised objects is undertaken. If sections of performance are regarded in a similar way to frames of Hockney's work, both as being possessed of individual matrixes and also as part of a larger 'whole', then it is possible to set up a system of signs whereby the 'meaning' for each section is resident within its relationship to, *and position with*, those other sections which are located before, after or even at the same time as the section itself. This is the nature of theatre direction and the essence of montage, but approaching direction in a fashion analogous to Hockney's serves to foreground more directly the semiological connections that combine to form systems of signs.

In *Joiners*, just as a number of photographs are presented, so "different ways of seeing come into prominence and recede."[5] In a similar way, Hockney's creation of a grid, which is only apparent by the positioning of individual photographic images, creates a template for the ways in which *At Last Sight* might be constructed. Ferdinand Saussure posited the theory that individual 'units of meaning' only ever gain whatever meaning they possess when they are held in comparison to other signs.[6] To the extent that "any individual element is meaningless outside the confines of that structure."[7] In the same way, the scenic elements that make up the performance event of *At Last Sight* will derive their meaning from the relativity of their position to the bracketing created by the proximity of other scenes. The 'scenes' are thus offered as individual units at the same time as they are joined (to use the Hockneyesque term) by their relationship to the whole.

It will be useful here to ascertain the sense in which certain terms used in these introductory remarks is offered. Notwithstanding the broad familiarity, which most students of Drama have of the area of semiotics, it is apparent that the language itself is prone to a degree of ambiguity.[8] With regard to the notion of systems of signs, there will be evidence in the following pages of a debt to Saussure, for whom the sign is composed of two parts, a material *signifier*, a word, spoken or written, an image, and a *signified*, a concept. There is no essential relationship between signifier and signified, only a culturally agreed link. In this way, signs are seen to operate as part of a *system* and their meanings *(sic)* derive directly from their relationship to the other signs within the system. They are unable to function as individual *logos* of identical, or even similar, meaning if they are isolated from that system. In subsequent paragraphs, I will refer to the *referent*, a term employed to considerable effect by Roland Barthes. 'Referent' means the actual object, image or action which is referred to at any given moment in the work: so that, whilst a performer is always herself, she is also, although not *always*, a referent for something (someone) else. Already it seems as though I am predicting a production wherein the independence and autonomy of each 'moment', when located in a sometimes contradictory or juxtapositional relationship to other moments, will lead the spectator towards a questioning of the overall 'meaning' of the work.

It may be the case, and a part of me clearly *intends* it to be so, that the spectator is also invited to question the extent to which it is possible to derive any conclusive meaning from performance at all.

Within this projected method of rehearsal, the biological presence of the one who refers is as important as that which is referenced. The created performance of *At Last Sight* is of a no greater consideration than the exposed pattern of signs contained in the production in both its 'moments' and its entirety. As the eye shifts through time so the spectator will be encouraged to see the scenes as singular signs. The referent images (of scene, of sense, of *other*) are fractured and the signifiers and signifieds may confuse or even bar the way towards 'understanding'. This will result (and I am aware of the dangers, and contradictions, of speaking of 'results' at the start of rehearsal) in the raising of questions as to the possibility of deciding upon any stable meaning whatsoever. At this point, I should perhaps turn towards a post-structuralist view, to better see how it is that the reduction of emphasis on the signified, and the increased focus on the signifiers, will provide indications as to a spectator's *directed* reading of *At Last Sight*. If the meaning of each sign within the system is dependent upon its difference to other signs, then the overall creation or, indeed, identification of meaning becomes unstable. Each 'scene' within *At Last Sight* (I could say 'moment' or 'section') will have its own relationship to the surrounding scenes and its meaning will be identifiable by its difference to its neighbours. I can go further and say that each scene will gain its meaning or its concept (its *signified*) from its similarities to its neighbours. Each and every performative moment is a sign comprised of a signifier (the image) and a signified (the concept). Within its own specific frame a signified of its own small referent is offered, whereas when the spectator begins (or is allowed) to add these moments together the referent becomes larger and the network and interplay of signs begins to build into a system. The written script of *At Last Sight*, as it currently stands, has itself been constructed in this way.

The building of the system here will probably not, however, fully add up. The overall meaning of the system may emerge as somewhat greater than the sum of the signs, and aspects may well emerge in the work which are at once both within the system at the same time as they are unidentifiable as discrete and functional signs. As Derrida has written, "the movement of signification adds something ... to supplement a lack on the part of the signified",[9] and it is this added extra element, the 'transcendental signifier',[10] to use Derrida's term, that allows the spectator to become the ultimate creator of meaning. 'Sense' is thus defined by the way in which the signs are read and by the receptive weight given to the elements seen rather than by the semiotic potency of the signs.

The *At Last Sight* of this point of rehearsal is revealing itself as intrinsically postmodernist. It is not my intention to submit *At Last Sight* to its spectators as a paradigm of postmodern performance. Postmodernism has already passed into the *passé*, to the extent that formulaic lists of its tendencies have been published.[11] Where postmodernism still seems to possess vitality is in its refusal to fix and its disinclination to close down. If postmodernism is identifiable by one element, that element is contained in a shifting away from readily rationalised solutions. Where postmodernism has moved towards an awareness that the very tools and techniques we have been using to free ourselves from ignorance have themselves become enslaving doctrines it has left behind a philosophy that I remain happy to embrace. Postmodernism, although differing to a degree in terms of the specificity of some concepts and ideologies, can be said to subsume post-structuralism, and, as such, postmodern notions of performance making will be providing an umbrella underneath which this project is to be made.[12]

If we distrust and ultimately deny the idea of grand-scheme solutions, then we begin to see that the shift from a belief in something being an *original* to the awareness that everything is a *copy* leads inevitably towards a questioning of the validity and 'realness' of all things.[13] It is certainly the case that these feelings are informing my ideas for the work. This continues to be the case even though, at this point, all that has emerged is a vague idea of performers playing out the 'roles' of the performance with varying degrees of certainty, so that issues of 'acting', of 'being', of 'truth' and of 'lies' permeate the fabric of the work. Even in writing these words, however, I am aware of my own unspoken inclinations towards a type of essentialism. As though a belief in truth – in something that matters – is within me, despite my embracing of notions of simulacrum *ad infinitum*. Writing the word truth without the qualification created by inverted commas or italicisation leads to a heady sensation: a queasiness brought on by risk and *naivety* in equal measures. If a gnawing essentialism runs counter to postmodern *chic* then so be it. This book is not intended as a mantra towards the idols of our age. If I did not believe in some form of redemptive qualities in the making of art (I have more doubts as to the possibilities of redemption through spectatorship) then I would not be trawling my own past for the written material of *At Last Sight*. Richer and more profound material is all around. I believe in redemption and I believe in truth. What concerns me is my ability (or otherwise) to recognise either if or when they appear.

Notwithstanding this, I am continuing to work within and through an ostensible distrust of reality, just as postmodern performance strategies invite their audiences to deny authoritarian solutions through the adoption of a sceptically slanted gaze. If "the notion that our experience of reality is organised and determined by the images we make of it"[14] is a true one, then the sentiment is appropriate to *At Last Sight*. It is so inasmuch as the work undertaken in rehearsal is designed to create a production wherein ideas of reality are brought into question by a process of looking clearly and with *knowing doubt* at the images we are making of the performance. Baudrillard has attempted to remove our reliance on the word 'signs', replacing them with *codes*, which are seen to exist as unshifting points of reference. Although Baudrillard might follow the Saussurian concept that "no object exists in isolation from others",[15] this Baudrillardian 'code' is actually replacing the sign. It is not only the reproduction of the referent, it *is* the referent, and the two have become indistinguishable, indeterminable one from the other.

At Last Sight is thus a system of codes which, working in relation to each other, (re)produce the referent. Baudrillard forces us to stop searching for the referent: the search is futile as there are no 'real' originals and everything is already a reproduction and representation ... "the difference between copy and original is redundant."[16] *At Last Sight* is claiming that the referent can be viewed from another position, the position of the creation of meaning. In this way - and this is central to the starting position - the moments refer to the referent, but the referent *is* the referral. What the spectator sees then is image and comment in one ... the two phenomena exist interdependently and cannot be separated.

This ideological and directorial perspective has arisen out of a searching for a practical method of dealing with a shift that I have begun to recognise in my own thinking. The shift is from a search for explanations within the prescribed and directorial forms provided in performance towards a realisation that the referent's meaning always resides within the spectator, which is the very stuff of heuristics. The interpretation and decision of a performance is never other than individualised. It is a series of meanings to which no universal or standardised explanation can fully apply. That it is the 'I' of the spectator and not the 'I' of the director who determines meaning. Accordingly, my own directorial practice must strive, if I am in any practical sense committed to the idea of progression, towards an accommodation of this theoretical positioning. The difficulty occurs because of the realisation that these idealised notions of personal contextualisation are contaminated by the social and cultural determinants of thought that this book keeps returning to. In this way, the cultural circumstances which encapsulate every spectator's frame of reference will be what determines the interpretation. The director's role is subject to a deep and contradictory disturbance, for what is *it* that I am seeking to direct my individual spectator's attention towards? How can I *direct* the performers if I have so little idea of where we are going?

Clark Moustakis, in detailing the specifics of his own research procedures, also provides a telling treatise on creative, rather than interpretative, direction. If we substitute Moustakis' words

'learning' and 'searches' for 'direction' and 'directing' the similarities
emerge with immediacy

Learning that proceeds heuristically has a path of its own. It is self-
directed, self-motivated, and open to spontaneous shift. It defies the
shackles of convention and tradition ... It pushes beyond the known,
the expected, or the merely possible ...without the restraining leash

of formal hypotheses, and free from external methodological
structures that limit awareness or channel it, the one who searches
heuristically may draw upon the perceptual powers afforded by direct
experience.[17]

To add yet another complexity to the issue, my own
acknowledged determinants include Roland Barthes. It was Barthes
who, within the space provided by the short publication that was
Camera Lucida,[18] set up an *examination* of the nature of photographs.
In so doing he initiated a discourse on the principles of absence and
presence which has formed the mainstay of much subsequent writings
on performance. For Barthes, "a specific photograph, in effect, is never
distinguished from its referent,"[19] creating a tautological dimension to
photography in which the referent is always present. Indeed, Barthes
goes on to postulate that the referent is all that can ever exist, that the
photograph is invisible and absent because it is the referent that
consumes our gaze. Barthes' ideas of photographic absence are
important to the creative processes behind *At Last Sight*, which is not
to suggest that I have as yet located a comfortable method of dealing
with them.

If it is not possible to separate a theatrically constructed
image from its referent, if there is an inextricable binding together of
the two. Then the successful attempt to remove the referent (if such an
act is possible) would be to render the image as referentially neutral, as
nothing other than itself. It follows then that in applying Barthes'
views to *At Last Sight* (or to generic performance) it would be possible
to remove the problem of assigning signifiers and signified to the
performance event. In so doing it would turn the spectator's gaze to
the referent, to the performer as communicator and communicated.
The compositional element of each performed image can and will
consist of signification, inasmuch as an aesthetic directorial
(directional?) control will be in evidence.   But in allowing the

spectator to see that every scene within the production is the result of a conscious decision, of *choice*, a suggestion will be made that it is that choice which is significant rather than the ideas that are contained in the referentiality of acted 'other'.

Hints of phenomenology are emerging here. At least to the extent that we can recognise that "phenomenologists like to pick up objects ... turn them around, examining them from all sides ... (and that) this cannot be accomplished by viewing them frontally as they are embedded in the rest of the experiential world."[20] If there is an underlying conceptual distinction between semiology and phenomenology it is that whilst with the former everything relates to something else (we could even say that everything *is* something else) in the latter case everything is nothing *but* itself. In this sense, a phenomenological position is informing the notions I have of the way the rehearsals of *At Last Sight* might develop towards performance. It is impacting on the ways that I would wish the work to be read; although we would do well to remind ourselves that phenomenology allows research without *direct* experience, whereas heuristics demands a full experiential engagement. Seen in this way, a phenomenological approach may be of value to a spectator in much the same way that a heuristic approach functions for the researcher/maker who has experienced an ongoing contact with the work.

Before proceeding further with this, however, I need first to make some decisions as to how this is likely to happen. In stating this I am recognising, as has been pointed out in earlier sections of this work, that the onus of analysis is already inclining me towards ways of working which are not normative within my own previous experience. What I mean by this is that I have never in the past, when working on productions, sought to document directorial inclinations in the way that I am attempting here.[21] A consequence of this is that notions of the work on *At Last Sight* as constituting a case study of a *production* from idea to realisation are flawed before the event. What is being undertaken is an overt example of practice as research, which differs from practice for the sake of practice itself.

Phenomenologically then, it is possible to approach *At Last Sight* as a developing object in its own right, to see it as a part of the empirical world, and to look at it in those terms. We can analyse *At Last Sight*, for example, in the same way that one could study a pebble or a blade of grass, not as elements of a coastline or a field, but as nothing more or less than the things themselves. Alternatively, we could say that *At Last Sight* will exist in a co-present state, whereby the empirical world is put on hold. In this way we accept that the production is at once an attempt to seduce the spectator into a suspension of belief in reality at the same time as it activates a belief in the illusionary. It is this second approach that most powerfully engages me as a theoretical 'ideal' that might, perhaps, lead the work into an interesting location. In this way, at least in my directorial imaginings, the spectator will be invited not so much to make an empirical inspection of the performance as to provide an imaginative intuition of it. If this is in any way successful, if it results in an ability to view *At Last Sight* as an event removed from its cultural and empirical connotations and if it frees the spectator to regard it as something which exists within its own frame of reference … then the work will have achieved much of that which is being targeted. That in art all things function as they are perceived and that the event's relation to the percipient is ultimately the only one that matters.

In this, phenomenology flirts with postmodernism, at once embracing an absence of mass meaning at the same time as it prioritises individual absorption. Bert O. States tells us that it is the "first four seconds" that are the most vital in our process of determination.[22] That the empirical world is put on hold as we trust only our connection with that which we see. And yet, it is this previously experienced outside world which has provided us with the library of seemingly intuitive references, which in their own turn allow us to arrive at the 'immediate' and untrammelled perceptions of States' understanding of phenomenological immediacy.

What a phenomenological approach does provide is a position whereby the debate as to the location and efficacy of signs becomes an irrelevance. The act of negotiation leading to meaning emerges as the sole responsibility of the percipient and it is s/he and s/he alone who must create a signification between performative moments and their relationship to a referent as and when they occur. Having said this, it should be pointed out that *At Last Sight* contains its share of semiotic indicators, some of which are deliberately misleading … or deliberately 'leading'.

After discussing these ideas of 'truth', 'lies' and 'belief' with the group (inverted commas again: the absence felt like too much risk) we have decided to advertise the group as a collective of lovers, current and ex, and to include this false fact in any and all pre-production publicity. (It is important to note that this is the first time I

am able to use the word 'we' in this book without any feelings of
trying to conjure up a false sense of democracy.) The decision was not
a whimsical one and neither was it intended to cause mischief. In
terms of theatre, we are strongly predisposed to believe what we read
about the company in question precisely because the written
information is seen to exist beyond the frame of performance. This is
so because the power of the written word is derived in part at least
from its permanence. If I read that Goat Island is a performance
collective from Chicago, I believe it because I have no reason to doubt
it, and also because printed words afford the claim a different and
more pressing type of authority to words uttered in performance. If the
sleeve notes from Gavin Bryars' *Jesus' Blood Never Failed Me Yet* tell
me that the voice heard is that of a homeless man in London, now
dead, I not only believe them whole-heartedly but the experience of
listening to the compact disc is radically affected by that belief.
Similarly, if programme notes exist to tell me something of the genesis
of the work I am about to see, then why would I distrust them? A
woman tells a man, in performance, that she loves him ... it is
performance *ergo* I (have to) doubt the voracity of the sentiment. If the
same woman is described in a programme as being the same man's
lover, I believe it entirely and without question.

    The decision to advertise the group thus has opened up
what appears to be a new way of working: simple activities and
encounters are 'loaded' differently and the performers' on-stage
behaviour seems suddenly much less mannered. Certainly, I feel more
confident about the piece now that it is (and we are) set to sail under
this new and false banner. It carries with it the assumption, and it may
be one that I make overt, that the group has been formed because of
their emotional connections, rather than as an auditioned and selected
troupe. As such, it may be the case that spectators read the work as
something other than performance in the pursuit of polished
excellence. It is much more of a salve here to my own insecurities than
any damning critique of the performers *per se*.

    The students and I are attempting to extend the frame of the
performance to the extent where, in effect, the spectators are unaware
of the point where the work starts and finishes. There seems little
alternative to this. If the spectators were to know that the information
they receive is untrue, then the frame would still be extended but the
rationale behind it would be ruined. It is still too early to foresee the
implications of this deceit on the way the work of *At Last Sight* will

develop. The vagaries of student-timetabling, alongside my own teaching and tutorial commitments means that we have only met as a group on seven occasions - but I have no doubts that the lie will drive the piece in directions we had never previously considered.

This raises the question of the extent to which my words on these pages are to be believed by the reader. As a self-confessed dealer in 'lies' in one form, that knowledge will compromise the integrity of 'truths' in another. The assumption of honesty afforded by the reader may have been lost in the last few paragraphs. All I can hope is that a distinction can be made between telling the truth about lies and disguising lies as truth. As this book is not about 'explaining things' so much as analysing my own processes as they relate to *At Last Sight*, I make no claims for (or against) one approach over another. We - the group and I - are telling lies to our hosts. I am attempting an honest documentation of the process of making *At Last Sight*, even when that process involves dishonesty. The reader can trust the tale if not quite still the teller.

In writing about general issues of making work with students I am aware that I am avoiding the matter of specifics. Perhaps what it is that has pre-empted this unwillingness to write in any detail about the ways in which the group functions is no more than a primitive type of caution. A fear that to say too much about the students is to invoke the wrath of the idealised ensemble. There is also the feeling that to be critical in private - inasmuch as none of the students will have access to the tenor of these pages until long after they have graduated - is an invidious form of hypocrisy. That it is a praising in public and a subsequent carping in the seclusion of an office after-hours. Writing about a sense of 'team spirit' was never my intention, and, in fact, I can state that the recognition of this has only arrived with the typing of these words. It is dawning on me (and I am more than a little embarrassed to realise how late) that my use of the term 'the group' has been used exclusively to refer to the seven students, never to the eight of *us* who are pooling our resources to one end.

This is because we, as a group, are now much more aware of the vocabulary of the performance of *At Last Sight*. Whereas at the start of the academic year it was very much a sense of the group being directed it now seems as though the piece is being devised. I write this with a knowledge of the fact that distinctions between 'devising' and 'directing' are awkward and confused, and that the idea of devising is much more commonly associated with work where no script exists as a dramatic blueprint for performance than in instances such as ours, where the script, being all we had to start with, was imbued with prominence.[23]

The approach undertaken in this particular example of practice-led research is diachronic, in that the written elements of the book are moving through time in a similar way to the practical element of *At Last Sight*. Accordingly, this chapter moves now some six weeks forward ... a new phase if not quite a new chapter.

Many changes have happened, one of the most immediately identifiable areas is that of autobiography ... of *At Last Sight* as a project which is driven by my own desires for a work which leads towards catharsis for the artist.

If at the start of the project my intentions were geared towards the performative articulation of 'truth', of selected aspects of my own history given voice through the mouths and movements of others, then that desire has been diluted by the group's emerging 'ownership' of the work. Accordingly, a high degree of that which we can call catharsis has already been achieved.

If I am unable to regard the work with anything approximating to an 'outside eye' then I am no longer sure of my role. This feeling of increasing redundancy at precisely those moments when my knowledge of the work should (?) make me most necessary and useful is not a new one. I have experienced similar states whilst working on previous projects; however, in the past I have always seemed able to draw on something which provided me with a location from which to stand outside and view the work. Here, because I am working in a way which is new to me, I have no responses to trust other than my own. For example, the issue of lies and truth, which could be said to have initially prompted the work, is one that I am coming to with no theatrical experiences to draw from. In effect, the 'rules' of the performance are being drawn up alongside the piece and I have no way, other than by a series of estimations, of knowing the extent to which the choices I am making will hold good.

This feeling is a tacit recognition of the ways in which the making of *At Last Sight* has been approached. I have utilised a way of working which has allowed me to 'improvise' throughout the process. What is *not* meant here is improvisation in terms either of the Mike Leigh approach or of that made widespread by the publication of Keith Johnstone's 1981 book, *Impro*.[24] Rather, it is an approach towards directing which has allowed for the consideration of any and all interventions and shifts in emphases during the work's construction. This has been characterised as another kind of control towards the achieving of relevant form and not as a wilful and arbitrary procedure.

Relevance is measured from two points of view. Firstly, in as far as it fulfils my own acknowledged need not to work from a pre-determined plan but to create 'intuitively' throughout the making of the performance piece, and secondly, to be able to effectively communicate this approach in written form. In these ways, we can say that the practical aspect of the research work undertaken is experimental, in as far as intuitions are tested out and remoulded in relationship to those tests (which is, in fact, the very stuff of rehearsal) in order to create appropriate solutions for performance. It is comparative as well as theoretical inasmuch as certain observations are made and conclusions are reached (as a consequence of these comparisons) about the nature of performance practice within the work of one individual practitioner (myself) and how this may subsequently be read as a valid part of the practice as a whole.

Therefore, certain conditions which remained - or sought to remain - constant throughout the research have proven themselves too slippery, elusive and restrictive to maintain. Two examples serve to establish this point. Initially, for instance, and notwithstanding notions of heuristic methodologies, the research was intended to remain predominantly retrospective. The retrospection was intended to function inasmuch as I was operating, at the time, with the thought that this would avoid the situation wherein the creative work undertaken would be pre-emptively sullied by analytical concerns. It is also true (and it makes an obvious connection) that an early and unsustainable distinction was made between the activity of making and that of reflecting upon that making. These two issues were clearly interrelated and interdependent, but nonetheless were believed to have their own unique identities. What has *actually* happened is that the research has managed to become intertwined with the practice. There is no distinction: the process of thinking and writing, talking and doing feeds off itself without, as yet, any sign of exhaustion.

Not only has it emerged that it is impossible for solitary reflection on one rehearsal to do anything other than inform work on the next, it has, with the benefit of hindsight, become crucial that it this cyclical pattern is encouraged, given space and licence to evolve.

Because research within the practice of performance, of practice as research, is a relatively new discipline, it has been necessary to develop an effective means of carrying out the analysis needed to document the work. These means have borrowed, at least in part, from observations of non-theatre based disciplines.[25] Notwithstanding its scarcity within the field of performance, the relevance of using an individual's own practice as a means towards an understanding of how artists work is not in itself new. It may, indeed, be the only way for an artist to examine the situation of the making of practice. For how else can the observer know more than he or she observes? Clark Moustakis found this to be the case in his study of loneliness *as a subject*, precisely within his own situation as the lonely subject,[26] in much the same way that Igor Stravinsky's series of published lectures, *Poetics of Music*, contains the following progressive disclaimer

> What I intend to say to you will not constitute an impersonal exposition of general data, but will be an exploration of music as I conceive it. Nor will this explanation be any less objective for being the fruit of my own experience and personal observations.[27]

Stravinsky continues by saying that because he tests his observations through his own experiences, he is not offering opinions so much as findings, which, accordingly, are as valid for him as any others. Stravinsky's observations are echoed by the artist, David Smith, who writes

> I make no attempt to generalise dispassionately. My statements are coloured and prejudiced by my own concepts and experiences.[28]

We could say that whereas music, as Stravinsky's paradigm, occurs through and organises time, David Smith's sculptures exists in space, organising that space through material and process. As a hybrid form, performance can be seen to function at the interface between sound and object, between time and space, duration and location. Something of the difficulties of the two extremes is there, just as much of the licence enjoyed by each form is present in the ephemerality of live performance. I write this because the work that *At Last Sight* is 'becoming' is starting to 'feel' like it should be an installation. The fact remains, if only by dint of its inclusion at a festival of theatre and in a traditional theatre space, that the work will resist this pull, remaining a piece of work which moves through time whilst staying firmly rooted on the theatrical stage.

However, I will speak, if only very briefly, about why the pull towards installation is a strong one. Firstly, we know that theatre deals with metaphorical space: the stage masquerades as a drawing room, a battlefield, a palace; just as the theatre lights are signifiers of (an)other time, atmosphere and location. In short, the theatrical space seeks (usually) to invest its on-stage world with values and features of elsewhere. Even when the work is an overt reaction against naturalism, we are still likely to witness the invocation of 'other'. Peter Brook takes us, or at least our *minds*, to Arjuna's chambers. Bertolt Brecht takes us to Arturo Ui's dressing room; Steven Berkoff to a mythical East End of London out of Sophocles' Thebes. Installation, on the other hand, tends to utilise its own *actual* space, drawing on both the historical/cultural *ambience* of the location and its concrete physicality. In this, there exists a type of 'truth' in installation. A truth that is more or less denied to theatre. For whereas an installation can move towards the highly theatrical a theatre piece is hemmed in by its own artifice ... the truth can go on to lie, but the lie can never then tell truth.[29]

There is another, less philosophical and more pragmatic reason why the notion of developing *At Last Sight* into a work of installation is so tempting. Theatre requires and feeds off variations in pace, rhythm, mood and meaning, amongst a host of other phenomena. The spectator is taken on a journey by the creator(s) of the theatrical product. The nature of *At Last Sight* is that it has developed its own somnambulistic pace ... its inner energies are overtly contemplative rather than dynamic. Re-working, or developing the piece into an installation would allow for the continuance of a lethargic pace inasmuch as differences in the receptive experience of the work would be determined by the spectators' activity of moving physically from one space to the next.

At Last Sight will maintain its theatrical essence, which is not the same as saying that the emerging interest in subversion *via* installation is something that cannot impact on the work. If nothing else has been learned by this stage it is that we cannot delete from the mind, and that *all* thoughts and ideas of the performance will inform the performance in one way or another. Indeed, we could say that the chief value of this book, as its title suggests, is that it is seeking to trace and document these very changes of mind as and when they occur. Any awkwardness in the reading, therefore, is a mirroring of this process of making.

This is research on my own processes. It has excluded
other approaches and is not concerned with the making of
comparisons between my own and the practice of others. The research
of performance practice does not lend itself to statistical averages, as
the practice is designed uniquely in each case. One of the guiding
principles of the research, and it is one which has remained
throughout, is the notion of appropriateness. Of research which is not
carried out primarily for its own sake, but for the development of
research itself, of a *way* of researching, which is relevant to the wider
practice and understanding of performance. This implies that the
research will be at once unique - different to that which might be
carried out by somebody else, elsewhere, looking at different work - at
the same time as it is capable of dissemination amongst my colleagues
and peers.

A reading of 'explanatory' works from artists practising
across a range of media suggests that the use of aesthetics or any kind
of theory is ascribed a differing value *at the time of creation*
depending upon the working practices of the artist. A feature of much
postmodern work, for example, is the relationship *with* theory *through*
practice.[30] With a number of other approaches, although theory is
clearly regarded as having a valuable role to play in post-creation
analysis, it is not always deemed useful *in creation*.[31] As Claude
Debussy was wont to say, 'theories do not make works of art';[32] and
Picasso, famously, refuted all notions that his art product was driven in
any way by a theoretically motivated mind.[33] My own experiences,
however, suggest a broadly postmodern line; which is not the same
thing as stating that my work on *At Last Sight* amounts to the creation
of a set of rules or code of practice which would be true for all
practitioners and for all time. The subject of theatre may be taught in
this way, but it is seldom practised like it.

What is meant here is that the theatricalisation of theory
has become a feature of my theoretical reflection on theatre. During
the early stages of this project, my own process of working might, with
hindsight, have been described as lateral rather than linear. I was
seeking to address a number of aspects of constructing the discrete
elements of performance in order that they might be later brought
together into one final 'whole'. In later months, as the work
developed, these processes evolved into a procedure wherein each of
the processes was combined.

The path of inquiry to this point has by no means been in a straight line. Rather, it has been comprised of a series of exploratory meanderings by means of which I have acquired valuable experiences – and continue so to do - as well as gaining an increased understanding of my own artistic personality during the process of making a work of performance. 'Artistic personality' may be at once the clumsiest and most pretension-laden of terms, but it is offered here as one which seeks to encompass something of the distinction between the 'I' of everyday activity and the 'I' as observed during the making of art. The edges are blurred and indistinct, and ideas of art 'intrude' at times when the mind is at its least expectant or inviting.

The fact that the inquiry has not followed a straight line has been a consequence of my undertaking of rehearsal as a process of creation rather than repetition. This has brought with it a rejection of certain lines of inquiry alongside the picking up of new ones, and dealing with these rejections and attractions will form much of the content of subsequent chapters. Relatively early changes were apparent in my rejection, or my move away from, initial ideas about autobiography, in favour of a more complex negotiation of truth and lies within an equally complex written frame. A new language was beginning to evolve which brought with it a dialogue between myself and the problems that I had created, both for myself and for the group - and, by wider implication, for any spectators of the work.

Where choices have been made, they are not offered here as solutions for every practitioner working on every project. My earlier comments sought to distance myself from such a claim (or charge) and I can only reiterate that to suggest a series of all-encompassing answers would be misleading in terms of understanding the practice of making performance. That which is documented in these pages is no more or less than an articulation of the individual choices, which have, come to function as elements within a composed and evolving structure, which *this* practitioner has formed for *this* project. What is chosen is up to the individual, but those choices are controlled by the language and assumptions which every practitioner holds in relation to the practice they are undertaking.

Notes

[1] In this, my approach to making work is antithetical to Elizabeth Lecompte's processes with the Wooster Group, where she urges the performers on to greater speed whenever she gets bored with rehearsals. See Savran, D. *Breaking the Rules: The Wooster Group*. UMI Research Press, Michigan, 1986.

[2] Clark Moustakis' contribution to the field of heuristic research methodology is considerable, and his writings have informed this book no less than they have impacted on my approach to lecturing. In addition to Moustakis' paper in J. F.T. Bugental's *Challenges of Humanistic Psychology*. New York: McGraw-Hill, 1967, other influential works read in the period leading up to the undertaking of *this* particular research project include Moustakis, C. *Loneliness*. Englewood Cliffs, New Jersey: Prentice-Hall, 1961 and Moustakis, C. *Loneliness and Love*. Englewood Cliffs, New Jersey: Prentice-Hall, 1972. The three texts, taken together, will provide any reader of this book with a thorough overview of heuristic research processes and will articulate and contextualise the area in ways which this writer cannot hope to match.

[3] A consequence of this is that I feel I need to provide clues as to the potential shape of the work when I would rather let the project evolve in its own way. It is at this point that I am beginning to recall some of the negative aspects of working with a group. The fact that they care enough about the work to care about the way that it will (probably) be made is reassuring, but their collective need to know is out of sync with my own.

[4] Reinelt, J & Roach, J. *Critical Theory and Performance*. Michigan University Press., 1992

[5] *ibid.* p. 109.

[6] Pierce, C. S. *Writings on Semiotics*. University of North Carolina Press, Chapel Hill & London, 1991. pp. 47-54

[7] Lechte, L. *Fifty Key Contemporary Thinkers*. Routledge, London and New York, 1994. p. 150.

[8] See Pierce (1991).

[9] Derrida, J. *Structure, Sign and Play*. University of Chicago Press, 1978. p. 289.

[10] *ibid.* p. 111

[11] Martin, J. *Voice in Modern Theatre*. Routledge, London, 1991. p.119.

[12] For an analysis of the ways in which the two approaches differ and overlap see Sarup, M. *Post-Structuralism and Postmodernism*. Harvester Wheatsheaf, Hertfordshire, 1993.

[13] I am using 'we' here as a reference to spectators, critics and readers of book, rather than the 'we' of the *At Last Sight* group. In fact, I am not convinced at this stage of the project that the members of the group share

these views at all. That it will comprise a way of working does not mean that it will create a way of thinking.

[14] Simms, S. *Postmodern Thought*. Icon Books, 1998. p. 95.

[15] Lechte, L, 1994. p. 234.

[16] *ibid.* p. 235.

[17] Douglass, B and Moustakis, C. 'Heuristic Inquiry: The internal search to know. *Journal of Humanistic Psychology*. Vol. 25(3). pp. 39-40.

[18] Barthes, R. *Camera Lucida*. Vintage Books, 1982.

[19] *ibid.* P. 5.

[20] Reinelt & Roach, 1992. p. 354.

[21] Production work feeds into one's teaching, just as teaching feeds into subsequent productions. The relationship is, in my experience, rich and rewarding. What distinguishes the approach being taken with *At Last Sight* is that the processes are being made subject to analysis, which is both immediate and reflective. Connections that might otherwise be made casually are, in this case, demands I am making on myself.

[22] States, B in Reinelt & Roach, 1992. p. 371.

[23] See Oddey (1997).

[24] Mike Leigh's use of improvisation as a means towards the creation of character and plot has been evidenced most emphatically in his critically acclaimed productions for stage and screen. A critical referencing of his processes can be found in Clements, P. *The Improvised Play: The Work of Mike Leigh*. Methuen, London, 1983.
Issues of improvisation in terms of theatre exercises are contained in Johnstone, K. *Impro: Improvisation and the Theatre*. Methuen, London, 1981.

[25] Books such as Gordon Graham's *Philosophy of the Arts*. Routledge, London & New York, 1997, cover the work of many artists working in many forms. Performance references are notable through their absence. Graham's work is not alone in this regard. Other than through references *via* Plato and Aristotle, no mention is made of performance in Shepherd's *Aesthetics* (Oxford University Press, 1987) or Cothey's *The Nature of Art* (Routledge, London, 1990). It is as though something of the ephemerality of performance is carried over into analysis of its making. Nothing remains of one and precious little remains of the other.

[26] Moustakis, 1961.

[27] Stravinsky, Igor. *Poetics of Music*, 1970. pp. 7-9

[28] Smith, D. in Gray, 1968. p. 137

[29] Something of the relationship between installation and theatre is explored in *Performance Art Into the 90s*. Hodges, N (Ed.) Art & Design, London, 1994.

[30] See Whitmore, J. *Directing Postmodern Theater* University of Michigan Press, 1994 and Birringer, J. *Theatre, Theory, Postmodernism*. Indiana University Press, 1991.

[31] As the bibliography will reveal, the writings of artists working across a number of disciplines have been considered in the construction of this book. Many of these examples have been found in the pages of broad-spectrum publications such as *The Philosophy of Art, an Introduction to Aesthetics* (Graham, G. Routledge, 1997), The *Principles of Art* (Collingwood, R. G. Clarendon Press, Oxford, 1938) and *Philosophy Looks at the Arts* (Margolis, J. (ed.) Temple University Press, Philadelphia, 1987).

[32] In Graham, G (1997). P.86

[33] *ibid* p. 95

Chapter 3:
Text into Performance

The writing now is post-performance. More accurately, this writing occupies the space between one performance and another. This creates room for both reflection and projection.

What follows then is my reading – my *documentation* – of the way that the performance moved from the rhythms of rehearsal into the pace of performance. For better, for worse and as ever, all did not go as planned.

It was clear that the programmes issued to spectators were instrumental in the ways in which the work was read. This is more than mere assumption on my part. Immediately after the performance the cast members were embroiled in a series of conversations with impassioned spectators. The concern was with of off-stage 'relationships' within the cast and the ways in which these relationships had been seen to impact on the performance. To a strong core of spectators, the lies contained in the programme were taken at face value. Of the spectators who spoke with either the students, or myself none seemed to have even the slightest doubt that the information given was anything but true.

For myself, this created something of a Catch-22, as I had no real wish to extend this aspect of the fabrication beyond the performance ... it had functioned, to my mind, as a method of extending the performance frame, but it had only done this really as a way in. Consequently, I had a strong inclination to 'come clean' with the truth and rationale behind the misinformation in question as soon as was appropriate. The cast, however, thought and felt differently. For them this was a wonderful and only partly unexpected opportunity to engage in an extended process of invisible theatre. To this end, they continued the 'performance' by developing the story of romantic and emotional involvement, to the point where they were manufacturing arguments, 'tiffs' and intimate encounters in front of those people who had begun to form an unknowing and partly unwilling audience.

There are a series of ethical issues at work here, which I am seeking in a hypocritical way to distance myself from. There is a sense of duplicity, inasmuch as I am raising questions of ethics at the same time as I am claiming to want to divorce myself from any ethical considerations. In this I am aware that my approach to analysis is on one level consistent with Gay McAuley's

> Insiders reporting on their own culture ... raises a very important methodological issue in terms of rehearsal analysis. Should the observation, documentation and analysis of rehearsal process be undertaken by the artists themselves? Is this possible .... Who has the right to tell the tale? Who sees more of what is going on?[1]

This consistency, however, is only temporary. When McAuley develops her argument, suggesting that "there are serious methodological problems for someone who has a major creative involvement with the production also attempting to observe and analyse the whole of the process"[2] I have to disagree. Indeed, *Tracing the Footprints* comprises a challenge to her claims.

Ethical considerations then *are* an issue within the work at the same time as they *are not* an issue within my analysis. Whereas McAuley's idealised and non-participant observer might be inclined towards a rationalisation of the ethical implications within *At Last Sight* I am not. As McAuley recognises, "documentation of any sort necessarily involves selection and is, therefore, already in itself a form of analysis".[3] Accordingly, my decision to raise an issue and then side-step it is an integral part of the documentary process. Having agreed within the group that any and all aspects of the making and performing process are likely to be used as grist to the mill of this book, the ethics of making and reading are taking care of themselves. Where ethics become questionable is in the act of telling lies within a framework that only exists for the tellers. And yet to hesitate at this point would be to deny *At Last Sight* what is becoming its central concern. The stretching of the frame of performance is now *the* defining feature of the work, to the point where I am able to say that the way the work is being made is what the work is about. What more apposite way of dealing with truth and lies than to develop the work itself into a position where lies are themselves read as truths?

This is not to ignore the issue of ethics altogether, as though a refusal to discuss the matter would make it disappear. In fact, the 'problem', such as it is that at all, is connected to ideas of invisible theatre *per se*, rather than to the specifics of *At Last Sight*.

At best, I have a cautious cynicism towards invisible theatre; at worst this cynicism threatens to become overpowering. It has always seemed to me that there are enough incidents occurring in the world at large, without actors, be they students or professionals, adding their own inventions to that mass. 'Terrible is the temptation to do well', as Brecht warned us, and that temptation seems never more terrible than when we come to regard performance as some sort of medicine for the masses. As a means of showing people how to live their lives according to our own intrinsically patronising notions of 'good' and 'bad' behaviour. If that accounts for the cynicism, let me state that the caution comes from the notions of accountability and consequence. If an action takes place within the recognised confines of performance, then, broadly speaking, the propagator of that action is not likely to be held accountable beyond the metaphorical bringing down of the curtain. We accept that the act encountered is a lie and that, as such, it has no direct consequence on or in the outside world. Subsequently, we are able to recognise a dysfunctional form of over-empathy in those instances when - for example, as is the case for certain television soap actors - members of the public loathe or love the actor according to the on-screen activities undertaken and displayed. To this end, I have never been tempted by ideas of bringing theatre into the realm of the real, so much as I have been, and remain, fascinated by the possibilities of bringing the real into the realms of theatre.

Notwithstanding this, it was interesting to observe the ways in which the cast so obviously relished the notion of - at least in public - living out the lies created by and through *At Last Sight*. What was perhaps of most interest was the fact that the absence of any characterisation based on an emotional and psychological rationale, which was a feature of the 'production' of *At Last Sight*, was so fully subverted by the off-stage behaviour of the group. It was as though, having acted as ciphers within the performance, the students were possessed of an eagerness to engage in forms of invisible realism within the elastic parameters of the performative frame. There was both more to it and less than this, of course ... on one level, I have no doubts that the group took pleasure in what really amounted to a type of flirtation without consequence. For if the idea of observers as 'audience' imbued the behaviour of the group towards each other with a high degree of consequence, then, conversely, the students themselves were able to flirt openly (and, it should be said, at times quite outrageously) with impunity. To engage in flirtation with an absence of consequence. Their behaviour was legitimised and licensed from both sides: from the spectators' and also their own.

In terms of the performance itself, *At Last Sight* could be said to have held together well in production terms. By this, I mean that the work had an internal coherence that ensured a correspondingly coherent 'style'. The individual student's endeavours were carried through to a high standard, to the point - and this often seems to be the acid-test of curriculum-driven work - where I was able to observe the group as 'performers', rather than being reminded of their status as students. There is, however, a large 'but' here. The fact that I was pleased with the way in which *At Last Sight* played does not mean that the piece is not also in need of a considerable process of overhaul and revision. The levels of energy within the piece meant that the pace was at times somnambulistic. The notion of deconstruction was so heavily applied that that there was no real sense of what it was that was being deconstructed. Conversely, the ending was too neat ... reading like the stitching together of something hitherto unseen. The space was played with too much width, meaning that performers simply getting into position took up an inordinate amount of time.

It is often the case that any full weekends of rehearsal are only used closer to the date of performance, when, effectively, the work is already 'set'. Short rehearsals mean that problems with pace are less readily picked up on. As directors/tutors we see short sections of the work, often with several days in between, and may only recognise a predictability in pace at precisely that time when we tell ourselves the all-too readily acceptable lie that 'all we need now is an audience'. It is at this point, that this book, this reading and recording of the practical processes involved in making work for performance, moves into a new direction. Whereas the work of the previous chapters has been reflective only inasmuch as the written words have reflected on performative decisions already made, this chapter has to deal with reflecting on reflection. For it is clear that in the time between now and the next performance a number of key changes will need to be made. Shortness of time means that all of the changes need to be worked through with expediency. A challenge to change comes from the positive feelings of the group members. There is a strong sense of satisfaction within the group, and deservedly so; which means that change may well be resisted from within. Whilst it is in the nature of the work that our rehearsals remain organic and progressive, rather than repetitive and fixed, it is in the nature of the group, as we have created it, that all of the opinions offered are listened to and respected. Whether this means, as I suspect it does, that I will (simply) attempt to introduce the notion of change as though it is part of a group-decision, remains to be seen.

I am aware of the possibility that I am introducing change primarily (or even purely) as a research device. As something that is done in order to assess the reaction of the students as well as my own ways of dealing with their responses. The reader may wonder whether I am suggesting change for these reasons and that my stated perception of 'artistic concerns' is functioning as a smokescreen. It is a question I am unable to answer with any authority. Certainly, I can discount the idea of change as a research device in any 'pure' sense - and I can say the same thing about the word 'primarily' – but this is not to suggest that any easy dislocating of research strategies *per se* from the subject of the research can exist. My actions and decisions stem from my interests, and my interests are located as firmly within the concerns of this book as with the construction of *At Last Sight*. I am not only *unable* to separate the researcher's role from the practitioner's, I am *unwilling* to do so. If, as I have suggested, the way that the work is being made is what the work is about, then the complexity and overlap of my role is central.

What I can hope for is that any decisions stemming from a drive towards research are strengthening rather than diluting the creative product of *At Last Sight*. But even within this hope there is defiance. The work is, after all, a research project. As has been pointed out throughout this book, *At Last Sight* was never intended as a process, as an *event*, which would then be made subject to analysis. This remains a key feature of the study.[4]

My roles have been complex and overlapping from the moment that this project was conceived. That this complexity is being negotiated *in the here and now* does not add to the initial level of complexity. It only takes it from the private and inarticulate into the public. The first point 'public' is the group.

The group met for our first post-performance rehearsal. I took this opportunity to discuss with them my feelings about the work, along with some of my ideas as to how the work might be further developed. As I had anticipated, this caused something of a schism in the group, with some members resisting change and others more happily embracing the idea. There is, in fact, an almost even spilt, although it has to be said that those who are most emphatically opposed to change appear to be so inclined because of pressures of time rather than any strong aesthetically driven disagreement.

We began the process of modification by introducing more elements of narrative. Not in order to give the piece a stronger sense of linear progression, so much as to provide the spectators with more clues as to what it is that is being fragmented. In its first performance *At Last Sight* felt like an ultimately straightforward exercise in deconstruction and on-stage/in-situ *assemblage*, rather than an experiment with form and narrative, truth and lies, experience and invention. The inclusion, therefore, of additional encounters between performers is intended to bolster the fictional thematics, which were always at the core of the origins of the written script. In fact, it is through going back to the script of *At Last Sight* that these encounters will almost certainly emerge and take shape. I have no real desire to create a series of new 'moments of business' in order to flesh the work out, when there are a number of sections of the text where the germ, at least, of narrative-enhancing moments already exists. I have no real desire to engage the audience's attention through dialogue. So what is left? *At Last Sight* can be regarded as occupying the spaces between expressivity and imitation. Between abstraction and intimacy. Without expressivity and the imitative, we are left with only four modes of performance: indication, metaphor, description and actuality, and it is to these modes that *At Last Sight* must now look.

Within these self-imposed limitations some options already exist, and these are as follows. Dialogue can be placed at a greater distance from the audience ... and can be utilised in such a way that the potential for empathetic engagement is undercut. The consumption of bottles of wine within the production can be ritualised in some way, in order that, at the same time as the reality of the alcohol is blurring the divide between fiction and fact, the activity of drinking can be used to comment on courtship. And the ordering of those events which currently exist and which we wish to keep can be reconfigured in a way that augurs against a neat conclusion to an otherwise fragmented experience.

Although this may seem like a going back to Square One ... as a peculiar return to a point of beginnings, this is not the case. Telling the students that the work thus far allows us the luxury of change with a minimum of risk was no mere platitude. The work undertaken so far will enable the group to re-create from a position of relative knowing; for just as I, from a directorial perspective, can see areas that would benefit from change, so the students, as performers, are increasingly aware of discernible weaknesses within the piece. The palpable fear of change is not a response to the notion of change itself, so much as to the pressures of time ... to the temptation to settle for 'good enough'. It is a measure of the group's desire to produce a piece of work which stretches them both academically and creatively that they are willing to suspend these temptations and re-work with a renewed vigour. If anything, the 'success' of the first performance has made the group even more determined to work to their utmost.

This notion of 'success' is a vexed one. By what criteria could the work be so considered? By the volume of applause received? By the level and manner of spectatorial discussion? By the feelings of satisfaction inherent in the performers (informed as it undoubtedly is by their collective reading of the response)? By the layers of complexity within the work, over which the group feel they have established a high and surprising degree of control? There are no satisfactory answers. All that I can suggest, with a reasonable impunity, is that the performers feel a greater sense of satisfaction at this moment in time than do I.

This in itself is a common enough feeling. From a performer's perspective, presenting the work to an audience will often bring with it an attendant sense of satisfaction *via* ownership: in performance the work seems to belong solely to the performer. Individual nuances are introduced, pace alters according to one's reading of the mood of the audience and the hours of rehearsal, of preparation, are brought to a conclusion for the duration of the piece. Speaking from my own experience, I can recognise that in my capacity as a performer within other projects, I have been satisfied with my own contribution to a given production even when or if that production is patently unsatisfactory to an audience. As a director, one has an overview that seeks at least to encompass the work as a whole. This is another reason why the idea of revision at this stage has not been an easy subject to broach: the performers pleased with their individual contributions, as am I ... and to introduce change is to inevitably change something of these sections. It is difficult, therefore, to praise the performer's efforts and accomplishments on the one hand and then be critical on the other.

An example of a need for change, which may meet with resistance within the group, is a 'kissing scene' between two of the performers.

This began as an exercise in 'staging the real' but has since taken on a rather gratuitous feel. Not least because there is evidence of a strong physical and emotional attraction between the two students. Nothing has been said - at least to me - by any of the group, but a perceptible feeling of voyeurism has descended whenever these two work through this scene. This in itself offers a curious element of role-reversal, as the scene was initially created in order to suggest voyeurism to the spectators. As long as the two were 'acting' the kiss, no matter how seemingly authentically, we in the group were happy to watch it; now that we feel it may be driven by desire we are distinctly uncomfortable. I say 'we' with a degree of authority, and notwithstanding the absence of any hard information, as the evidence of my own eyes tell me how awkward others in the group are feeling. There is a palpable discomfort, which is, I should stress, not aligned to any notions of imposed morality. It is at once much simpler and more complex than that. We are beginning to feel like 'Peeping Toms'.

Being outside of their 'relationship' we have become spectators rather than collaborators and this is leading to a sense of unease, which is separate from any shared happiness we might be feeling at two people who we care for who are so clearly enjoying each other's company.

This raises the much larger issue of developing relationships within the group and the extent to which this quite common phenomena will impact on the ways in which we work. Even existing as a 'suspicion' it appears to have done so already. The group has always been friendly *as a group*, rather than as a collection of cliques, and I have a relaxed relationship with each of them. There is a common bond of humour in the group, which makes for a pleasant informality and which goes some considerable way towards undercutting the pressures of making and presenting performance.

I have to question as to the extent to which the nature of *At Last Sight* should be held accountable for the developing relationship between these two 'kissers'. My instincts and experience tell me that to credit (?) the production with bringing people together solely because of its insidiously seductive themes would be a mistake. It is in the nature of making performance rather than in the nature or theme of that which is made that result in romantic pairings. Working anti-social hours, often late into the night or at weekends, means that any socialising which is done tends to remain within the group. This, together with a shared interest and the emotional investment which comes with commitment to a project, can often result in relationships which might not have occurred under other, less intense, circumstances. Whilst it is true that this is the case, it would be naive of me to suggest that an on-stage or in-performance intimacy is not possessed of the capability to bleed into off-stage lives. Certainly, *At Last Sight* is a project that draws its strength from the advertised fiction of individual relationships within the group and it is easy to see how the edges between *that* reality and the one that takes place in a non-performative privacy might become blurred. It is enough, perhaps, to recognise that *At Last Sight* has been a catalyst for this particular change within these two lives and to leave it, at least for the moment, at that.

The ending of *At Last Sight* is at present too neat. As it stands, the spectator is presented with an overly sentimentalised view, which none of us within the group feel is appropriate to the work. An emotional response seems to be called for from the spectators without the work having *earned* that response with an emotion-inducing structure. It reads as though *At Last Sight* is seeking to cloak itself in the status of wistful memory and nothing else. The end-scene has only survived this long because of unwillingness on my part to let go of the words. Words which appeal to a mawkish aspect of my own personality, and which only being heard uttered within the context of full performance has taken me to the point where I can see the necessity for excision.

I have to address here the fact that my interest within *At Last Sight* is to *deal with* sentimentality, whereas my own subconscious predilection draws me towards a sentimentality that simply *is*. It is as though the process of performance making functions as a form of exorcision, forcing a degree of control onto certain aspects of my own life. I am aware of the distrust of sentimental art, both in academic and aesthetic circles, a distrust that says that sentimentality *per se* must be treated with a type of ironic distance for fear of falling into a *Mills & Boon* world of handkerchief-wringing romance. I can recognise in my own responses to sentimental material a willingness to engage uncritically which might seem to sit uneasily with the cynicism of my adopted (?) pose of world-weariness. Notwithstanding this, I do not regard this as symptomatic of any dishonesty on my part. Rather, I feel that the two aspects of sentimentality and cynicism find a balance in the creation of performance. For it is only at this place that the battle is in any way joined. Elsewhere in my life the two are able to function through a separation which is as comfortable as I could hope for. In this way, I am able to respond to a film such as *The English Patient* with tears which would never fall (would never be *allowed* to fall) if the same piece of work were to be staged in a theatre.

Seen in this way, *At Last Sight* emerges as a rather different type of cathartic experience to that which I had originally envisaged ... if 'originally' can be taken here to refer to the beliefs I held at the start of both this project and this book. Whereas I had believed - however many thousand words and hours and thoughts ago - that the autobiographical content of *At Last Sight* was central to this notion of catharsis for the artist, I am now beginning to realise that what has been more important has been the relationship between that written content and this realised form. The catharsis, such as it can be said to apply in this case, is arrived at *via* a balancing of romantic ideas of redemption (my own) and the recognition of irredemption (also my own) when the past bleeds pentimento-like into every aspect of the present. *At Last Sight* stands then not as a staged diary of what was, so much as the staging of what is. Encountered in this way, the entire piece becomes a necessary coming to terms with two aspects of my own personality.

Jung said that "the work in process becomes the poet's fate and determines his psychic development. It is not Goethe who creates *Faust*, but *Faust* which creates Goethe."[5] If this is the case, then *At Last Sight* has been, and remains, an indication, albeit unclear, of who I am. The process of creating the work began with a vague and confused intimation of a potential resolution; a resolution that would reveal itself as the piece progressed. In this, I can see now that there was considerably more intimation than determination. There was always a sense of inspiration, of a discernible type of impulse which has kept *At Last Sight* moving along, but this inspiration has never been harnessed to a projection of how the piece might appear in performance. At this point, I am still in the process of creating, at the same time as that which has been created up to now has given me a strong sense of how the work will look when it is next performed. It is almost as if the group is now engaged in a process of interpretation rather than devising. The 'text' to be interpreted is the text as it was presented. The canvas is no longer blank, making choices easier, even in the midst now of a compromise to earlier freedoms.

Now that the work of *At Last Sight* is partly formed, it seems easier to write about the processes leading up to it. It is as though the concentration on creation worked against analysis even if *at that time* the analysis did not seem particularly problematic.

Analysis might be thus seen to have diluted something of the tension necessary to create a production. In endeavouring to express the aims of *At Last Sight* it may be the case that the practical work itself has drifted too far towards becoming (little more than) an exposition of concepts. This is not to say that *At Last Sight* has suffered from my twin role as artist and analyst. The work is what the work is and can never be anything other than that. What has happened, and is still happening, is that that which would ordinarily remain subconscious has been summoned to the fore more than would be the usual case. In this fashion, the pages of this book can provide the reader with a series of insights that may be of some assistance in determining what happens during the processes of making performance. The book is adhering then to what it set out to be: not a general survey of performance-making - although it does contain that wider implication - but as detailed a reflection as is proving possible of the concerns noted during the making of *this* production at *this* time.

While it remains the case that *Tracing the Footprints* has an intended application in the field of performance, it is being written - just as *At Last Sight* is being created - within a belief that the 'old' ideology which had it that all of the arts were subject to particular forms suggested or even imposed by works within the same field, is being replaced. It is being replaced by a conviction that any creative work, of any type, can lead us towards a meditation on the process of creation itself. Such a cross-fertilised approach to study is not forced. In the same way that any maker of art who wishes the process to remain as something alchemical is unlikely to find comfort in this book.

Some makers of work will instinctively feel that a process of analysis is little more than an attempt to undermine the powers of creativity; that artists are meant to know their art through the making of it and through that making alone. There is a certain logic here. But only if one considers logical the notion that an inordinate period of analytical pre-requisition would effectively curtail all action. If, for example, one were to refuse to participate in the action of breathing until such time as that person had made a detailed analysis of the nature of breath s/he would asphyxiate long before the dissemination of any findings. This may well be the case. But this book is not concerned with the holding off of the breath of performance. On the contrary, it is only through attaching a high degree of importance to the analysis of creativity that we will be able to contemplate the act of making with the same level of discipline that we have for centuries applied to studies of that which has already been made.

We can find a ready example of this in the work undertaken on *At Last Sight*. What we have seen is evidence that a number of decisions made during the 'making process' have been arrived at out of a state which I can now recognise as alternating between self and other. By this, I refer to that state whereby the 'self' of the creator is tempered on occasions by the 'other' of the spectators-to-be. In other words, that which the self of the director creates is always already modified, or mediated, by an advance awareness, or at least a prediction, of the judgement of others. Of the work's spectators. It follows then that any assessment which I am able to make, either now or at some future time, of *At Last Sight* will inevitably necessitate the opting for one or other of these mutually exclusive positions. They are inclusive in the process of making and exclusive when it comes to an assessment of that which is made. If I intend to analyse *At Last Sight*, I need to first be able to make a distinction between an investigation into the creative processes involved in making the work and an analysis of the work's values as a production. I can only consider *At Last Sight* either in relation to myself as a director/writer/creator or in relation to my perceptions of the work when I am positioned as a spectator.

Where this collapsing of roles is an integral element of spectatorship, it is one which I, in my chosen role as maker, reader and writer, need to maintain some considerable control over. This is the nature of research into practice. In examining the nature of making, one also casts a new light on the made. This is not about homogenisation. All processes are different, in degree if not always in kind. History has revealed to us, for example, that Mozart thought out symphonies, even entire operatic scenes, and then transcribed these 'completed' ideas onto paper. Beethoven, on the other hand, wrote fragments of themes in copious notebooks, which he worked on and developed for years before formatting them as symphonies.[6] One artist plunges into the moment, the other treads warily around the edges. This book attempts no documented hierarchy of approaches, any more than it is suggesting that the processes involved in *At Last Sight* are somehow preferable to those sanctioned in any other project at this or any other time. Just as one can regard that which has been produced by either Mozart or Beethoven through the lens provided by a knowledge of the tools of their own creation, so any all work can be enhanced by an analysis of how the piece was made.

Performances may be made in many different ways and all creation of performance is to some degree automatic. But there is at certain times a very full consciousness of the process, or at least of such of its aspects as are open to introspection. Notwithstanding this, there are, as far as I am aware, no thorough accounts of the production processes of specific works. With *At Last Sight* I am able to say that the script was a beginning. Although it would be undeniably true(er) to regard this script itself as a stage along a process long ago commenced. The script still stands as a reasonable place to start. Reasonable, that is, inasmuch as its genesis has been dealt with in Chapter One. I can see now that early drafts of the script were weak, in that they failed to establish a diverse enough balance of moods and images. The structure of that early script gives few, perhaps too few, clues to a subsequent director ... even when that director is also the writer.

The work undertaken on *At Last Sight* up to this point in time has been an aspect of an *act* of understanding, and also an *attempt* at understanding. It can be described as the effort of a man to present an account of his relationship to a world that allows him little certainty and vast regrets. This account has been at once performative and public. The structures engaged in were created with a predominance of forethought, even at those times when I was perhaps unable to see which way certain rehearsals and ideas were going. I would hesitate to regard these aspects here as completely accidental, although they were often informed by the random. The processes undertaken in the rehearsal process *made space* for the random to occur, and this in itself comprised a deliberate form. Because of this, I can see that *At Last Sight* has arrived at the transitional point that it now occupies through a series of *intentions* rather than *calculations*. There has been a strict, even a rigorous intent, which has allowed the separate elements of the work, as in Hockney's *Joiners*, to merge into one another without any absolute demarcation ... often being possessed of multiple functions. Being one thing at the same time as they are also another.

Historically and currently, the making of performance has a practical aim. The standard question tends not so much towards an asking of 'Where did the work come from and why was it made?' as to 'What did the performance achieve?'. The Why and Where of the first question are never usually taken beyond the guessing stage, precisely because, in the language of those who most often will it to be so, performance is not easily made subject to the conditions of the scientific laboratory. Experiments can never be repeated, because the conditions, the human conditions of performance are never even remotely the same from one experiment to the other. Performance is creation. It moves and transmutes, even as we watch. It amounts to a type of knowledge that one could not be in possession of before the fact. We can say, therefore, that *At Last Sight* is not comprised of knowledge *about* something else ... *At Last Sight* is the fullness of its own knowledge. It is what it is, which is not to say that it is not, in its Joineresque aspirations, always also referring to the world of something else.

If, at the outset of this project, I considered myself to be engaged in the theatricalisation of an abstracted version of my own history, I have since come to realise that what I have (or had) to tell is not nearly so important as the process of telling itself. There is no goal. Whatever it is that I thought I knew, that I felt such a strong urge to tell has become increasingly unstable, unfixed. The edges have blurred to the point where I am no longer sure where practice ends and analysis begins. I am giving myself over, increasingly, to a state of knowing nothing in advance. Not the next line, not even the next word. What I am developing as a consequence is a faith in my own ability to articulate the process of making, and to embrace the confusion therein with a genuine relish. The mystery of the sentence to come (of the rehearsal to come) is always there, but the *existence* of that mystery is no longer mysterious in and of itself. Understanding, it seems, is not about solving the mysteries of making work so much as accepting that these mysteries are simply so.

This book is about the ways in which writing relates to performance. Where this results in non-linearity, with sections shifting from documentation and reportage to analysis and supposition without warning, the writing is at its closest approximation to the practice of making *At Last Sight*. By this I mean that the structure of this book is flexible enough to move with thoughts and ideas as they occur, rather than compartmentalising them into passages which, whilst appearing coherent, would actually give a false flavour of the process of making the performance project. Where this results in obfuscation rather than clarity the reader is asked to accept this as a necessary by-product of writing which is engaged in during rather than after the fact. The process is intrinsically elliptical in that spaces are left open, only to be filled in at a later stage. This is a deliberate act, for if the *process* of making *At Last Sight* is the object of the research, then it is appropriate that that process is articulated as much through the form of this writing as it is in the content. Words that might more comfortably sit within a concluding chapter are presented as part of the fabric of *making* because they are an integral part of it. They are, in fact, not so much 'conclusions' as moments of insight, which are wont to occur at the least expected times. To record them in note-form as a prelude to a later 'writing up' would be to create a record of the production-process which augurs against the slippery nature of the creative activities undertaken.

Confusion does not emerge, therefore, as the consequence of an unclear treatment so much as the inevitability of an unclear act. An act(ivity) within which certainty is sacrificed to a faith in doubt. Written documentation is generally regarded as an exercise in left-brain thinking. It is logical, rational and systematic. Creative activity, conversely, is a right-brain dominated process. As Stefan Brecht tells us

> The brain is functionally asymmetric .... It has been known for a little over a century now that it is the left brain that all in all, - linguistic and manual dexterity being coupled – is the linguistic, - has the powers of speech and speech-comprehension, writing and reading: but during the last thirty years, the right brain has emerged as particularly endowed with visual powers, the seer .... It seems clear that as naming is the left brain's tool of analysis, so the right brain's syntheses are spatial metaphors.[7]

If the documentation of *At Last Sight* is to contain an awareness of the contradiction between writing and doing, at the same time as it is seeking to dissolve some of those contradictions in the writing itself, then a simple and clear record of the event is entirely inappropriate. Working in the way that it is this book stands as an attempt at avoiding the status of unchallengable 'evidence', even in the midst of its reliance on the evidence of experience. The fixed nature of a book works against the fluidity of approach that is central to the making of performance. As soon as a book is typed, bound and presented as an artefact of learning, it acquires a quality that the process it is trying to articulate never had. We can go further than that and say that the qualities expected of an academic text are at odds with the spontaneous and accidental qualities employed and encountered in devising performance. That which exists as one of a series of possibilities runs the risk of calcification through ink into a specific set of actions, as though that which happened could only ever have happened in the way that it did.

The question then is 'How can this process of creative slippage be documented?' How can the documentation avoid the pitfalls of closure, when the practice it stems from is seeking an open and free interaction between spectator and performer, between the watcher and the watched? One way - and it is the way of this book - is to recognise the writing as a dialogue with the self. The activity of writing is an inevitable disseminating agent, but that which is written is primarily comprised of a making sense of making work. It seems logical then to see *Tracing the Footprints* as being as indicative of a concern with my own understanding as it is with the understanding of any future readers. Which brings us back to Jung's reading of the symbiosis between Goethe and his *Faust*. The core of this book, as indeed one could speak of the core of *At Last Sight*, is the maker's address to the being made ... which is in a constant state of slippage.

Other researchers might adopt a more overtly divisive approach to the same relationship, separating out in a cleaner way the distinctions between action and analysis. In this way, writing a series of descriptions, followed closely by an attendant and thorough reading of those actions - by the construction of an event and its subsequent deconstruction - a clear(er) communication would emerge. But that clarity would disguise its own insidiously coercive intent.

In much the same way, any once-held distinctions between objective and subjective responses have been exposed as invidious and false. Everything has emerged as illusive. There have been, throughout the process so far, no solid facts to address, other than the facts of writing, rehearsal and performance ... and the factual nature of these phenomena have been compromised, and permanently so, by my own interests and prejudices. In writing this book, even such deformations and distortions which exist are not, however, necessarily *untruths*. The realisation that fiction and invention are the very fabric of life means that those elements infiltrate even the most scholarly and well intended of pursuits. In performance, as in other forms of art, it can be said that one adopts a mask in order then to tell the truth. But when the line between truth and false is so unclear (if it can even be said to be there at all) then how can the writer's words be trusted? All that can be said is that the words 'lies' and 'truth' have lost much of their presumed currency at the same time as this book and *At Last Sight* are beginning to establish their own.

Even those memories that have been regarded as 'inspiring' the text are not necessarily trustworthy. How accurately can I trust my memory, even before the activity of selection and of poeticising take their toll on truth? How can I trust this report as a truthful rendition of that which has occurred? How can I trust my memory of this morning's rehearsal and this afternoon's thoughts?

If a flawed and increasingly suspect memory continues to prove central to *At Last Sight* - inasmuch at least as the work began with the structured recollection of certain of my own memories - then we can also say that memory is the mainstay of art.[8] We can say this because all imaginative thought is in one vital way an exercise of memory. We are not able to imagine anything that we do not already know.[9] Through this we can suggest that the ability to imagine is actually the ability to remember. We remember that which we have already experienced and we apply it to a new situation. Creative imagination is thus comprised of an ability to harness memory to invention. It is an action of the mind that produces a new idea or insight from out of the known. Looking at *At Last Sight* like this I can recognise a startling deficiency in my own utilisation of memory. I can identify a weakness that tells me much, now, about the ways in which *At Last Sight* is operating. My own subconscious approach to memory has been to seek to reproduce that memory rather than to exploit it in some new way. My memory is thus inclined to stay resolutely in the past. Where somebody else might be able to fashion the same memories as mine (if the reader will allow this flight of fancy) into a new situation, I have so far been unable to achieve this. The domestic nature of my memories has not been transformed into other than a domestic treatment of a domestic theme. Unable, or unwilling, to turn *how it was* into *how I would now choose it to be*, I find I am repeating history. I am, I feel, too often offering memory in place of imagination.[10]

This realisation - and it is one which has occurred to me only during this session at my desk - has evaded me during four full months of rehearsal and some eighteen years as a student, practitioner and teacher of theatre. If evidence were ever needed of the importance of reflection on one's own practice then it is surely provided here. Whether or not I am able to act on this realisation is a different matter; but this difference in no way negates the value of the discovery. The die of *At Last Sight* may well be cast too far to re-assess the ways in which the group (for let us not forget that all decisions made are made within the certainty of *group*) are either willing or able to act on this 'new' knowledge. Assuming, that is, that the words written here are fed constructively back into the practical work.

What is occurring most emphatically at this point in time is an informed (re)consideration of the project that was, is and is becoming *At Last Sight*. On one level, I have a confidence in the work, which stems from my own feelings about the ways in which the piece has progressed, and also the ways in which the 'product' seemed to be perceived. By this I refer to the belief I have that the work thus far has contributed to a new and valid insight into the language of performance. That is a large claim. It is one I need to justify. A part of that justification is a sense of how well the work – the research-project – builds on practical and theoretical approaches currently at large.

Joseph Kosuth has suggested that "Art 'lives' through influencing other art, not by existing as the physical residue of an artist's ideas",[11] and the Standing Committee of University Drama Departments (SCUDD) has defined practice as research as being that which will "lead to new or substantially improved insights".[12] According to these criteria, it would appear that the analytical approach to the work of *At Last Sight* is moving things in the right direction. Despite the fact that I am not yet able to affirm that the production/book *has* influenced other art, I have a growing confidence that it *will*. On one level I can relate this to my own future work ... for how could I make work after *At Last Sight* which would fail to draw upon the work of its own past? But this is to subvert Kosuth's statement to too great a degree. It is more acceptable to suggest, and indeed to aspire, to the idea that a significant proportion of readers of this book (and spectators to the practice) will elaborate in some way upon the ideas encountered therein. My role as a university lecturer means that this presumption is made more watertight than might otherwise be the case. My teaching has already been influenced by the work undertaken on this 'project' and it is inevitable that a number of those students who are made subject to my teaching are going to be 'influenced' by my approaches.

This type of influence, however, is not determined by any intrinsic quality. It is a fact of education that a tutor's own bias will infiltrate even the most rigorously exclusive curriculum. In this way, the 'influence' of the work done and the 'residue of an artist's ideas' become almost impossible to separate. The residue of ideas could, albeit somewhat harshly, be said to define much of what passes for research-driven teaching. Accordingly, if I talk long and hard enough to my students about the contents of this book then I will undoubtedly sway (some of) them, if only through insistence, towards a belief in the sanctity of these words. This is influence through persuasion ... through indoctrination. In some ways - actually, in *key* ways - this book acts as its own defence against influence-by-rote. If there is anything constant within the pouring out of words it is that provocation is prioritised over prescription. *Tracing the Footprints* is thus always in one way arguing against itself. The solid appearance of the lines on the page is undercut by the fragility of any faith in the lines' own worth.

In this way, the book is locating itself as postmodern in its form, rather than the modernist analysis of a postmodern form.

Postmodernism has been described by Jean-Francois Lyotard as a working without rules in order to establish the rules of that which has been made. Arguing against the 'solace of good forms', he suggests that postmodern practice is a

> ... search for new presentations, not in order to be able to enjoy them but in order to impart a stronger sense of the unpresentable. A postmodern artist ... is in the position of a philosopher: the ... work he produces (is) not in principle governed by pre-established rules, and ... cannot be judged according to a determined judgement, by applying familiar categories to the text or work. Those rules and categories are what the work of art itself is looking for .... Hence the fact that work

and text have the characters of an *event*; hence also, they always come
too late for their author.[13]

Taking this criterion we can make a case that its application
is central to notions of all creative activity. When we say that an artist
is creative, we do not do so because s/he has demonstrated an ability to
obey rules which were known before the work was made, so that the
artist only succeeded in doing that which had been done before. We
acknowledge as creative those artists whose work is seen to embody
something that did not exist before. This is an implicit recognition of
the creative artist as the originator of the rules s/he followed.
Afterwards, other artists might deliberately follow these same rules
and thereby achieve a similar 'success', but these artists are not
engaged in the same level of creative activity.

The creative artist - like Lyotard's paradigmatic
postmodernist - does not know what the target is. Although there is a
degree of 'aiming', the artist is unlikely to know precisely where this
aim will lead until *after* the event.[14] Creativity in terms of making
performance is not then a model of a purposive activity ... that is to say
it is not indicative of an activity which is engaged in and consciously
controlled so as to produce a desired result. At the time of making the
performance of *At Last Sight* for its first performance, I was impelled
to engage in that type of creative activity, but I was unable to envisage
the results of that endeavour. The performance that occurred was, to a
large extent, unimaginable when I first met with the cast. This also
applies to the performers themselves. None of the group had any real
sense, from day to day, of the ways in which *At Last Sight* would
develop in subsequent rehearsals. Each day was a making without
rules in order to establish the rules of that which was being made. Our
collective activity has not then been controlled or shaped overmuch by
a desire for a predicted result.

This is not to say that the group has not been conscious of a
certain direction, however vague this direction has been. We have
known that our work has been heading towards a series of public
performances, for example. The sense of direction has actually been
more acute than this. Without any idea as to whether certain decisions
were 'right' or 'wrong', I would have been unable to develop the work
directorially through rehearsals, and the performance suggestions of
the cast would have been considerably less valid than they have been
in practice. Creative activity in the making of performance can be
defined then as an activity which is subject to an applied critical

control by the artists involved, at the same time as this control does not amount to any imitation-seeking foresight regarding the work to be made.

The ability to discriminate between levels of appropriateness in terms of the input of group members has required, of all of us, a certain fastidiousness in ongoing critical judgements ... and these judgements are more focused now than at any time previously. Each of the participants has developed a vocabulary of discrimination to the point where rehearsals now have a discernible coherence. We are becoming aware of the *direction* that *At Last Sight* is moving in only now that the piece has arrived at its first venue. The rules have been established, at least in part, to the extent where we are perhaps every bit as effective as we have ever been, but rather less creative than in the early stages of the work. In the same way that I am now able to use the past tense to describe certain processes, *At Last Sight* is both done and undone ... completed in one sense and also liable to significant change. The shift in tense is therefore both deliberate and inevitable.

The 'product' that has been is informing the ways in which the 'product' to come is now being shaped. This brings with it the possibility of new directions. Of the establishment of new rules of making, informed now by our developing understanding of the old.

The performance artist, Chris Burden has put the argument that functionalism in art amounts to no more than propaganda, suggesting that the act of functionalism is intrinsically antithetical to creativity.[15] There is a sense of an anti-functionalist approach in *At Last Sight*, inasmuch as only in a very qualified sense would I be able to say that I had before me any 'problem' which I felt that the work could provide a solution for. Perhaps it would be more apposite to say that any functionalist value which might be ascribed now or at any future time to *At Last Sight* would not be the result of a response to conditions set before the work was commenced. In terms of its artistic creation, the formulation of problems and the solution to those problems amount to one and the same phenomenon. The process of making the work can be revealed as at once creating the work and discovering that which the work has to say. The process is comprised of inseparable elements. The event thus created is a product of art, in that it is as new and unexpected to the maker(s) as it is to its audience. This creates a seeming contradiction. *At Last Sight* is presenting itself to the creating group as an event which has controlled our activities and which has resisted a great deal of our own attempts at control, and

78 Text into Performance

yet it is at the same time the product of a working through of tensions which we can recognise as being our own. It no more or less belongs to the group than we do to it.

In the course of writing this chapter, one of the performers has left the group. Her reasons for doing so do not impact on this book - or indeed on the remaining rehearsals for *At Last Sight* - so much as her absence now necessitates a re-working of the piece, which will go beyond the relatively straightforward changes suggested at this chapter's start. It also provides me with a valuable bringing down to earth. Just as I have been exercising certain theoretical positionings within the pages of this book, so an unforeseen act has brought with it a reminder of the power of the random. In the midst of feeling that all is going well, something has happened to undercut that complacency. To say that the flow of this chapter is broken is to state no more than the reader will already know. But this has come at a useful time. It serves as a cautionary notice that this book is a response to the work of the production, and that the production itself is still too unfinished, too unmade, to attempt to write about it as though it were now in the past.

The irony of discovering this student's departure at the same time as I was writing about the group belonging to the work and the work belonging to the group is harsh. That the practical work is demanding now of renewed energies on the part of all its remaining members is apparent. What this will do to the spirits of the group is impossible to predict with any accuracy, although my suspicions are that they will respond with the same level of maturity, adaptability and positivity that they have shown since the project began.

Notes

---

[1] McAuley, G 'Towards an Ethnography of Rehearsal' in *New Theatre Quarterly* Vol. XIV, Part 1 (NTQ 53) February 1998. p.80.
[2] *ibid.* p. 81.
[3] *ibid.* p.76.
[4] The importance of this cannot be overstated. The process of documenting *At Last Sight* from within denied the possibility of analysis being something 'apart'. The here-and-nowness of the analysis was intended to show the processes of making work in a way that other forms of documentation disallow. A consequence of this approach has been an identification of the ways in which performance making is beset by blind alleys and emphasis-shifts which *at the time of making* appear to possess promise. The

documentation of the processes leading to *At Last Sight*, therefore, has been concomitant with the processes it describes.

[5] Jung, C.G., cited in *Critical Reasoning.* Thomson, A. Routledge, 1996. p.161.

[6] See Spender, S 'The Making of a Poem' in Ghiselin, B. *The Creative Process.* New American Library, New York and Ontario, 1952 pp.112-125

[7] Brecht, S. *the Theatre of Visions: Robert Wilson.* Methuen, London, 1994. pp. 9-10.

[8] Williams, B. *Problems of the Self.* Cambridge University Press, 1973. p. 13.

[9] *ibid.* p. 17.

[10] Chaos, contradiction and confusion are central features of contemporary practice, and the ways in which these aspects are made manifest in writing about work is addressed in this book. In many ways the book is an attempt at articulating the tensions between chaos and order. Chaos and order, like the here-and-now of memory and the there-and-then of the remembered are not contradictions so much as vitally important aspects of the creative process.

[11] Kosuth, J. *Art after Philosophy.* 'Studio International', October 1969. p. 78.

[12] *Guide Lines for the Submission of Practical Projects in Drama, Dance and Performing Arts as 'Works'.* Standing Committee of University Drama Departments (SCUDD). Published April 1995.

[13] Lyotard, J.F, *Answering the Question: What is Postmodernism?* In 'Innovation/Renovation', Hassan, I. and Hassan, S. (eds), University of Wisconsin Press, Madison, 1983. pp. 81-82.

[14] As with the performance, so it is with the book. The fact that I did not know where the book would develop from one day to the next is not an accident or weakness of the methodology; uncertainty was written into the research as an inevitable and positive aspect. The book is not an analysis of an 'experimental performance'; it is an experimental activity in and of itself. It is in this way that *Tracing the Footprints* develops a new way of writing about performance.

[15] Burden, C. in *Talking Art*, Searle, A. (ed), Institute of Contemporary arts, London, 1993. p. 25

Chapter 4:
Performance Critique 1

The appraisal entered into here is hindered as much as it is helped by access to video footage of the first performance of *At Last Sight*. It is helped in that I am able to watch what happened in order to refresh my memory; it is hindered in that what I am watching on video is not what 'happened'. As Gay McAuley remarks

> A video recording of theatrical performance will be misread by people who see only through their experience of television, or who expect a 'replacement performance' rather than an analytical document.[1]

Whilst my role as joint-creator of *At Last Sight* means that I cannot be regarded, in this instance, as one who sees only through an experience of television, it is true that

> Video ... impose(s) the single perspective of the camera's eye ... while the camera also 'sees' much less than the human eye. In visual terms, theatrical expressivity depends crucially on the simultaneous functioning of detail ... the detail of objects and interactions and the ever-present reality of the performance space as a whole.[2]

There is a sense wherein watching a videotape still reads to us as the thing-as-it-was. We know this to be false at the same time as we are seduced by the images before our eyes. We feel this to a much lesser extent, I think, with still photographs. Performance photographs provide a distorted record, equal in distortion to video. But, perhaps for no greater reason than the fact that photographs offer an overt and unmistakably *fixed* picture of an event that happened through time, we regard them as partial traces of the documentation process and the video as a 'true record'.

At Last Sight was filmed with one camera only, which may prove to be problematic. McAuley believes that the use of three cameras allows for a type of integrity through synchronisation

> ... so that the tapes will play together. It is entirely feasible for a spectator to view three images simultaneously, scanning from one screen to another in a way which may approximate the theatre spectator's pattern.[3]

Watching the video version available to me allows the eye to wander to a certain extent, but the manner of its filming suggests nothing of the deliberateness of this as a directorial concept within the live performance.

I wonder now, with the benefit of hindsight, whether I have ever really made my intentions clear to anyone in the group. A part of this is that I have never really had any 'intentions' in the first place. Much has happened instinctively, with the group developing a vocabulary of performance, which has, in its own turn, allowed us to develop the work through rehearsals. That which began as a difficult process of creation – effectively, making a performance without being able to articulate or even identify what it was that we were trying to make – has developed, smoothly, to my mind, into a process where we all (or nearly all) know the 'rules', without ever spending much time in their discussion. It is a process, which many that have devised performance will be familiar with.

I feel that I have *carte blanche* to write with freedom about any aspect of the performers' activities, attitudes or comments that happen during rehearsals or performance. I have the safety net of knowing (of *feeling*, of *believing*) that I will not be violating any principles of trust between us. This remains the case even at those times when the relationship between myself and a member of the cast is stretched to an almost intolerable degree ... as it was with one of the performers, whose role was radically reconfigured no more than one hour before the audience entered the theatre. Any readers will arrive at their own conclusions as to the validity of this decision, and indeed of the manner in which the decision was employed. Suffice, at this stage and on my own part, to say that it was a decision I regret and one where, with the benefit of hindsight, I think I acted neither wisely nor well.

Whereas the rest of the group-members are able to work through the inevitable disparities between thought and technique without breaking stride, one of the performers has always been compelled to stop and apologise. She has to make public the voices in her head.

This has led to problems in rehearsal. Increasingly, as the student has arrested her work in this way, I became concerned that she would do the same thing in performance. In many ways this in-and-out-of-acting is precisely what the performance piece is fuelled by; however, this student's public corrections are so obviously (and at times painfully) *real* that they are exposing as sham the *acted* 'corrections' of the other members of the group. I have talked with her at some length about this, and I have said that there could well come a point where I would quite literally pull her from the work if I felt that she was not achieving an ability to control these breaks. The student was, I think and hope, aware that I was not saying this as a threat designed to bully her into a different type of performance, so much as it was the articulation of my own genuine and increasing concerns.

By the time we got into the performance venue (a large theatre at a venue in Belgium) the student had not managed one rehearsal without halting her own performance to either apologise to the group or myself or to berate herself for 'getting it wrong'. Her friends talked with her about this, which resulted, it needs to be said, no discernible improvement. This has been particularly upsetting because the student in question's best work is really very good and she is always watchable. She has a type of presence which is exactly as it sounds ... she is present in the work. Her commitment and care are palpable and all she really needs to do is to believe in that. This may read like performance as self-help; as a blend of 1960's idealism and drama-as-therapy. If so, the words I am using are inappropriate and clumsy. What I mean to suggest is that this student's work is in no way particularly weaker than that of her peers, other than in her inability to move seamlessly through 'errors'. She is overly harsh on herself, and nothing the group or I can say seems to offset that.

What this is leading up to is the fact that during our final scheduled rehearsal, she was still unable to get through a run without stopping. As soon as our last rehearsal was over, I told her that her participation put the production at risk, and that I was going to pull her from the work. This was some two hours before the audience arrived. Even as I said it, I knew it was a mistake.

The student was, quite naturally, deeply upset. More, I think, with herself than with me; although this may be wishful thinking on my part. I believe she expected me to respond in the way that I did. None of the rest of the group argued with my decision. I think they could all see it coming and felt a type of powerlessness. In hindsight, I wish I had acted differently. My decision hurt and embarrassed one of the cast greatly, and I feel now that I should have put her feelings as a person, and as my student, ahead of my own concerns for the production. Perhaps an audience in front of her would have led to a different and more sustained type of concentration. I have no way of knowing whether this would have been the case.

The students went and sat in the dressing room as the rest of the group divided her sections up between themselves. I have to say that everybody dealt well with the consequences of this unplanned absence, and this included the ousted student herself. She was bitterly disappointed, and yet responded with maturity and more good grace than I had any right to expect. I made it plain to her that the events of today bore no relevance on future performances, and that I believed I had no real choice ... that to include her in the performance at this stage was neither fair to herself or to her peers. Her performance had become like an accident waiting to happen. There was such a feeling of inevitability to her lapses that the cast was on tenterhooks every time she spoke a passage of text.

The closer we came to the performance the more upset she became. She cried and was quite inconsolable. She sat in the audience space as we crammed in a last rushed rehearsal and her sobs acted as soundtrack for the performance. It was harrowing to experience. The emotion was so patently *real* that it functioned as a frame for everything on stage. I then asked if she would be prepared to sit in the performance space, during the performance, and just allow her feelings, her tears and her pain, to be integrated into the work. I am not proud of asking this. It was an exploitative request, and one, which I would have considerable difficulty in justifying on any sort of humanitarian grounds. It was not a calculated request in the literal sense, because I simply asked it as I thought it; but it was cold and perhaps it was cynical. The student agreed to do as I asked, as much, I think, as a means of being part of the production as because she could see any logic in my thoughts.

What happened in performance was something I had not anticipated. The new and temporary 'role', of a young woman seated at upstage right and sobbing, gave a charge to the entire work. Members of the cast would crouch next to her during the performance, touch her, dry her tears and share lit cigarettes. It was, on one level, as though *At Last Sight* had become her story. On another level, and much more emphatically, it read as though the sexual and emotional relationships within the group - which I had fabricated in the programme notes – were of such an intensity that the student, as an individual rather than as a 'performer', was simply unable to control her pain.

It was apparent to me at this stage, watching from the audience, that one of the male performers had an emotional connection with Sarah that went beyond friendship. The ways in which he touched and looked at her were of a different quality to the behaviour of the rest of the cast. I know now, from speaking with them after the performance, that they have, for some time now, felt a growing attraction for each other, which they have struggled against and which now seems set to develop into a love affair.

In writing these words, I am inevitably running the risk of moving into areas that are personal and, as such, are not the business of this book. However, it would be remiss of me not to record something here, which in its own turn cannot fail to impact on our future rehearsals. Affairs and sexual encounters between performers are common, no less so when those performers are students. In itself, it is generally no more or less than a consequence of late-night rehearsals and the close proximity, at times both emotional and physical, between people with shared interests. Performance is also always about looking. It provides one of the very few occasions in our society when we are invited and even compelled to watch each other. There is an unavoidable erotics to this. It would be alarming in its own way if the erotic nature of this did not spill over into some type of sexual *frisson* between performers. Some directors will counsel against this, believing that sexual relationships within the cast work to the detriment of the cast *per se*; that jealousies, petty squabbles and perhaps even the collapse of the relationship will create problems. Others may feel that the group is what and who the group is. If they are lovers, so be it. If people in the group do not get on with each other, so be it.

With *At Last Sight* there is an irony to the fact that the lie of lovers is now becoming true. It is an irony, which I am happy to embrace. I feel no moral responsibility for their actions (or intentions), any more than I would if this were a production of *Julius Caesar*. The work is neither responsible nor accountable for any desires or passions within the cast. The group members are adults and are capable of arriving at their own decisions as to who they wish to be involved with and why. If the two students involved become lovers during the time between now and the end of their time together in the group then we, as a group, have to live and deal with that in the same way that we are dealing with another student's departure. It happens. On a positive level, I would expect their feelings for each other to be explored (exploited?) in future rehearsals and future performances. The work is as much about who the group members are and what they are feeling as it is about the words and actions we are seeking to present. I have written earlier in this documentation of my cynicism with regard to 'invisible theatre' as a tool for social change, but as a theatrical device, and *in this instance*, it was effective, and, as such, successful. The lies in the programme had been told in order to see whether an audience would believe what they read for no better reason than that those lies were being offered in a 'truthful' form. If the experience of performing the work in Belgium stands in any way as 'evidence' - and I believe that it does - then the work is opening up possibilities for interventions that I had never, prior to this project, even considered. We can tell the truth in performance and the form makes that truth read as a lie; we can tell lies in the programme and that form makes those lies read as truth. The potential for future projects is immense. For anybody interested in truth and lies (and how can any of us make art and not be?) then this intervention provides a frame within which a seemingly endless series of explorations can be made. For if we are able to subvert and displace the idea of certainty even before the spectators take their seats, then perhaps we are more able to tell the truth about the lies of performance than if we were to perpetuate the belief that the world beyond the performance is somehow fixed and factual.

In a key moment of the performance, one of the performers addresses the audience directly, explaining that she will be speaking in sign language for part of the performance. Some time later, whilst other members of the cast are presenting action and dialogue on stage, this student begins to whisper to a male spectator. She asks him why he is watching her rather than the performance *per se*. She asks whether he likes looking at her. She tells him she has noticed that he has been watching her. The words and the delivery are overtly flirtatious. In fact, the words are no more than a development of an earlier section where she has asked the audience whether they think that her lips are painted red for their collective gaze. Structurally, the only difference here is that the spectator is alone and is made complicit in that gaze: it is being returned. Emotionally there are a great many differences. The student is an attractive young woman. She is aware that she is exploiting this in this scene and is comfortable with the complexities of speaking in these whispered tones to a male stranger. The fact that this stranger may well not understand any of her words should not diminish the effectiveness of the encounter. It is loaded with whispered intimacy and invitation.

It is perhaps a crude means of playing with notions of the gaze. It came about, like much of this work has, by accident. During one rehearsal, the student was sitting on the floor in a down stage position when she began whispering to me. The words were only whispered because other members of the cast were still performing and this performer did not wish to upset their concentration. The words themselves were inconsequential: she was asking if she could leave the space to make a pre-arranged phone call to a letting agent. Two things were interesting. The first was that I felt drawn into the world of the performance by the initiation of a dialogue with one of the cast whilst the rest of the performance continued. It was as though I were no longer invisible, which was a strange realisation, because we had never been operating with any notion of the 'fourth wall'. Whispering my own response to the student only served to enhance this feeling of participation ... of a being in at the same time as a being out.

The second was that I was made aware of the intimacy of whispers within a public space. There was nothing salacious about the content of our dialogue, yet the form imbued it with a kind of secret sharing. In terms of performance this is exciting because within a whispered relationship there is the possibility for empathy born of a primarily somatic engagement. The body can fool the mind. As an example of this we can say that if performer **A** were to prod performer **B** in the chest repeatedly there is a possibility that performer **B** would become angry, even though s/he is aware that performer **A** is only acting. The body's responses can over-rule the more reasoned responses of the mind. In this way a performer whispering to a stranger might lead to an emotional engagement on his part. This engagement would exist in spite of the fact that he would know, logically, that the words were either part of a prepared text or else were negated by the context within which they were being uttered.

This may not amount to a 'legitimate' working through of the idea. Certainly, I grasped the idea almost as it came with little thought of any problematic consequences. Fortunately, there were no problems with this section in (or following) the performance. According to the student (I was too far away to bear reliable witness to the exchange) the spectator, a Belgian male in his thirties who spoke English well, responded to her words with whispers of his own. He said that yes, indeed, he had been watching her more than any of the others, and that yes, he was enjoying looking at her very much. According to her and also to other members of the group, this same spectator spent the remaining fifty minutes following the student with his eyes, ignoring everything else that occurred on stage.

I am able to trace this interest I have in on-stage whispers to a production of *A Winter's Tale* at the Everyman Theatre, Liverpool in 1987. Before the performance could begin, the director came out on the stage and addressed the audience. She told us that the actress playing the part of Paulina had lost her voice and would have to whisper the part. The audience duly applauded this spirit of 'The Show Must Go On'. When the character of Paulina first spoke, and indeed she did so in a whisper, I was drawn in to her words to a much greater degree than had she proclaimed them in the manner (and at the level) of the rest of the cast. The words carried easily. No sounds came from the audience and the acoustics of the space ensured that every word was clearly heard. After a few moments, the actors sharing scenes with Paulina (the performer's name escapes me) began to moderate their own voices until before long every performer in the cast was whispering.

I did not particularly enjoy the 'play'. The direction did not impress me and the set, costumes and actors were ordinary. Had it not been for the whispers I suspect that I would have forgotten the experience almost as soon as the evening had passed. As it was, it remains one of the most powerful examples of theatre I have ever witnessed. Years later, when watching a production of *Othello* at the Young Vic Theatre, I can remember aching for some of the unplanned for whispered restraint of the Everyman *Winter's Tale*. Willard Whyte, as Othello, bellowing his speech over the dead Desdemona as though he were shouting instructions across a parade ground and in a high wind had little to offer. When the audience had been invited to listen attentively in Liverpool we had done so. We had listened in the way that one listens to conversations through a hotel wall. The fainter the words the greater our urgency to hear. There had been more intimacy, more sharing and more engagement in that straining to hear than in any of the Young Vic projection.

Whispers then have long been an aesthetic device I have wished to utilise. The intimate nature of this performance has allowed me to explore this aesthetic without feeling that the device is either arbitrary or ill conceived. Again, it is a guess. What works for or appeals to me may not work for an audience. It will certainly not work for all members of an audience. As ever, all that one can do is make guesses based on the blend of judgement, experience and instinct that we each carry with us. If a whisper is also possessed of a certain filmic quality, of an eavesdropping on the part of the spectator, then that too is appropriate to the work, which has always been driven by a sensibility born of a love of film.

In writing these words, I am coming to realise that all of my best guesses are really wishes dressed up as strategies. They are hopes and very little more: and in this they are at least as optimistic as they are informed. That this is the nature of creating work does not make its realisation any easier to accept. It makes the creation of performance more of a lottery than I would normally care to admit. The very absence of any 'rules' of success, which makes the commencement of each project such an exciting leap in the dark, is the same thing that leads to experienced practitioners feeling every bit as vulnerable as the new. We move bodies in space and time and light, and sometimes give them words to speak, in the hope that something of our original intentions will find a way to speak to strangers seated in the dark. We play – or I am playing here – with issues of redemption towards a decidedly unstable end. The spectators no more share my world-view than I feel any desire to make a work that seeks to show them how to think. Which makes the construction of the work seem somehow shallow and without purpose.

I can recognise these doubts as a direct consequence of reflective analysis. In tracing my intentions thus I am also inevitably recalling something of my fears. When a project has no clear function other than as an example of an 'interesting' way of making work, then there are times when one's faith in the interest of spectators is stretched too thin to bear. With this project the absence of any obvious function places an almost intolerable weight on the success of the work according to purely aesthetic criteria. When there is no 'message' all that can remain is the hope – or at best, the *belief* – that the work will be sustained through the internal logic of its own construction ... that the aesthetic qualities displayed will be enough to make an audience attend.

There is a Catch-22 in my own argument here ... which exposes my concerns as no more than a wishing for protection *via* the very criteria for theatre as a tool for social reform that I am resolutely disinclined towards. For whereas issue-based dramas can take solace in the assumed worthiness of their causes, be they stated or implied, work such as *At Last Sight* has no such safety net. Offering audiences no more or less than an 'interesting take' on performance, the project almost invites criticisms of esoteric and elitist self-indulgence.

There is a perversity to my mood now, as we enter what are the final stages of making the work. The first performance was a success, according to my own terms and expectations. The piece went well, the cast pulled together and the response from spectators was sufficient to make the entire group feel a genuine confidence about the project.

This last point is an interesting one, because the words spectators offer to makers of performances are not always accurate responses. I know this to be so by the dishonesty of many of my own post-performance comments to actors, directors, dancers, musicians and writers. To say that a spectator enjoyed any given production is an impossible claim to support: the comments made by spectators are simply not sufficient to be afforded the status of evidence or proof. Notwithstanding this, we continue to believe the good things that we hear from spectators, just as we seek to discredit and dismiss the bad. A desperate triumph of hope over experience.

The lies we told in our programmes served their purpose, and indeed exceeded our expectations in an entirely positive way. The work contained an interesting blend of the at-risk and the well rehearsed. We are left with enough time now to work through any changes we feel necessary. Why then these self-doubts? I suspect that they are nothing more than the usual concerns, exaggerated here by their inclusion in a written documentation. Under 'normal' circumstances, by which I mean the making of a performance project, which would not be accompanied by a written discourse, there would be precious little time for such doubts to emerge. Other tasks take up other times and any concerns that do exist would be reconciled in the rehearsal space rather than at the desk. This does not mean that a process of reflective documentation is to be avoided. I have no doubts that this performance is and will be better and richer than would have been the case if the 'making' were not so closely aligned with reflection and explanation. But the process is draining. It provides no respite: one is rehearsing or else one is writing.

The result of this is a concentration that borders on the obsessive.

A consequence of the performance thus far is that the group feels an ownership of the work. Any doubts they may have harboured as to the ways in which it would be read seemed to be allayed by experience of performing the work in public and by the immediate and subsequent responses of spectators. They feel now as though the work is *theirs*. And, if truth be told, I feel threatened here by the very thing that I have so strenuously sought to achieve, and which the group has so clearly attained. This makes me wonder whether I have only been seeking the *illusion* of collaboration, whilst secretly (as a secret even to myself?) wanting to maintain a directorial control which would subjugate the cast to the status of breathing puppets.

What I do know is that I trust the group. I have every faith in their individual and collective abilities to develop the work constructively; which leaves me with the bleak realisation that any concerns I have are not for the work as much as for myself. That I care less about the changes they may make to the work than the ways they may change how they care about me.

I do not think that the cast members are aware of this, and I hope that they are not. It was not something that I was aware of until such time as I sat down and wrote the words preceding these. I wonder whether a part of this is tied in with the feelings I often have of anti-climax when I see work I have directed being performed. I say this not because the work itself fails to match up to my hopes or expectations (that it singularly does so is another issue altogether) so much as because a part of me is sitting in the audience and envying the performers. This envy is not connected to the quality or otherwise of the work they are in; nor is it because I regard myself as an actor *manqué*. The envy exists, I think, because the work is passing out of my hands and into theirs. The pleasures ordinarily felt by performers during and immediately after a performance only serve to highlight the emptiness of this director's role. One becomes redundant after so many weeks or months of being in a position of control.

This may leave me with no alternative to the idea that a function of creating the work has been, for me, a means of satisfying some desire for control. Perhaps some oblique aspects of catharsis are being met by this exercising of control. Rather than seeking to hide from this in shame, perhaps I should simply be acknowledging it as an inevitable aspect of performance-making and as a (presumably) constructive and (hopefully) harmless means of giving vent to that which might otherwise emerge in everyday life. Whatever the wider ramifications, I am still left with the feeling that I have been deluding myself as to too many of the reasons behind embarking on the project. It concerns me that much of that which has felt good through the giving away has been no more than a sham. It is actually twice as false as it first appears, because in the first instance, my feelings of collaboration have disguised a number of submerged but no less strong feelings of control, and in the second I have never really given the work away. I am clinging to the work precisely *because* the project provides me with the tools for controlling the group.

We can go two ways with this. I can either accept this desire for control as something that exists and that can itself be made subject to control; or else I regard it as something invidious and beyond restraint. Because *Tracing the Footprints* has been driven from the start

by a reading of what *is* rather than by that which might *otherwise be* ...
by a commitment to working with the givens of the specific experience
of making *this* work, at *this* time and with *this* group, it would be
illogical now to bemoan the situation. The flip-side of an interest in
heuristics, of the process of research being as concerned with the
researcher's developing knowledge of the self as it is with a knowledge
of the subject, is that this 'self' may not be the type one would wish to
discover. Notwithstanding this, the recognition of any given aspect of
my own behaviour would only be more or less 'good' than any other if
this book were concerned with the valuing of self. Recognising my self
as one of the elements of the work means that I am also a subject for
the study that is this book ... even *the* subject. Which is not the same
thing as turning the book into a value-judgement as to my own worth.
To recognise it, to read it and to be able to make judgements as to the
impact it may be having on the work is one thing, to seek to subvert it
simply because the process of reflection has unearthed it is another
thing entirely.

Notes

---

[1] McAuley, G. *The Video Documentation of Theatrical Performance* in 'New
Theatre Quarterly' Vol. X No. 38, May 1994. p. 184.
[2] *ibid.* p.186.
[3] *ibid.* p. 189.

Chapter 5:
Performance Critique 2

We are looking here and now at the way things will be for the next performance. A number of changes from the presentation in Belgium are unavoidable. The cast is one down on this time six weeks ago and the need to alter the work has thus been imposed on the group. As ever, it seems, a certain *caveat* exists. There will be no easy distinction here between the process of revision through rehearsals and the process of evaluating subsequent performances. In writing at the time of making there is a progression from one to the other, but this will not be articulated here under headings such as 'Revisions' and 'Evaluation' or 'Process' and 'Product'. Rather, the two will collapse in on each other even as I write.

There are certain 'givens' for the revised production: many elements that will not change. Thus, the process of revision is also always in part a process of projection. No matter how radical the changes to the piece may be, I have a firm idea now of how the work will emerge. I cannot isolate my developing familiarity and understanding from this period of re-evaluation and revision. If *At Last Sight* were never to be performed again, I would still be able to make an assessment of it as a *thing done*. As a publicly presented event. This changes my role. I am no longer engaged entirely in a process towards an end, so much as I am moving from one realised end towards another. How it *was* is a part of my thinking now, in the same way that how it *will be* is.

The shifts in wording from the 'original' working script, through its various transformations reveal much about the process of revision. Much of the spoken text was deliberately inaudible, consisting of whispers between performers and from performers to spectators. In this way, no authoritative record of words spoken could ever exist. Increasingly, as the cast has come to regard the work as their own, they have been willing to provide verbal as well as physical ideas. Indeed, if there is an imbalance in terms of material, that imbalance now is even more noticeable in the ease with which the group is able to draw on a literary rather than a physical confidence. As such, rehearsals are still as prone to being word-bound now as at the start of rehearsals. The principle difference is that now we are aware of the changes that *need* to be made to *At Last Sight*, which is enabling us to force moments of movement, even at those times when we would all seem more comfortable with the further provision of words.

It is ironic that it is only now, when the work is being made for an exclusively English speaking audience, that we are beginning to make the work play with a visual coherence instead of a predominantly verbal one.

There are more significant changes from the performance in Belgium. Three new elements have been introduced.

The first is a section of text, which has been written as a type of American B Movie dialogue. The dialogue, which is concerned with an encounter between a man and a woman, has not been constructed with any sense of which gender speaks which words. We will work that out in rehearsal. I am making no claims as to the quality of the text as it reads. It is simplistic, even 'cod' dialogue. However, we have already begun to work the words into a scene, with the students doing the bulk of this without any great interference from myself, and it seems as though the section is developing into a scene of some pace, energy and action. A drink is thrown, a kiss is attempted, an embrace is made and the performance space is used both intelligently and well. The text was introduced because *At Last Sight* is suffering from an absence of encounters. It is as though we need to build more moments of dialogue into the work and take out some of the long(er) sections of monologue. Similarly, we need to exploit the possibility of physical contact between performers, which is made logical by the thematic structure of *At Last Sight* as at least partly concerned with a series of meetings between a man and a woman in a rented room. Without physicalising these *meetings* between performers (perhaps I need to swallow the false pride of postmodernism and say 'meetings between *characters*') the audience may not be receiving enough identifiable elements for them to engage in a readerly process of deconstruction. Too little is being placed before them for any engagement to take place.

This feels (or at least it may sound) like capitulation. Like an admission on my part that spectators need straightforward elements of narrative in order to attend to performance. I know this not to be the case. If it is an admission of anything it is of my emerging recognition that whilst others may possess the necessary skills to make work that functions adequately without recourse to a structure of 'story', my own skills are not at this level. The capacity for recognition may be a useful component of analysis almost in itself. However, in terms of making performance, I am still faced with the challenge of developing *At Last Sight* into the best work that it can be, and of doing this in the realisation that my own best may not always be quite good enough.

The way in which I am making an assessment as to the 'needs' of the production is no less a process of guess work now than it was at the first. The fact that I am able to respond to the production as it has so far been given is still exemplified by a faith, blind or otherwise, in my own reading of a situation. In many ways, directing can be seen as a placing oneself in a spectator's position: of making decisions based on one's own judgement and taste.

Adding the new scene feels right, and I am affording that feeling the status of a requirement. The work *feels* as though it is short of something, I *think* I know what that something is, and accordingly I can then say that the work *needs* something else in order to be put *right*. It is a process of assumptions wherein the language one uses (even if that language is no more or less than the language of thought) presupposes some kind of logical link between response and reaction. The reality may be no more than a stumbling in the half-light of the latter stages of making, rather than in the darkness of beginnings. 'Thoughts', in this sense and at this point in the process, emerge as combinations of memories, expectations and sensations; in the context of making performance they can be described as movements (or moments) which have not yet happened. Some are more fleeting and ephemeral than are others. The ones that last longest or arrive with most force are the ones most likely to be translated into action and transcribed into the performance text.

Because the brain is not like a computer - inasmuch as it is not capable of repeating its actions and it is equally incapable of preserving ideas in a vacuum – thoughts are subject to the vagaries of time.[1] The wonderful idea of today is exposed tomorrow as a sham device. This happens. Experience – or thought as memory – tells us not to worry overmuch about these shifts, for just as much scientific research concludes that its original hypothesis was fundamentally wrong, so the creation of performance is a fluid game of re-adjustments, re-negotiations and blind alleys. The only litmus paper we possess is the way we feel and think the work is shaping up. It is as imprecise an endeavour as one could ever encounter. Wittgenstein told us that problems are solved, not by giving new information, but by arranging what we already know, and this is a close approximation to the act of creative making.[2] We work with what we know, arranging that knowledge into a new syntax. A syntax that allows us to create a structure that is then able to convey more than the individual elements could hope to contain. We trust that this structure will work, and by 'work' we mean that it will communicate something of the maker's intent.

With work where the structure is complex, the maker might favour a certain type of spectator. Certainly, with *At Last Sight*, the work has been made thus far with a view to presentations to 'informed' viewers. The ways in which these spectators have been so informed (and the ways in which I hope future spectators will be) is in the sense of them constituting a 'guessing right' group. Every maker of work will have her or his own 'ideal'. John Cage, for example, has written that he is

> on the side of keeping things mysterious, and I have never enjoyed understanding things. If I understand something, I have no further use for it. So I try to make a music which I don't understand and which will be difficult for other people to understand, too.[3]

A cognitive process is required from spectators: one that allows for them to piece together a positive response out of their own experiences of non-narrative theatre forms. Just as my own processes of making are guesses, so then do spectators undertake the processes of reception. Writing specifically about spoken language, Sue Savage-Rumbaugh nevertheless goes some considerable way towards articulating the process of making work for public reception, alongside the attendant process of receiving, when she states that

> Comprehension demands an active intellectual process of listening to another party while trying to figure out … the other's meaning and intent – both of which are always imperfectly conveyed. We know what we think and what we wish to mean. We don't have to figure out 'what it is we mean', only how to say it. By contrast, when we listen to someone else, we not only have to determine what the other person is

saying, but also what he or she means by what is said, without the
insider's knowledge that the speaker has.[4]
    We make performance in the knowledge of this imprecision
because, as Lewis Carroll's Dodo says to Alice, it is generally the case
that the best way to explain a thing is to do it. We can imagine 'perfect'
performances without ever being able to make them, just as we can
harbour dreams of 'perfect' spectators, who pick up on our every
nuance, no matter how subtle or strange. But the testing ground for
performance is performance. Written words are measured. They can be
corrected and refined. A draft is recognised as such in ways that
performances are not. When practical work in progress goes public it
does so, almost always, without the safety net status of a work in
transition. Weak work analysed well is still weak work, even though the
analysis may break new ground. We make work because we need to test
our own 'guessing right'. The results are only ever good for the time it
takes for the performance to run in the there and then. Perhaps not even
for that long, because in watching work play, we are already refining
and rethinking as we watch.
    As ever, it seems, within the pages of this work, this sounds
more bleak than it feels. *At Last Sight* is already as accomplished a
piece of work as I had ever allowed myself to expect. Perhaps there is
something in the nature of a reflective process, which is drawing me
towards an articulation that proffers gloom in *lieu* of the optimism that I
actually feel. Anybody who has made performances will realise that
certain of the issues arising in rehearsal are actually pleasant to work
through in practice and equally unpleasant to describe.[5] We need to
remember that the making of performance in the context within which I
am functioning is a choice and not an imperative. There is a joy in the
process, which the isolation of writing this book is at some odds with.
There have been no rehearsals that I have not been excited to attend; no
problems of where to go next that I have not been pleased to seek
solutions to. Even during those rehearsals when the work feels like a
game of Solitaire in which the shuffling of the deck has created a
situation where no possibility of 'success' is possible, something
positive remains. For, unlike the imposition of order on a chance
configuration of a hand of cards (where each new configuration is
indeed 'new') every 'failed' rehearsal is always also a success. I can
recognise from this that the stages of the creative process undertaken to
this point have involved preparation, incubation, inspiration and
evaluation, and that any divisions between the stages have been elastic.
    One of the central ideas of *At Last Sight* is the conflict between
truth and lies. To this end, differing perceptions are actively

encouraged. A truth may be read as a lie and *vice versa*. There is, I hope, a tension in this which is more than glib and ironic. When detachment and engagement are being sought in this way, however, it is difficult to envisage any distancing from that same postmodernism where irony is seen to reign. *At Last Sight* is about representation, and it plays with representation in a self-conscious way. It is about an erosion of fixity and a distrust of meaning. It is about the recognition that everything spoken is always the already said. It is concerned with the slippery relationship between 'I' and 'You'. It wants control and it wants to be given away. It seeks indeterminacy (and is determined to have it). It strives for originality within an absence of faith in originality as a realistic aim.

I write the above as reminders to myself as much as pointers to the reader. I write because, like the performers in *At Last Sight*, I am no longer sure of the distinction between the truth as it was and the truth that I have subsequently invented. Like Alice, I am losing and finding myself in a strange place. For me, that place is the Wonderland gap between the past events of rehearsal to performance and the present event of performance to rehearsal. Derrida's assertion that nothing can exist outside of the text is becoming all too painfully real. Lost in the text of *At Last Sight* I am no longer able to see a way clear. I am not sure whether *At Last Sight* is a fact or an event. Whether this book is the experience itself or merely a trace of the experience of the performed other. As Laura Marcus states in *Auto/Biographical Discourses* 'The self does not pre-exist the text but is constructed by it ... the self 'finds' itself in its acts of self-expression.'[6]

I know that the work's proceeding without a clear plan is no handicap. What *At Last Sight* may have been hindered by in terms of its having no blueprint for a route by which to progress, has been equally fortuitous in that that same absence has provided space for progression, which was impossible to predict. The educational philosopher J. P. Guilford recognises this as being paradigmatic of divergent thinking

> In tests of convergent thinking there is almost always one conclusion or answer that is regarded as unique, and thinking is to be channelled or controlled in the direction of that answer.... In divergent thinking, on the other hand, there is much searching about or going off in various directions. This is most obviously seen when there are no unique conclusions. Divergent thinking ... is characterised ... as being less goal-bound. There is freedom to go off in different directions .... Rejecting the old solution and striking out in some direction is necessary.[7]

The process of creating *At Last Sight* is an example of divergent thought ... although at times this seems like too complimentary a term to describe that which *feels* so chaotic.[8] Bertrand Russell's *Enquiry into Memory and Truth* tells us that for a journey of investigation to have any worth it needs to be commenced with inarticulate certainty and concluded with articulate hesitation.[9] Allan Owens writes in *Mapping Drama* that whilst the most overtly problematical educational states are ignorance and certainty the single worst case scenario is always encountered in 'articulate certainty'.[10] If the process of making *At Last Sight* is demonstrable of a faith in anything at all then it is of a faith in doubt. In the concept of uncertainty as a thing to be clung to and sustained. Kenneth J. W. Craik embraces doubt as a positive phenomenon

> If I ever conceive of any original idea, it will be because I have been abnormally prone to confuse ideas ... and have thus found remote analogies and relations which others have not considered! Others rarely make these confusions, and proceed by precise analysis.[11]

There is also the issue of group. Not in the sense of the feelings of power recognised earlier, so much as in the pleasure of working with people who share a commitment to making work *work*. The feelings of camaraderie are at times quite intense. As a teacher, I take pleasure from introducing ideas, which the students will be encouraged to learn from and through. As a part of the group, I take even more pleasure in the erosion of the teacher/student relationship that exists elsewhere within the curriculum. A part of this has been formed by the trip to Belgium. We travelled together, took our meals together, drank together and talked for extended periods of time, all of which would be impossible within the 'normal' structures of timetabled contact on campus. Accordingly, I feel that I have come to know the cast well, and to like them as people at the same time as I can acknowledge their accomplishments as students.

How far can this go before it reads as a *clique*? How openly can I state my emotional attachment to the group and still function in my professional capacity as a lecturer? Although I will not carry out the assessment of the *At Last Sight* group, I do teach a course in Contemporary Theatre Practice where members of the cast are my students. I am also likely to function as a second marker on the assessment of these and other members of the group on other courses. Whilst I may feel able to separate issues of affection from those of assessment, I need to remain aware that other students (and indeed my colleagues in the department) may not be quite so sure. Perception is important, and it would be foolish of me to think that the opinions of others did not matter so long as my own conscience was clear. As far as the students in the group go, I am confident that they share my faith in dispassionate marking. They know (I hope) that being pleased with their progress is one thing (I cannot mark *that* anyway, even if I were able to mark anything at all)[12] whilst being pleased with them (because I find their company pleasing) is another thing entirely.

What I would be distressed to discover would be any reduction in the recognition of the group's worth as students, for no greater reason than that they are working closely with a tutor for whom that close working relationship is inevitably spilling over into close relationships.

This is not to suggest that we socialise together outside of rehearsals. I do not meet with members of the group at times other than those we have arranged as part of the course. But it does happen that when I see them by chance in the department we are likely to stop and talk, in ways that are less likely to occur with 'other' students. To a certain extent, this is happening with each of my colleagues who are working on productions. The closeness is a part of the process. In making work together, we reveal much of who we are, and in so doing an intimacy is created. Without some sort of trust, much of the work made would never (*could* never) emerge. With *At Last Sight* this phenomenon is writ large because the work is intrinsically dealing with aspects of self. Just as the cast has had nowhere to hide from the exposure of much that makes them who they are, so I have been unable to avoid witnessing these acts of revelation as and when they have emerged. As we have seen through Grotowski's work, this revelation is at its most acute when performers play their characters by playing who they are. They 'must not illustrate but accomplish an act'.[13] In so doing they 'express as fact the fiction of their narratives'.[14]

These last few paragraphs will be regarded as either a deviation from or a development of my *rationale* for the new scene, depending upon the views of the reader. For my own purposes, the thoughts are developmental, in that the process of description and explanation is perpetually interlocking. One cannot be separated out from the other, so that pages of 'what' are followed neatly by pages of 'how' and then still more discrete pages of 'why'. The rehearsal process of *At Last Sight* is the same as this. We throw ideas around and are as likely to sit down and talk the ideas through as we are to get on our feet and try to work them out practically. The thinking is as central to the work as is the doing. If this is regarded as a 'luxury' – and I am sure that a great many directors working professionally with only a very limited time to create would feel that it is – then it is a luxury that is receding as the time between the now of rehearsal and the then of the final performance is collapsing.

The second idea is that the consumption of alcohol as a part of *At Last Sight* needs to be ritualised in some way.[15] There seems to be something innately British about drinking such vast quantities in such a brief time. The fact that it conforms to one of the abiding stereotypes of British behaviour is making me feel that we should exaggerate the actions somehow. There are also the ongoing issues of energy and pace. I have been wondering if some sort of drinking game (which again seems to be a quintessentially British pastime) would not provide a means of investing the work with pace at the same time as that pace is arrived at *via* an activity that is appropriate within the performance framework already in place.

In the rehearsals leading up to the performance in Belgium, the cast worked with non-alcoholic drinks, rather than wine.[16] We had only one full rehearsal where wine was used. This was a matter of cost as much as anything else. In the spirit of a questioning of the currency of performative truth, we have considered using either non-alcoholic wine or coloured water in performance. Although this is something we have currently decided against, it is not ruled out for some time in the future. At the moment, the drinking, and the ways in which that drinking impact on individual performances within the work, are features of *At Last Sight*. This was never likely to be a production where the imitation of an action was going to be favoured over the presentation of an action itself. To borrow again from the traditions of Grotowski: "The performance is not an illusionist copy of reality, its imitation ... The actor does not play, does not imitate, or pretend. He is himself".[17]

Whilst the performers will not be 'acting drinking', they will be drinking in a performative fashion. I have written a series of words and numbers, for which I am planning to create corresponding 'ways of drinking'. The cast will inevitably develop these 'ways' further. There is no overt logic to the movements themselves. The words written are as follows:

1: Absolution.
2: Redemption.
3: Ephemera.
4: Solace.
5: Isolation.
6: Indicative Thought.

How the words and the actions come together, even if the idea stays, is not yet known.[18] I am imagining a concentrated burst of activity. A wild drinking game, where the rules seem to make absolute sense to the performers and absolutely no sense to the spectators. So that one performer might start the 'game' by calling a word - a literal cue – and then the cast drink themselves into near-oblivion, perhaps until another cue is uttered, or perhaps until all of the wine is consumed. What I do not want any more is the leisurely drinking of the Belgian performance without something more *urgent* that lifts it. There is an obvious analogy to be drawn between drinking and forgetting. I like the idea of this forgetting being twofold. In the first place, it is consistent with the content of *At Last Sight*, inasmuch as the content is thematically concerned with love and loss. In the second place, I will be interested to see what effect swift drinking has on the performers' ability to remember the words and actions still to come. It is a means of denying the performers the chance to drink at their own pace and also of a giving away of control ... of my control as a director and of the students' as performers.

I have talked some of this through with the group and we are already looking at ways of working this scene and of a point in the work where it might best fit. We are also discussing the possibility of allowing any one member of the cast the opportunity to start the scene at any time that she or he chooses. Leaving it, if not entirely to chance, then at least to the instincts of the cast, rather than to the decidability in advance of the director.

The third intervention is a piece of music, *Lullaby*, recorded by Shawn Mullins.[19] I played the song to the group in a rehearsal and at some considerable volume. The song became an instant soundtrack. We played it whenever we reached moments in rehearsal of not knowing where to go next. The words of the song are delivered in a laconic fashion (the words themselves tend towards the maudlin) apart from the chorus, which comes in with a rush and lifts the track.

In Belgium we used a radio, tuned in as part of the performance in order to allow the random to infiltrate the work. We all liked this idea, although we probably liked the reality rather less. Not only did the tuning in take some time, it also happened upon some dour-sounding stations just at the moment when the piece was so in need of an injection of pace and volume. At one point, I had wanted to use the sound of a radio playing softly all the way through *At Last Sight*, as though the sounds the spectators and performers were hearing were the sounds of a radio through a hotel wall. Like the whispered words of *A Winter's Tale*. We lost that idea somewhere along the way and the piece now feels like it does not need it. It smacks now of too naturalistic a device, as though I had been striving for an imitative 'other', rather than seeking to exploit the space as it is. Using *Lullaby* in place of the radio takes us away from our original idea. Notwithstanding that, I strongly suspect that we will end up using the track.

One of the male performers, Andrew, has created a piece of text that centres upon an appeal for a partner. The words are not without a sense of desperation. When he read them out in rehearsal, we all felt that they should be included in the performance. It seems appropriate for this performer to speak this section immediately after either a session of manic drinking, or the section where he forces his own head under water. This may, of course, have no logic whatsoever. It may be no more than another guess. Be that as it may, watching and listening to the student's delivery sparked these connections and they seem to make sense within my own reading of the structure of our work. Andrew seems to want to place himself at some emotional risk within *At Last Sight*, and I like the idea of this emotional risk coming after the physical risk of the drowning scene. The moment where he puts his head under water does bring its own risk. Rather than holding his breath, he attempts to breathe the water, to take it deliberately into his lungs. To force himself to drown.[20]

A female student's section on the female orgasm is being reworked. The way the scene works now is that whilst the student, Sarah, is in the process of speaking in a dry and informative manner, pointing to a prone and shrouded fellow performer with a cane, another student, Elizabeth, is mirroring the words with actions of her own. She is doing so in an equally deadpan way. As she says that 'nipples become erect', Elizabeth points to the chest of a male student, Glenn. The two are seated side by side on the bed at this point; when Sarah speaks of the vagina contracting, 'adjusting to circumstances', Elizabeth closes her own fist in front of Glenn's groin. Whilst this is going on, Andrew is plunging his head into a basin of water. In rehearsal, at least, this compression of three previously discrete scenes into one collage is playing effectively enough for us to run with the idea. Learned text, a disturbing level of risk and deadpan humour are placed side by side in a recurring montage. The eye of the watcher is drawn around the space in ways that seem to exemplify the freedom of watching live work, and the layering of sounds and images is creating a constructive cacophony.

Sarah knows that she will have to work hard to attract and hold the spectator's attention, which is giving her more of a challenge than was previously the case. Andrew's plunging (which is a development of an earlier scene where his head was held under water as part of an interrogation that never really worked in rehearsal) does now play as an attempt at suicide. Andrew emerges from the water gagging and coughing, only to thrust his head back under. There is something deeply disturbing about the action at the same time as it is fundamentally absurd. Sarah is ignoring both Andrew and Elizabeth and is playing only a response to the spectator's displacing of attention. At the moment, I am the only spectator. Sometimes I am joined by other members of the cast, Chris, Laurent and Anke. We find the scene funny and moving in turns, and the performers involved enjoy playing it. There are no doubts that we will use it in the piece. The only concern I have is that it may look as though we are expecting a certain response. I do not think that this is the case anywhere else in *At Last Sight*. What I want to avoid are moments where we run the risk of failing in public to match up to our directorial and performative intentions. During the rest of the work, our conceits are less overtly displayed than they might be here.

Increasingly, the work reads, I think, as elusive, as a thing almost but never quite accessible. The scene I have just described feels a little like we are going for broke, pitching a mass of energy into one extended moment as a type of climactic *dénouement*.

The work is becoming multi-layered, to the extent where the thinness of certain layers is disguised by a number of other (perhaps equally thin) layers. Whereas I was able, much earlier on in the process of making, to refer to Hockney's *Joiners* as a type of blueprint for *At Last Sight*, the grid-like placing of images side by side has shifted now towards a more appropriately performative overlap. One of the strongest things to have emerged in recent rehearsals is this sense of simultaneity. It is as though the running orders we have been so keen to create, as a means of confirming structure, have worked against us up until this point precisely because they have located actions sequentially. Our running order still exists - and we still value the sense of structure that it brings – but we are much more inclined of late to see scenes bleeding into each other. *Joiners* was useful as way into *At Last Sight* … the problem, I feel, has been one of knowing when to let *this* work break free of *that* structure.

The running order we have now is one which, although it will be inevitably subject to change (and overlap) nevertheless serves as an indication of the ways in which *At Last Sight* has shifted since its presentation in Belgium.

Whereas the first version of *At Last Sight* began with the cast removing the traces of previous performances, subsequent performances will begin with the cast milling around as a French language tape plays. The removal of traces *looked* fine, but I was always concerned that it was beginning the work with too much that was overtly illusory. The space was new to us and the traces were faked. Ironically, because our next performances will be delivered over a four-night period, the traces of rehearsals and previous performances will be real. Notwithstanding this, the on-stage eradication of evidence as a starting point no longer possesses the currency it once did. What we have now is the cast *behaving* rather than *acting* naturally. Having no prescribed movements to engage in means that they are able to initiate a performance wherein the lines between 'ordinary' and 'performative' attitudes are immediately introduced. As director, I have no idea of who will do what and when. They move amongst themselves and into the audience as they so choose.

The French language tape is one that was played by my wife at our home. My wife is currently taking a French evening class. The formulaic banality of the text amused us both: a customer in a bar ordering a coffee; a traveller, lost and asking for directions to the railway station; an encounter at a Lost Property desk, with an enquiry about a mislaid camera. The dialogue is delivered in so flat and colourless a fashion as to drain all of the emotion from the words. The tone is monotonous in the extreme, but the context of the tape subverts this monotony, changing it from weakness into choice. Listening to the tape felt a little like the experience of watching *At Last Sight*. It was both similar to and different from. Using the tape at the start of the show provides a type of clue for the spectators. It suggests being somewhere far from home, where the rules are not quite the same and have only been half-learned.[21] It communicates everything necessary to comprehension and nothing that is needed to feel and to emote. In this way, it is both a parallel to *At Last Sight* and its antithesis.

The French language tape is replaced with another cassette. All of this is done in full view of the audience. The lights are 'theatrical', but basic. A general wash of light across the space. The only change to this state now is towards the end of the piece, when the lights are taken half way down, paused and then taken to black. At all other times, the lights stay as they are. The new tape contains dialogue between two of the performers. Glenn and Liz have a brief conversation about commitment. We hear a crash, a chair breaking, which signals an abrupt end. The next voices we hear belong to two female Japanese students. They speak in whispers, urgently. The tape shifts then to a section where the cast members were recorded talking in restaurant. This conversation cuts out and a telephone conversation between Glenn, and Sarah Skelton, fades in.

During the Japanese section, Sarah Skelton walks off-stage, through a swing door and into a shower and toilet area. She showers, fully costumed, as are all of the women, in a white shirt and blue jeans. The men are all in dark suits and white shirts. All are barefoot. Sarah re-emerges as the telephone conversation ends. The tape is clicked off and thrown to one side by Glenn Robertson. Sarah speaks falteringly, using a type of half-invented sign language as an attempt to add to her articulation. She is wet through during this section. The sentences she speaks are sometimes no more than one or two words. The tone is sombre. At one point she takes a Polaroid photograph of the audience. She lays down stage right, holding this photograph.

The running order we have is full enough for me to be able to go through each of the elements and provide a commentary and explanation, which would run to several thousand more words. The running order is currently comprised of fifty seven separate sections, and to describe and explain each one would be perhaps not the most purposive way of providing the reader with a developing sense of the work. Better then to use this space to underpin and theoretically contextualise my current feelings and thoughts about the work, *and also about this stage of making work.*

I will describe the thinking that is driving *At Last Sight*. Like the project itself, this thinking has changed and developed. I am less inclined at this point to be satisfied with an inability to articulate (even to myself) the *rationale* behind directorial and/or writerly decisions. Where I was, only a matter of months ago, prepared to accept creative making as a thing driven in part at least by untraceable stimuli, I am now inclined towards a searching for the origin. This does not mean that the search is always successful. But it does mean that ideas that cannot be comfortably traced can be made subject to the same level of analysis as those ideas that can be seen to stem from a logical body of theory. At times, this might result in the articulation of incomprehension. Where this occurs, I am confident that this articulation is as valid as any other. It is not the job of this book to prove that the writer has the 'correct' answer to every challenge thrown up in the activity of making work, so much as it is to document a particular process in a manner that is as thorough as it is informed.

To argue thus - for an analytical framework that can be applied to the creation of a performance event - does not amount to an attempt to fix meaning. Rather, it allows me to identify the various elements of

At Last Sight that exist for analysis from the perspectives I am choosing to employ.

The next version of *At Last Sight* is likely to contain more elements of narrative, and indeed more of a narrative drive, than did the *At Last Sight* of Belgium, and there are certain (broadly postmodern) notions of narratology that inform the work. It begins with an acceptance that one's identity is determined by the narrative elements of one's own life. By this I mean that the best, perhaps even the only way to establish an identity is *via* the telling of story. We could better describe this as an ordering of episodes in such a way that one's life can be read as a narrative. What we do is thus who we are. Events, which we might regard as having a particular significance, are organised in ways that allow us to understand who we are. In this way, narrative provides us with the opportunity to conceive of self.[22]

Any and all narratives have a point of view, whether concealed or overt. The narrative itself goes some considerable way towards determining the location from which the spectator/reader experiences events and the narrative will always seek in some way to exert a control over the spectator's ways of perceiving. (At this point, I will abandon references to 'readers' and use 'spectators' as an all-encompassing term). By controlling, or guiding, the spectator's perception of *At Last Sight* I am attempting to suggest an identification with a certain way of watching. I am asking the spectator to engage in a particular type of watching, one that allows the spectator to believe that s/he is making of the work whatever s/he feels, at the same time as this process is actually set up and controlled by the maker. It offers a freedom from a directorial 'directing of the gaze', which is actually quite false. In creating a performance wherein the spectator's eye can wander without shame, I am still very much seeking control. We can recognise this as being in relative accord with notions of Althusser's 'interpellation', inasmuch as it is "a process which is controlled by the text, yet the reader is under the illusion that identification is freely entered into."[23]

At Last Sight abandons the idea of an audience as a like-thinking mass, since the product will be played in the knowledge that spectatorial identification and the reading of our played out narrative will differ from one person to the next. It is also being created with a faith (a faith in right guessing?) that enough of the audience will respond in similar ways to certain sections. For example, there are points when I want them to make certain connections, even at the same time as I cling fast to their freedom to choose. *Theoretically*, I want freedom; *directorially*, I want control. The narrative of *At Last Sight* is also the narrative of this tension.

Notions of the male gaze are explored in *At Last Sight* (in both the version for Belgium and subsequent versions) and issues of gender in terms of the way we play and the way we watch have always been a concern of this work. It is a commonplace reading of the way performance is generally constructed to say that narratives are split between the passive, and often eroticised image of women and the more active portrayal of males.[24] Men are doubly active in performance, in that they are usually the people who make things happen – the pro-actors to the women's reactors – and they are also the active lookers. This gaze provides the male spectator with a different type of identification with the narrative in question from females. This results in a situation where males are afforded a narrative and visual pleasure, whereas women are more likely to associate themselves most strongly with the passive and prettified object of the gaze. The old idea (of old art) is an illustration of this, where we see galleries filled with paintings by men of female nudes.

Male performers often function then as surrogates for spectators. We could describe this as an activity where men are subjects and women are objects. The narrative of *At Last Sight* subverts this. The text was always written without gender specification ... partly as a consequence of not knowing the gender breakdown or number of students who would sign up for this project, but primarily because I did not want to write certain lines or situations for men and others for women. Keeping the written text open in this way affords the cast the opportunity to impose gender on words simply by dint of the choices they make. In this way, either Sarah Skelton or Andrew Proudfoot could have elected to read the parts of **A** or **B** in the newly scripted section. The fact that Andrew has by now opted for **B** and Sarah **A** may or may not be the most appropriate choice, but it is *their* choice. The imposition of gender was not of my making.

In terms of the ways in which the gaze could be said to rest on a person as object, I have attempted throughout to avoid a situation where women are disproportionately passive. The ways in which this has been achieved (and I think it *has* and *is being* achieved) are not through a counting up of situations, so that a passive female here is replaced by a passive male in the next 'scene'. What we have done is to make all of the cast viewers of their own and their fellow performers' actions. By this, I mean that each scene within the performance space created by the chairs, back board, sound desk and lights, is observed by the rest of the cast, whether these observers are actively engaged in the scene or not. At its most successful – if by 'successful' I am referring here to the success of the subverting of the male gaze – the entire performance and all within it function as both object and subject. We watch the performers making the performance and we watch them watching the ways that it is made. The members of the cast adjust their positions as they go.

At times, the issue of gaze is treated more directly. When Sarah Skelton asks a male spectator why he is watching her at the expense of other performers, she is at once identifying herself as the passive subject *and* the active watcher. In returning the gaze she shifts the balance. At another point in the performance, Sarah, in the midst of applying lipstick, says to the audience: "And now you watch me.... Are my lips painted red for you? Is this done for your gaze? Am I becoming someone else for you? Well, I'm still Sarah. Some of you know me. I'm twenty-one years old. I'm Sarah."

The only time that a photograph is taken of the audience, it is taken by a female performer. Again, this is Sarah Skelton. This is no accident. In opening the live text of the re-worked version of *At Last Sight*, and then laying on the floor, to be looked at by the male performers as well as the spectators, Sarah is the most likely of the females to be regarded as 'object'.[25] Further to this, she describes a female orgasm and is subsequently photographed by Glenn Robertson as she lies on the bed. It is important to me that this objectification is challenged in the work.

Perhaps three quarters of the way through *At Last Sight 2*, as the running order currently stands, three of the men, Glenn, Andrew and Chris, sit on the bed and contort their bodies into positions that approximate to pornographic images normally associated with women. The women move into the audience and watch this section, with either Sarah Robertson or Elizabeth Hague taking a Polaroid photograph of the men and then pinning the picture up on the board. It is perhaps in every sense of the word too crude an indication to the audience. Nevertheless, it serves I think a useful purpose. It is an image I would never consider asking female students to adopt (I should point out that the men are clothed throughout). The chief reason for this, even if the context of the work made the request 'reasonable', would be my own position of power over the cast. As a man, such a request would be likely to read as precisely the type of active gazing at an eroticised female passivity that I am seeking to avoid.[26]

At Last Sight is attempting to raise the issue of sexual identity through the impossibility of any fixing of the subject ... not least the 'subject' of Sarah Skelton. When she is presented within the piece it is done - in almost every scene that she 'drives' - in a way that turns her into both the reader and the read: as a spectacle and also as a spectator.

Inasmuch then as the spectator is refused a permanent position from which to view, the very process of perception is rendered unstable.

Issues of gender are central to *At Last Sight* and I am pleased that the ways in which it is being treated are consistent with my views at the start of the process. Other things have changed. I am aware, for example, that I am referring increasingly to 'the audience', instead of 'the spectator' of earlier chapters. Again, I put this down to the same tension between the theory of ideas and the practice of action as was mentioned a few paragraphs ago. There are inevitable compromises between intention and application, which mean that one's beliefs are tempered in part by the process of working collaboratively and in part by the absence of the safety net that libraries and offices provide. Performance can be unforgiving of theory (Brecht told us that a good idea badly presented dies a long time)[27] just as in its own way theory can be unforgiving of performance. Ideas of gaze-subversion and authorial redemption may be all well and good, but the pragmatics of making a performance mean that many ideas that are sound in theory are sacrificed in rehearsal.

Within the narrative of *At Last Sight* there has been an attempt to match what is being said with the manner of its saying. The written language of the performance itself could already be said to have form, even before it is made physical in practice. By this I mean that the manner of the writing carries with it a certain formal implication: it is episodic, it is fragmentary and it is possessed in certain sections of a particular melancholy. We cannot then refer to it as content without form. By the same token, the form of *At Last Sight* is also a type of content. The ways in which the work is constructed and the elements that make up its parts are sympathetically inclined, to the point where any attempted separation would be invidious. Similarly, it makes less sense to refer to 'narrative elements' of *At Last Sight* than to regard the entire work as narratological.

Just as a life is contained in a series of episodes, which we string together, overlay and juxtapose in order to obtain an overall image, so the sometimes-disparate elements of *At Last Sight* combine to make up the narrative of itself. We can take this further and suggest that the narrative of *At Last Sight* and my reading of it here in this book are identical. As Derrida would have it, any standing outside of the text is impossible.[28] This may mean that the work is so self-referential that I am unable to read it at all. My own theorising would thus become not so much a critical practice beyond and outside the performance, but an indivisible element of the (critical) performance itself. Am I able to refer any longer to *At Last Sight* as a performance in time, which is discrete, and this book as words, which occupy space and are separate? I feel not. The project is no longer *that* and the writing *this*.

Any shift from theory into practice - such as my own movement from full-time immersion in academia to a sustained attempt at making performance – has the potential to lead to a type of self-contemplation that in turn renders performance theoretical.[29] I can recognise *At Last Sight* as a performance that is at once a discourse on narrative and a narrative itself. Just as I would be unable to describe something 'postmodern' as 'original', so this work is emerging as a revisiting and rereading of its own (*my* own) past. *At Last Sight* seeks to alert or remind the spectator to the fact that it is itself an artificial construct, and it does this through an abandoning of representation (mimetic or otherwise) in favour of a self-referentiality where nothing is ever fully fixed. That it does this in the same space and at the same time as it offers the 'reality' of the rapid consumption of alcohol only serves it seems to foreground these issues of deconstruction and undecidability. Deconstruction is always an issue. From the start, *At Last Sight* has been assembled in a way that has invited deconstruction, and it has done this because its structure reveals something of its own knowledge of certain deconstructive theories of performance. The work thus advertises itself as an appropriate site for deconstruction. It does this through the lack of 'plot' and the irregularity of the authorial voice. Its openness to deconstruction is taken further still by the disjunctive distinction between the illusory nature of certain events and the non-illusion of others - for example, the illusion-breaking activity of consuming considerable quantities of alcohol - which combine to create a world of slippage rather than of meaning.[30]

This slippage exists within the words as well as the actions of *At Last Sight*. The appropriation of certain extracts of text from, for example, Hartley's *The Go-Between* (spoken variously by Glenn Robertson, Andrew Proudfoot and Elizabeth Hague) and Montaigne's 1580 dictum on the presentation of self as 'a work of good faith' (delivered, with a name-change by Chris Roberts) sits uneasily alongside 'original' words, such as those composed by either the cast or myself. When fictional films by famous directors are described *as though they exist*, and when these descriptions are intercut with descriptions of 'genuine' films, which are *described in the same manner*, then any comfortable acceptance of either 'truth' or 'fact' is denied. The cast are 'advertised' as lovers (two of them are now openly so), assuming that the spectators believe that to be true, then they will be inclined in future performances, as they were in Belgium, to puzzle over which embraces are 'real' and which 'false'.[31] Everything slides

out of place. The wine and cigarettes are 'real' and the Polaroid
photographs provide evidence that certain events did indeed take place.
And yet the performers embody no 'characters' with whom the
spectators are allowed to engage and the work's fictionality is
consistently exposed by the deliberate visibility of stage lights and
control boards.

The aim is to produce a persistent destabilisation of
expectation. The work purports to be about truth, yet it deals in lies (and
lies in the way that it deals with truth); it foregrounds its status as a
theatrical construction, and thereby as something false, at the same time
as so much of it is seemingly 'real'. What *At Last Sight* is doing then is
exploring the relationship that exists between the spectator and the
work. The spectator is being asked to enter into more than the
customary 'suspension of disbelief': s/he is being asked to 'believe' and
to do this in spite of the fact that much of the performance is blatantly
false.[32] I would argue that in this way the spectator is afforded a huge
importance. The importance of spectatorship is not here that a particular
response to *At Last Sight* might be more or less profound or incisive
than any others, so much as it is the individual spectator's *own
response*. The 'you' of the spectator becomes as vital as the 'I' of the
instigator of the action or the text. Furthermore, this 'you' is
considerably less vexed. For whereas the 'I' is problematised by the
difficulties of establishing any fixed sense of where the 'I' resides, the
'you' is always and only you the spectator, regardless of the text's
chosen mode of delivery from one moment to the next.

In the continued use of 'I' in the text for *At Last Sight*, the
spectator is reminded that any identification between the watcher and
the watched is troubled. Who, after all, is the 'I' that one is seeing?
There are no character's names, other than Arabella and Paris, and these
are decided within the context of the performance. "You can be
Arabella," Glenn Robertson tells Elizabeth Hague, "and I can be Paris."
The identities are fictionalised even within the fictional frame of the
performance. Elsewhere, Glenn is Glenn and Liz is Liz. What they are
saying to the spectator is that this is one layer of performance within
many others. At its most mimetic, then – and the Arabella and Paris
section is played very naturalistically – the process of imitation is
subject to its most emphatic exposure. What can be trusted here? When
Andrew Proudfoot and Sarah Skelton work through the B Movie scene
they do so with texts in their hands, long after they have learned the
words. It is though *At Last Sight* is fearful of giving in to any type of
empathetic engagement on the part of the spectator. This is both true
and false. When Andrew tells the audience how lonely he is (and his is

a loneliness that is true at the time of writing) I certainly do want an empathetic response from the spectators. What I do not want is empathy through fiction. If the spectators want to care, then let them care about truth (or at least a kind of truth) rather than about the lie of lines written by another hand and learned.

The truth, though, cannot be easily tracked down. If the text tells the spectator that it is dishonest and this statement is seen to be true, then that truth belies the claims of dishonesty, even as they are being made. Equally, if *At Last Sight* is true, then its assertion of its intrinsic dishonesty is shown to be incorrect and false. The only claim for truth that can be made is that the work is never fully one thing or the other. Its journey from truth to lies and back is such that I am no longer able or even inclined to keep track of where truth starts and ends. I am not sure now that I ever was.

If we accept that realism is generally seen as something that has as its aim a type of mimetic transparency - so that its spectators witness an imitation of an action, which is 'life-like' without ever being really 'like life' - then *At Last Sight* can be seen as a work that sets out to foreground that very fakery. Theatrical devices are made visible and the language of the text tends towards opacity. Where words can be said to be imitative of particular experiences, the delivery of these sections is such that the very act of imitation is exposed. This self-reflexivity is a theme of postmodern performance ... it could even be said to *define* particular performances *as* postmodern. Linda Hutcheon explores this aspect in the chapter 'Historiographic Metafiction' in *A Poetics of Postmodernism*, where she argues that self-reflexivity is a positive force in the construction of text

> ... provisionality and uncertainty (and the wilful and overt construction of meaning too) do not 'cast doubt upon their seriousness', but rather define the new postmodern seriousness that acknowledges the limits and powers of reporting or writing the past, recent or remote.[33]

I can draw parallels between Hutcheon's notions of postmodern self-reflexivity and *At Last Sight*, as performance text, as performance and also as this book. The three aspects each explore issues of identity and subjectivity, of representation and reference, of intertextuality and appropriation, of the implications of the reading of one's self. A narrative voice that is subjective will inevitably draw attention to itself. The pronoun 'I' is likely to be used; the location and time of the text's construction will perhaps be made evident. This subjectivity is a feature of all of the work engaged in on this overall project, and it would be possible, and simple, to pull sections of writing

from both the book and the text of *At Last Sight* as a means of exemplifying this point. In fact, the prolific nature of the references to person and place is such that the extrapolation of examples would be almost entirely unnecessary. The 'I' is everywhere in the work.

If received wisdom tells us that acting is about recreating truth from accepted words and repeated patterns of words, then the performers in *At Last Sight* are not acting. Clearly, they are. One can draw distinctions between 'performance' and 'acting', as indeed this book has attempted elsewhere, but these distinctions are often no more than tendentious exercises in the justification and promotion of one approach over another. Michael Kirby's continuum of acting, which he describes in *On Acting and Not Acting*, serves as a useful reminder that whereas 'acting' will generally function within a number of matrices, each of which combines to create the illusion of 'other', 'performance' can exist with no matrix whatsoever.[34] What Kirby's continuum does not provide for is the fact that a matrix is as likely to be internally as externally applied. If, for example, Sarah Robertson invests elements of her performance with an emotional and psychological underpinning at the same time as Laurent Ruggeri might be doing no more (?) than speaking remembered lines at given times and in certain spaces, can we say with any authority that one is acting and the other is not? If we accept that acting is as concerned with a state of mind as it is with any physical activity, then it becomes impossible to make any externally imposed distinctions between acting and performance that will hold true.

Conversely, if we believe the shifting state of 'acting' to be definable only by the 'actor', then we are denying the spectator any status as a valid provider and creator of meaning.

Because I am unable to monitor the states of the performers' minds at any given moment of any rehearsal (even if the students themselves were able to recognise the shifting ways in which they are attending, engaging and *pretending* from one instant to the next) I am unable to make any usefully distinctive determination of an 'in and out of actedness'. In effect, the performers are presenting their own agendas, within a text that also announces my own presence, and it is doing so at the same time as I am physically absent from the performance. In this, they are in one way indistinguishable from the performance *per se*. Their performances are ironic imitations in much the same way that *At Last Sight* is an ironic imitation of a performance. The performance, like the performers, and like this book, adopt different attitudes to self-narration. In the performance, certainly, there is evidence of a denial of truth, which runs simultaneously with a contradictory assertion and of signs that function as little more than signs of signs.

It will be apparent to the reader that *Tracing the Footprints* is troubled by time. I am not able to write about what might take place in any given rehearsals at the same time as I am writing about the thinking that is informing the work. Not within the form of notation adopted in these pages. Perhaps the only way to have achieved this would be to have written the words in overlapping boxes. This would result in a situation where the very thing that is designed to transmit comprehensible information would be rendered intelligible. The overlap inherent in the performance of *At Last Sight* is impossible to recreate on the printed pages of a book. This would not be the case with technology available on the World Wide Web. We are advised that

> Literary theorists ... are predicting that in the twenty-first century people will be so used to receiving messages in non-linear forms that they will no longer think of writing continuous prose as the default means of conveying meaning.[35]

As a document with roots in the twentieth century, regardless of its twenty first-century publication, *Tracing the Footprints* remains predominantly prose-bound and continuous.

The book itself is moving through time, as is the process of rehearsal, and yet its written form is a denial of the multiple layers of simultaneous occurrence experienced in practice. This results in a collapsing of time. The reader is aware of the point in *actual time* that rehearsals of *At Last Sight* have reached, because *that* time of the making is also *this* time of the writing. Recording the date on which each section of this book is being written would provide information about the stage in the process. However, it would also suggest many periods of inactivity, when in fact the thoughts and events to be documented are perhaps being thought about at length. Reading may be being undertaken, or rehearsals may be so intense that time for writing is limited.

This is the case. The pressure of getting *At Last Sight* ready for a new audience has caught up with the writing. It is, in fact, in danger of overtaking it.

Notes

---

[1] See Calvin, W. H. *How Brains Think: Evolving Intelligence, Then and Now.* HarperCollins, New York, 1997. p. 146

[2] Wittgenstein, L. *Philosophical Investigations.* Harper, New York, 1953. p. 89.

[3] Cage, J. *Conversing with Cage.* Richard Kostelanetz (ed). Omnibus Press, London, New York, Sydney, 1989. p208.

[4] Savage-Rumbaugh, S. and Roger Lewin. *Kanzi: The Ape at the Brink of the Human Mind.* Wiley, 1994. pp. 111-112

[5] This is recognised by H. A. Simon in his study of 'trial and error leading to breakthrough', 'Scientific Discovery and the psychology of problem solving' in R. G. Colodny (ed.), *Mind and Cosmos: Essays in Contemporary Science and Philosophy.* University of Pittsburgh Press, Pittsburgh, 1966. pp 73-86.

[6] Marcus, L. *Auto/Biographical Discourses.* Manchester University Press, UK, 1994. p. 180

[7] Guilford, J.P. 'Traits of Creativity' in *Creativity and its Cultivation.* H.H. Anderson (ed.) Harper, 1959. p.48

[8] J. P. Guilford in *Creativity.* McGraw-Hill, New York, 1967, pp. 110-133 proposes two general types of thinking: 'divergent thinking' and 'convergent thinking'. In convergent thinking the thinker is expected to 'converge' on the 'appropriate' answer to a problem. Convergent thinkers, therefore, have a preference for problems that require a single, correct answer. Divergent thinking, however, involves producing a variety of possible answers to a problem; thus, divergent thinkers prefer open-ended questions that allow for a range of possible answers. We can deduce from this (as we can from the making of *At Last Sight)* that the making of performance, which has no prescribed outcome, is suited to an approach where divergent thinking is allowed and encouraged.

[9] Cited in Owens, A. *Mapping Drama.* Carel Press, UK. 2001. p.50

[10] *ibid*

[11] Craik, K. J.W. *The Nature of Explanation.* Cambridge University Press 1943. P.98

[12] There is no possibility, within the module these students are working on, for an assessment to be made of 'Process'. This is a controversial issue within the department I teach in … as it is within many institutions. On the one hand, it seems inappropriate to take no notice of the distance travelled by a particular student, rather than focusing entirely on the point arrived at. We all know that practical work for students involves considerably more than 'merely' giving a good performance 'on the night'. However, there is a counter-argument. Many academics feel that assessing process is a recipe for disaster. It cannot, for example, be scrutinised adequately by an external examiner, and it lays tutors open to allegations of favouritism. 'Good Process', after all, might be regarded by some tutors as the willingness of a student to do as he or she is advised. It is a difficult area.

[13] Grotowski, J. *Towards a Poor Theatre.* Methuen, London, 1969. p 213.

[14] Mitter, S. *Systems of Rehearsal.* Routledge, London, 1992. p. 79.

[15] The consumption of alcohol by the students and *within* the performance has always been an intention, and it was realised during the performance in Belgium. Part of the reason for this is an interest in aspects of 'control' and 'out of control'. I want to see what happens when, in the midst of the high levels of concentration required for performance, one's faculties are affected by the rapid consumption of alcohol.

[16] The consumption of alcohol by students as an assessed part of their studies raises some interesting ethical dimensions. The university I work at does not possess any published documents, either in terms of teaching or research that throw specific light onto this. The committee responsible for 'Ethics and Research' has stated that 'No activity should be entered into that causes – or intends to cause- harm or offence to the public'. Because the students are not, in this sense, regarded as members of the public, this *caveat* does not apply. A further statement from the committee informs staff that (wherever possible) 'Students should be advised of the content and nature of modules prior to commencement.' In this sense, my approach to working with this student-group falls within the regulatory guidelines. The fact that alcohol - particularly when consumed in the quantity and at the pace that it is – is a mind-altering substance does add complexity to the matter. I am Health and Safety trained and have been on a First Aid course; this, alongside my head of department's full knowledge of what is happening and the students' willing participation in the activity, means that I have done all that need be done in order for the work to go ahead.

Ethical issues of another kind are raised by the lies I am telling to members of the audience. This could be regarded as causing offence to members of the public. However, the fact that this 'public' needs to enter willingly into a theatre space in order then to read the programme and see the subsequent work changes their status, if only inasmuch as they are offering themselves as participants in a creative exercise, albeit without knowing the extent to which their own participation is crucial.

On an individual level, I have few, if any, concerns about these matters. The spectators' unknowingness is an important element of the work and it is difficult to think of a way in which they could 'not know' and still not be lied to. Similarly, my interest in changing the physical conditions of the performance, and of the performers, contains within it the necessity to engage in practice that places the participants at some (very minor) risk, whether this be through exertion, duration or drink. It should be noted that I am always with the students when they drink alcohol in this piece, and that I am always sober.

I am aware that the education sector is becoming increasingly aware of its responsibilities, both to its immediate clients and the wider community, and it is in this spirit that I offer the above observations.

I suspect, in defence of the work, that this module is the first time that the students involved have been put in a situation where ethical issues have been considered at any length. From this perspective, the approaches taken could be regarded as vital to their studies.

[17] Flaszen, L. in Mitter (1992). p. 89.

[18] The words were chosen by the members of the group, myself included. We all made suggestions, only retaining those on which we were all agreed.

[19] Mullins, S. *Lullaby*. Columbia/Sony Records. Sony Music, 1998

[20] The idea of Andrew trying to breathe water, rather than holding his breath, came from watching him in rehearsal. Holding his breath brought with it a sense of predictability: he would remain motionless for a minute or so, only to emerge gasping. Asking him to open his throat and gulp the water as though it were air means that Andrew's body is racked and he emerges retching. Watching Andrew doing this in rehearsal seemed somehow familiar, and then I remembered reading about a Chris Burden performance, *Velvet Water*, in *Chris Burden: Beyond The Limits*. Peter Noever (ed.), Cantz Verlag, Germany, 1996. Looking at the book in my office immediately after the rehearsal, I read the following statement by Burden: "Today I am going to breathe water, which is the opposite of drowning, because when you breathe water, you believe water to be richer, thicker oxygen capable of sustaining life.' p. 164.

Because I had the idea without a *conscious awareness* of Burden's prior performance I can regard it as 'psychologically creative', as opposed to 'historically creative'. This is a distinction suggested by Margaret Boden in *Dimensions of Creativity*. Boden (ed.), MIT Press, Massachusetts, 1996. In Boden's words, "to be historically creative the novel product would have to be one that had never been seen or thought before. p. 17.

This raises the question of originality, and the extent to which something 'new' is also (*might* also be) something previously known … *even to the secondary thinker*. I feel no less a sense of ownership of Andrew's drowning scene now that I am able to recall Burden's earlier project. The idea was not knowingly derivative. Seeing Andrew's work reminded me of reading about Burden's, not *vice versa*.

[21] The language tape also provides a thematic link with Hartley's words re the past being a foreign country, which are spoken by Glenn Robertson early on in *At Last Sight*.

[22] 'Identity is not within us … it exists only as narrative. The only way to explain who we are is to tell our own story, to select key events that characterise us and organise them to the formal principles of narrative.

This gives narration at large the potential to teach us how to conceive of ourselves.' In Currie, M. *Postmodern Narrative Theory*. Macmillan Press, UK, 1998. 'The Manufacture of Identities' pp. 17-32

[23] Althusser, L. *Lenin and Philosophy*. Trans. B. Brewster. New Left Books, London, 1975. p.31

[24] See Burchill, J. *Girls on Film*. Virgin Books, London, 1986 for an analysis of the ways in which women are consistently portrayed as passive in cinema. Michelene Wandor's *Look Back in Gender*. Methuen, London, 1987 provides an analysis of the same phenomenon in live performance.

[25] Sarah Skelton's performance is the most overtly sexualised of the women's. This is a performative construction, which was developed through Sarah's own construction of self. *At Last Sight* has been created out of the performers' own notions of who they are and of what they wish to show. In this way, Sarah's

desire to be seen as desirable (even more than her level of physical attractiveness) has resulted in a preponderance of on-stage actions, which are suggestive of sexually charged encounters.
This is not to suggest that I have not had responsibility for the actions, words and images engaged in. As director of the work I have a considerable influence on the way that *At Last Sight* is both made and shown.

[26] I am asking the male performers to carry out an action here, whereas with the **A B** scene between Andrew and Sarah I was happy to let the performers decide on the way the lines were divided between male and female. I do not, however, feel that this results in a contradiction. The 'pornography scene' works *because* those carrying out the actions are male, and this has as much to do with my decision as do any notions of directorial and gender-based power. It would only be *if* I thought that the women working the scene would be more effective than the men that my notions of manipulation would be questioned (and exposed perhaps as false). It should be pointed out that this idea of not asking females in the group to do certain things has more to do with my role as their teacher than as director.

[27] Volker, K. *Brecht*. Marion Boyars Ltd. London, 1991. Chapter 34 'A Great Time Wasted' pp. 369-376

[28] The 'text' can be said to be the work that is *At Last Sight*, this book and also myself. James Olney's *Metaphors of Self: The Meaning of Autobiography*. Princeton University Press, USA, 1972 asserts that text is 'always a projection of the 'inner space' of the observing or conceiving self (and that) all forms of knowledge are in some way autobiographical' (p.3). It has not gone unnoticed that the intention to make *At Last Sight* self-revelatory has been transcended by the self-revelation that is this book. This is only in part to do with the collaborative nature of making the performance as opposed to the solitary practice of writing these words. Fundamentally, I feel, it is about the fact that 'you must have a self before you can afford to deconstruct it.' Jouve, N. W. *White Woman Speaks with Forked Tongue: Criticism as Autobigraphy*. Routledge, New York and London, 1991. p.7. The creation of *At Last Sight* has thus provided a creating self that this book is able to deconstruct.

[29] Brecht commented that 'In practice the theatre does not fulfil its social function. At a time like this the really practical talents are relegated to the field of theory in order to remain active.' Volker, 1991. p.106. Whilst I would take exception to Brecht's use of the term 'relegated', his words are as relevant today (perhaps more so) as they were at the time of writing.

[30] 'Slippage' may be literal in this sense. After draining litres of wine and then spinning wildly there is every possibility that some of the performers will slip and fall. The only safeguard against injury is that the cast members know that they can stop their actions at any time they choose. The context of the performance allows and even encourages this.

[31] I am aware here that I am making assumptions about an audience, which is a trap I would normally wish to avoid. In this case the assumption seems a reasonable one to make, based not least on the evidence of Liege.

---

[32] This is a crucial aspect. In assigning a distinction between the 'real' and the 'false' I am seeming to ignore those same theories of 'constructedness' that I elsewhere embrace. This is problematic, and yet to deny it, to state that all aspects of the work are as 'false' as each other, would be to ignore those very notions that brought me to the work in the first place. Essentialism is not a fashionable term. Its insistence that there is something 'real' has been argued against so cogently that, on an intellectual level, I am convinced of its internal contradictions. I cannot help but wonder, however, whether Baudrillard would regard it as 'real' or not if he stubbed his toe on the edge of his bed and cried out in pain. This may be a facetious example, but the fact remains that I do believe in the existence of the real: *At Last Sight* is founded on that belief, no less than it is founded on a desire to explore the distinctions between the real and the false in performance. Indeed, if there were no distinction between one and the other, then what would be the point of any artists making work that abandons illusion? When Abramovic and Ulay walked the Wall of China it was the reality of the action that gave it currency, no less than when Chris Burden was crucified to the bonnet of his Volkswagen. Conversely, we can say that exposing artifice only succeeds as a premise if one accepts that the act of exposure is somehow *less artificial* in nature than that which is being exposed.

I came to this performance project partly at least as a means of working through feelings related to living apart from my children. This formed the catalyst for a work that dealt with loss. It is the *truth* of these feelings that provides a context within which the rest of the work is able to function. Perhaps it is my belief in the truth of feelings that is more important than any faith I might have in facts over fictions. The emotional content of *At Last Sight* (and the emotional content of this book) is a testament (at least to myself) of the truth of feelings. This has been developed into ideas, such as the consumption of alcohol, which stand as 'truthful' in and of themselves, rather than solely as metaphors for 'truthful' origins.

I can accept that my 'life' is made up of constructions, without accepting that my life is not 'real'. *At Last Sight* is an attempt at making art out of this. The 'loss' in the performance of time passing is not designed to stand in some equation to the loss of children to a father, but its elements of (at least) reduced illusion are necessary counterpoints to the overt illusion of reading lines of text in *lieu* of natural(istic) behaviour.

There is a reality to the fact of performers in a space, carrying out actions at a certain time, but this is not the *only* reality of the performance. The investment in the work is personal and it matters. The distinctions between real and false may mean more to me than to any spectator, and more than they do to the performers, but they do exist. If art is a part of life, rather than a representation of it, then why should art be denied the same freedoms as life? *At Last Sight* was fuelled by the real and has now become a part of my reality. Howsoever we engage with the theories of the day, we live our lives with the intrinsic and *essentialist* regard for the real. What price parenthood if feelings are not real? What price this book if its words are false?

[33] Hutcheon, L. *A Poetics of Postmodernism*. Routledge, London, 1988. p.117

[34] Kirby, M 'On Acting and Not Acting' in *Acting (Re)Considered.* Routledge, London, 1995. pp. 43-58
[35] Clark, R & Ivanic, R. *The Politics of Writing.* Routledge, London & New York, 1997. p. 16.

Chapter 6:
Performance Critique 3

The previous chapter moved from the beginnings of a description of change and on through a rationalisation of those changes according to aspects of postmodern theory, to a position where *At Last Sight* was almost ready for performance ... and that movement was swift.

So swift, in fact, that the paragraphs to come will relate to a reflection on *At Last Sight*, rather than as a type of preparation. In these last few days, the pressure of bringing the work to its optimum state is denying the opportunities to write that existed when the rehearsal schedule was more leisurely. It is not just about the time spent on rehearsals, and on full-time teaching. It is about the necessity for some time spent away from *At Last Sight*. So that time spent away from rehearsals becomes time spent away from this book. We pause here, not to gather breath so much as to preserve any breath that remains for the production. Our pause is a pause in the time of the writer, if not quite the reader. For the reader, we move immediately here into a reflection on the subsequent performances of *At Last Sight*.

In writing here about *At Last Sight* as something finished, I am aware that the word 'finished' may be misleading. The work is clearly ongoing, not least in the sense of a series of performances that are still some months away. Notwithstanding this, it was always the intention that the footprints that this book would trace would be those leading up to a specific series of performances and not go beyond this point.

It almost goes without saying to report that the work was different on every night. The human material of performance, in the sense of both performers and spectators, ensure that no two occasions will ever match up. The opening night audience was responsive. Laughter, where it came, came freely. It was, for the cast and myself, an ideal start. We felt, after only a few moments, that the production was a 'success'. This book is not focussing on the certain dynamics of audiences, so there is little point in a deviation here that moves in any detail away from what happened and on to the ways in which it was or was not received.[1] It is enough, perhaps, to recognise that the relationship between spectators and performers is such that each is as likely to be termed 'good' or 'bad' as is the other. From a performance perspective, a 'bad' audience is often no more than a group of people whose collective response suggests that the process of guessing entered into by the performance group was misjudged. As makers of work, we seek confirmation from spectators of the wisdom, appropriateness and inventiveness of our decisions. An audience that fails to confirm this wisdom will be regarded as 'bad'. In this way, a totally silent audience can be interpreted as 'good', as long as their silence is possessed of the capability of being interpreted as attentiveness.

According to the above criteria, the audience for *At Last Sight* was good. Each performance had its own flavour, and each of the performers was happier on certain nights with aspects of their own performance than they were on others. From the Monday through to and including the Wednesday, there were qualities and weaknesses in everybody's performances. For example, Sarah Robertson was visibly shaking when she was waiting for the audience to settle at the start of the performance on Monday. This was noticed by a colleague of mine who was in the audience in his role as assessor, and it is difficult to see how this shaking would not have been seen by every spectator. The shaking was prolonged and difficult to watch. As soon as Sarah was engaged in more overt 'performing', the shaking stopped as suddenly as it had started. The fact that this shaking was the physical manifestation of nervous tension made it something that was beyond Sarah's control. Notwithstanding this, she was eager on Tuesday to demonstrate, not least to herself, that she was able to assume a degree of control. Chris Roberts stumbled over lines on Tuesday in ways that were not apparent on other evenings;[2] Elizabeth Hague's performance was more powerful on Monday and Wednesday than on Tuesday and Glenn Robertson was physically sick on Wednesday. That he was able to walk quickly out of the auditorium and on to the toilets situated in the corridor meant that the spectators were unaware of his purpose. When he re-entered the space, I suspect that most of the audience felt that his leaving had been no more or less than a further example of the performers' freedom to behave naturally for much of the duration of the work.

The performance on Friday was the most effective of the four. To my mind, *At Last Sight* is a stronger and more internally coherent piece of work now than it was in Belgium, which meant that every one of the recent performances was a vindication of our decision to initiate a process of reconstruction. Be that as it may, the performance on Friday, May 21st saw *At Last Sight* at its best. It was a powerful point for this stage of the project itself to end, and I am aware that the group will need some lifting if they are to recapture the qualities they displayed on the last night of the recent run. The audience was not set up to be supportive. The performance had sold out, but this was the case with every one of the performances. Perhaps the feedback that the group had received from audience members on the previous evenings had filtered down to subsequent spectators, so that they arrived with a positive anticipation. Many of the spectators were returning for a second sight.

As this book has progressed, it has become increasingly difficult to engage in analysis that is not second-hand. The key moments in *At Last Sight* remain key moments, despite the fact that they have been discussed elsewhere in this work. This does not make them any easier to revisit.

At Last Sight became, in performance, something that belonged almost solely to the cast, and in reflecting here on some of their own experiences of the project I will make reference to all six of the Level 3 students' essays, which were submitted post-performance. I refer here to their essays because I am convinced that, like this book, they form part of the critical project that was and is *At Last Sight*, rather than as discrete critical commentaries. At times, the students' readings of the work will be challenged. When this occurs, it does so within the spirit of ongoing dialogue that has been a feature of the group since the very start. It should be stressed that these essays were not written with any sense of being made subject to analysis *via* publication. They are essays written by students to satisfy certain module criteria. Each of the students has agreed to their work being discussed in the pages of this study.

The essays did not require titles, although each of the students in this group gave their work a name. These titles give a strong indication of what the students believed *At Last Sight* to be about: *'Truth' and 'Lies' in Performance: At Last Sight* (Andrew Proudfoot); *At Last Sight: Alienating or Liberating the Audience?* (Sarah

Robertson); *'Art is a Lie which tells the Truth': Truth and Lies in At Last Sight* (Sarah Skelton); *Theatre is What Theatre Did* (Glenn Robertson); *At Last Sight: Truth & Lies, Reality & Fiction, Acting & Being* (Chris Roberts); *At Last Sight: Voyeuristic Intention?* (Elizabeth Hague). I am unable to disclose or discuss the grades awarded for these essays. What I can say is that the essays share what the assessment team took to be an intellectual engagement with specific concerns of the project.[3] My failure to reveal marks – like my decision not to include the actual essays in this book - is not done to protect the students from any embarrassment.

Before I begin to highlight here certain sections of these essays, in order to provide the reader with an insight into the perspective of particular students, I should note that the use of the pronoun 'I' is a feature of all of the work. None of these essays were 'tutored', in the sense that each of the students worked alone and without my guidance. Theoretical discussion was a part of the process of rehearsal, but did not carry over into specific assistance with essays. The work, when it was submitted, was as new to me as it was to my colleagues in the department. The use of 'I' is not then an attempt on any of the students' part to mirror in some way the 'I' of this book ... none of the students have seen any of this book and its structure has not been discussed. Their collective use of the 'I' is, I feel, a logical continuation of the prioritised 'I' of the production. Because their thoughts, ideas and feelings have been so central to the process of constructing *At Last Sight* it is only right and proper (as well as only natural) that this foregrounding of their own agendas is a feature of their written submissions.

Where certain modules undertaken by these students have an express concern with the 'inculcation of technique, rather than the pursuance of personal agenda' (and I place these words in inverted commas because they are, at the students' institution, so often used *verbatim*) this project has actively sought to reverse that concern. The work has been made to the students' agendas, and also, of course, to my own. Accordingly, their use of the personal pronoun is both expected and acceptable.

Elizabeth Hague's essay picks up on certain key moments in *At Last Sight* in order to explore the work's relationship with its audience. The way she cites these moments is indicative of the sense of ownership felt by the group. When Elizabeth writes "'Most performance is disguised autobiography, however, this autobiography is a disguised performance' (Andrew Proudfoot, *At Last Sight*)" she applies the authorship of that line to Andrew. In one vital sense, of course, this is true. Andrew authored the line in performance. But the reference removes the line from its written origins ... it becomes only performative. This performative authoring continues through the essay: "'In the room with her it is dark, and sshhhhh it is very, very late' (Liz Hague, *At Last Sight*); "'He wants to touch her' (Chris Roberts, *At Last Sight*); "'Am I doing this for your gaze? (Sarah Skelton, *At Last Sight*). No distinction is drawn between these lines and "'I'm alone, it's quite sad really' (Andrew Proudfoot, *At Last Sight*) even though this line was doubly authored by the performer in a way that the previously cited lines were not.

The sub-text of Elizabeth's essay then is as focused on the event of performance as its title would suggest ... although its subtextuality hinges on performative rather than spectatorial ownership. With an examination of the presentation in Belgium, the essay itself articulates a concern with the specifics of *this* performance and at *that* time. That it addresses issues of watching through reference to the comments of particular spectators and not through a blanket assumption that any one response was automatically shared by the audience *per se* is an indication of the student's sensitivity to the idiosyncratic nature of perception.

Chris Roberts' essay sets out to investigate the extent to which the selves of the performers informed *At Last Sight*. In precisely the same way as Elizabeth Hague, Chris apportions ownership of the text used in performers to s/he who speaks, rather than the writer of the work. This is evidenced most emphatically when Chris, in his endnotes, attributes words from the programme to Freeman, J. and words delivered by himself in the performance to Roberts, C. From this separating out we can assume that Chris is regarding performed words as something distinct from words about performance, even when those words have been penned by the same hand. When Chris writes that the group were afforded the freedom to choose "the lines, stories, speeches and moments for ourselves", he seems to be developing this freedom into ownership.

Chris Roberts' essay moves into a reading of *At Last Sight* within a context created by Wilshire's article on paratheatrical form. In citing Wilshire, Chris begins an exploration of the extent to which *At Last Sight* tested the boundaries between 'theatre' and 'life'.

Although Chris's essay does not touch on it directly, the issue here is one of consequence. Whereas events in life have ramifications beyond the event, it is usually the case that events in performance are removed from the consequences of any continued response. The actor playing Othello is unlikely to be berated in the bar for slaying Desdemona in performance. For Chris the performance brought about profound consequences. He ended one long-standing relationship and began another. His performative behaviour with Sarah Robertson may turn out to be the most consequential act of his life. Certainly, the couple has become *the couple* of *At Last Sight*.

Sarah Robertson's essay begins with an assertion of Derrida's notion of 'writerly' and 'readerly' texts. Using this binary oppositionality, for Sarah at least, *At Last Sight* was writerly. Sarah recognises the fact that a move away from the conventional spectator/performer relationship may be more difficult for the spectator to adjust to than the performer. She writes "audience members may feel more comfortable in the type of performance that restricts their behaviour, for example, where the fourth wall can serve as a protective device". Sarah's essay suggests that *At Last Sight* was more 'writerly' than I had believed. For Sarah "The intention of *At Last Sight* was that no interpretation should be ruled out." My own feelings are that this is too liberal a reaction. I do not believe that any one interpretation of *At Last Sight* would be as valid as any other. In fact, we created the work with the intention of taking the audience along a journey towards a broadly shared interpretation. The work was not created out of chance and directorial decisions were made in pursuit of a particular resonance. On Page 4 of her essay, Sarah quotes from the text and attributes the words to *At Last Sight*. On Page 9, four sections of text are quoted, with each being credited to the speaker/performer. On the same page, programme notes are attributed to Freeman, J.

There are two ways of looking at this. One is to regard it as an inconsistency and therefore a 'fault'; the other is to regard it as evidence of thinking, which is at once inconsistent *and* apposite. Thus, as the essay develops, so does Sarah's position in relation to ownership. This may be no more than my own attempt at an interpretation of the essay that suits my overall view of both the work and the group. In the cold light of reflection it does seem to be unavoidably so.

However, in my initial grading of the essay as the communication of thought I may be more critical (or critical in a different way) than when I now re-read the essay as a documentary artefact.[4] From my present perspective, I am more concerned with the thoughts contained in the essay than with the grammatical vagaries of communication.

'Truth and lies' form the basis of Sarah Skelton's essay. Like Chris Roberts, she refers to Bruce Wilshire; she also locates her own performative persona, and those of her fellow group members, within Michael Kirby's notion of a continuum of acting and not acting. The essay exposes the complexities involved in the idea of playing oneself. Referring to Andrew Proudfoot's invitation to any female spectator who so desires to meet him after the show for a drink, and whilst recognising that "Andrew almost certainly believes what he is saying to be true", Sarah nevertheless identifies Andrew's behaviour as actorly. In informing us that "Andrew is always aware of the presence of the audience and the fact that he is 'on stage'", Sarah points us towards the incontrovertible fact that Andrew is indeed "acting out his own emotions and beliefs … for the sake of the audience."

In the middle of her essay, Sarah quotes Nietzsche's maxim that "truths are illusions we have forgotten are illusions." It is perhaps the most succinct way into *At Last Sight* that one could imagine. The fact that I did not point any of the group towards Nietzsche makes the integration of his words into the essay even more telling than had I referred to him during rehearsals. Where my own book is seeking explanatory articulation *via* many tens of thousands of words, Nietzsche encapsulates all this and more in eight words. Ten thousand - fifteen thousand maybe - of mine for each one of his.

As with Sarah Skelton, Andrew Proudfoot attempts in his essay to explore truth and lies. For Andrew, and very interestingly, 'truth' is somehow inextricably caught up in spontaneity, so that the more a scene is rehearsed the less 'true' it becomes. Andrew's essay does not really explain why he believes this to be so, but as a document for my assessment *now* - now that I am no longer involved in an arithmetical assessment of the essay's 'worth' – it creates an exciting point of departure for new work. A truth twice told is less true the second time than it was on the first? A *matinee* is more truthful than a performance later that night, simply by dint of the fact of its status as 'prior'? The implications of this within performance are incredible. If truth recedes with each consecutive telling - and if 'truth' is an aim - then work must inevitably deteriorate from first rehearsal to performance. It seems to throw received wisdom on its head.

For Andrew, if my reading of his essay is reasonable, he feels that 'truth' happens once only and that what follows is the recreation of that same 'truth' in performance. As an example of this, he writes about a scene he had difficulties with, and the way that those difficulties were incorporated into the eventual playing out in public. As is to be expected in a relatively short essay, the issue is left unresolved, inasmuch as Andrew never explains why this might be so. Why a rehearsed 'truth' is less true than when it was unrehearsed. I think, perhaps, the issues here are of control and imitation. In the first instance (and I am referring here to Andrew's problem scene) the difficulties are beyond his control. This is what leads to the difficulty. In the performance, these same difficulties are controlled in that they have been fashioned into that which is an imitation of its original state. There is a sense to this. A sense we can trace back to Plato and to Aristotle. It relates to those imitation theories of art, which have influenced for centuries the way we feel about perception. What it does not do is address the issue of truth as a state in itself.

If I rehearse the delivery of biographical details about myself, they are no less true simply because, as time passes, my phrasing becomes more polished or my body language more contrived. What potency do we afford to repetition when we say that its very process leads to the irretrievable dilution of truth?

The last of the students' essays to be discussed here is Glenn Robertson's, *Theatre is what Theatre Did*. This essay differs from those of his peers in that it is an extension of a separate essay, *Theatre is what Theatre Does*, submitted for a taught module in Contemporary Theatre Practice. Glenn's essay differs also because it is the only one that does not credit words spoken in the performance to the performer.

In order to rationalise the lies told in the programme, Glenn cites Plato's belief that "the 'truth' of things did not lie in the way that they most directly appeared – not in the shadows on the cave wall … but in the figures who cast them." This idea of truth as something that casts a shadow – the shadow of performance – is central to Glenn's essay. He isolates a section of Andrew Proudfoot's emotional address to the audience as an obviously acted element, at the same time as he recognises that the relatively stilted delivery of this one line was disguised "in the way that a transition from 'acting' to 'non-acting' had already been made". For Glenn, what is of most interest is the fact that Andrew was using one truth (or one illusion of one truth) as a disguise for another. When Andrew delivered his personal plea, he did so in a way that allowed the audience as a mass to regard the words in one way, whereas he hoped that one specific spectator would recognise the words as aimed only at her. In this way, Andrew's 'truth' could be said to be the one thing he most wanted to conceal from most of the watchers. It was akin to the hiding of a tree in a forest. In offering up such an overtly generic 'truth', Andrew was concealing the specific truth at its core.

Taking his cue from the performance, Glenn allows his essay to answer nothing. As mentioned in my response to the rest of the students' essays, I am able to read their work in a different way now that the pressures of assessment have shifted from my role (then) as lecturer through to my role (now) as writer. In this way, many of my initial criticisms of the essays have disappeared. Rather than regretting the absence of any coherent line of argument, I am inclined now towards an acceptance of the essay as a collection of thoughts. Where one thought gives way to another without ever going deeply into an analytical *rationale*, the thoughts are still valid. It is better, perhaps, that the students feel able to ask relevant and difficult questions than that they provide easy second-hand answers in response to the already long solved.

Whilst it is true to say that *At Last Sight* had a life before the students' involvement, it is also true that their perceptions of making the work have become part of *At Last Sight* itself. Their essays are discussed here, not in order to make the group feel a part of this publication ... their involvement has been so total that their *not* feeling a part of it is unthinkable. The ideas contained within their essays have been included because they provide a further insight into the ways in which *At Last Sight* was made, and of the investigative spirit of that construction. Their essays functioned not merely as written submissions for assessment but as traces of perception. Just as each of the students gave more to the practical project than could have ever been expected or asked, so each of their essays reveals an equally honest trawling of the self.[5]

In the same way that *At Last Sight* has been informed by a collapsing of issues of ownership, so this book is informed by the thoughts of its key personnel. As the last words before *Tracing the Footprints* draws towards its conclusion, there has been evidence in this chapter of an accelerated concern towards a reading of the past of the project. Postmodernism would have it that whilst the past did indeed exist, knowing it today is an impossibility. All that we have to go on are the traces of the past and the way that we read them.

132

Notes

---

[1] For a focus on the role of spectatorship, see Beckerman, B. *Theatrical Presentation*, Routledge, London, 1990 and Susan Bennett, *Theatre Audiences*, Routledge, London, 1994.

[2] This 'stumbling' also occurred when Chris Roberts stumbled and fell during a prolonged bout of mid-performance drinking. He drank a litre of wine, spun vigorously and fell groaning to the ground. When he regained his footing he had no idea where he was in relation to the spectators, and he began speaking to Glenn Robertson as though he were a member of the audience.

[3] The essays were marked quickly, firstly by myself and subsequently by two of my colleagues. Three of the essays were passed on to an external examiner, who returned them on June 15th, 1999. The external examiner agreed the internal marks and in one case increased the grade.

If the haste of the internal grading system seems to augur against contemplative critical reading it is important to note that it was entered into as a consequence of rapidly approaching examination boards.

[4] I make no apologies for this. The essay, as part of an undergraduate submission, is not read in the same way as it is as a piece of the jigsaw of *At Last Sight* that is this book.

[5] The students' responses provide more than a contribution to the documentary *information* of this book. Including elements of their ideas passes part of the ownership of this book over to them.

Just as I have been both subject and observer so too have the students. Their responsiveness to the nature of the work has taken *At Last Sight* into directions that I could never have anticipated and their contributions have been creative and intelligent.

Every maker of any performance knows that the work could not be the work that it is with different personnel. That is the nature of collaboration. *At Last Sight* would have been the same in name only with different performers. That the group's involvement has gone deeper still than these words suggest should be apparent in every section of this book.

Conclusion:
Arrival and Departure

At Last Sight is now finished. 'Finished' is not an easy term. It is loaded. It carries with it all of the implications of practice as something fleeting and time-based at the same time as it suggests a clean delineation of process into product and thence into past. Inasmuch as the work of performance was always going to be an *event* and not an *object*, this is certainly true. 'It' happened. And having happened is now gone and gone forever. This provides me with a little distance ... a suitable distance. A necessary distance.

This distance allows the conclusion to begin with a recognition of *At Last Sight* as a part of history, at the same time as notions of 'history' will be somewhat undermined. Later paragraphs will articulate the position on performance as research which has been arrived at during the course of this project.

The work of *At Last Sight* is now history. It is consigned to the world of the gone. This imbues the piece with an accompanying status. A label. *At Last Sight* was a project central to my research. It follows then, if only within the narrowness of my own experience, that it has become a part of my reading of theatre history. Whereas the *performance* is past, the reading of that performance, of this book, is always in the present. It is thus history made known in the here and now. It is theatre scholarship through theatre history.

The history of theatre provides us with a terminology ... a terminology which often appears as a litany of movements, of an identifiable idea of 'progress'. Futurism, Dada, Surrealism, Modernism, Absurdism, Kitchen Sink, Political, Situationism, Feminism, Agit-Prop, Popular, Community, Invisible, Intercultural, Intracultural, Forum, Functional, Reminiscence, Documentary, Celebratory, Postmodernism, Performance Art, Happenings, Live Art ... the list, even of Twentieth Century terms, is seemingly inexhaustible. A procession of departures, each one defined by its distinctiveness from the rest. The terms are offered and perpetuated through the creation of a consensus. This over-simplification of tendencies into 'movements' disguises a far more complex reality. Most of us have been taught to believe that there were 'great' and 'classic' works of any given period: *Ubu Roi*, *Rhinocerous*, *Waiting for Godot*, *Mother Courage*, *Look Back in Anger*, we could choose from a really rather narrow field. Just as Jarry, Beckett, Brecht and Osborne are seen as lasting paradigms for their age ... and also, through that peculiar conceit of 'Theatre', as voices that continue to speak to our own present. What this canonisation does, whether by default or design, is provide us with a limited view of the same periods it purports to describe. If we consider work of the 1930s and 40s we can see that it is not in fact epitomised by the theatre of Brecht; just as British theatre of the mid-1950s was not exclusively determined by the programme at The Royal Court and the pen of Kenneth Tynan. We know how selectively theatre history remembers, at the same time as our shelves bow to the weight of the tomes in which that selective memory has been enshrined. The names of the great and the good function as little more than co-ordinates of a fraudulently received version of the past. Their larger than life status casts shadows over much that is equally worthy of consideration.

In recognition of this, I should stress that *At Last Sight* is not being historicised in this book in order that any future reader might come to regard the work as being emblematic of a particular 'style' or movement within Higher Education at a particular time and in a particular place. If the practical production was reflective of anything it was of an eclecticism-in-denial; of an appropriation and *assemblage* which took little heed of the restraints of cultural anchorage and/or heritage.[1]

The lens of historical perspective is both a way of seeing, to borrow John Berger's term, and a way of not seeing.[2] Of both inclusion and exclusion. With the exception of Barba's 'living links': the embodied and learned techniques of, for example, Japanese Noh theatre, when we look back at eras that happen to lie beyond personal memory and experience we become ultra-dependent on the gaze which is permitted by the borrowed lens of Theatre History.[3] This happens to the point where that which is not seen, that which has not been written about and subsequently bound, ceases to exist. Where the lens tells us which work we should know, remember, admire and emulate. This restricted view of the past cannot but fail to restrict the view we have of the present, whilst the wider terminology of theatre brings its own weight to bear, so that words such as 'significant' and 'logical' are regarded as good, whilst 'insignificant' and 'illogical' are held to be bad. We could chase this list down, taking to task such commonplace words of theatre-debate as 'coherent' and 'convention', to the point where the terms we use to describe the thing we practice are exposed as being firmly entrenched in value judgements. Judgements so deep as to have become seen now as part of the very fabric of theatre itself.

Contemporary performance, we would be led to believe by many historians, is a professional practice with its roots in the modernist avant-garde. As such, it is subject to measurement according to comparison. By its very definition then, theatre history is in the business of creating boundaries: on one side we are presented with 'High Art', while on the other side we are offered 'Low Art'. On one side is professional theatre, on the other is amateur; on one side is the mainstream and on the other the marginal. The practical reality is one of parallel developments, progressions and regressions, cul de sacs, confusions and conceits. Ideas of seamless progress and neat categorisations are fundamentally false.

For theatre history to have any real worth, it should be striving for a more inclusive definition of performance, alongside a more inclusive way of looking at performance ... a way which recognises 'theatre' as one element of 'performance', rather than seeing the two as oppositional and competing factors. For if the theatre of the twentieth century can be defined in terms of any one unifying theme, then that theme is of an insatiable quest for the new. It is a theme of influence and rejections, off cross-fertilisation and the hybridisation of different practices. This creates a splintering of views which cannot be packaged off into a tidy coherence of discrete 'styles'.

Theatre history presents us with the past of theatre as a parade of events turned into artefacts, each with its own date, director,

author and location within a specific movement or 'ism'. This book
may not be so immune to that as it wishes. The word 'postmodernism'
has already peppered its pages, and continues so to do. But whilst each
historian's artefact creates the marking of a point in the progression of
theatrical sensibility, it is hoped that *Tracing the Footprints* does
something else ... something rather more than this. Theory, after all, is
a 'schema of explanation according to which a diversity of phenomena
are accorded a significance'.[4] Seen in this light, this book is theory in
action. A work where phenomena encountered along the route towards
performance are regarded without hierarchical judgement, and where
findings are always discovered in the interconnected here and nows of
making and of writing.

        Just as *At Last Sight* as a live performance cannot be
adequately replicated in the writing and subsequent reading of this
book, so the formal evaluation of work which was unseen in its
intended manifestation remains problematic. As Peggy Phelan has
warned us, many 'performance critics realize that the labor to write
about performance ... is also a labor that fundamentally alters the
event.'[5] That which looks a certain way on paper may have looked
different in performance. Published words last long after individual
memories fade and universities are filled with lecturers speaking
borrowed 'truths' (those Kosuthian residues of ideas) to students who
will then go on to perpetuate these self-same claims. I speak to my
students of cultural differences between Eastern and Western
performance and, notwithstanding a modicum of directly experiential
evidence, I will often find myself passing on the thoughts of Schechner
and Barba, out of Turner and Savarese, as though their published
words stand somehow as a proven truth. At best, this is a fourth-hand
notion by the time the student comes to formulate a responsive
thought. I speak of Brecht, who died before my birth, as though the
words of Willett and Esslin were in some way metamorphosed into my
own.[6] The permanence of the ink and the weight of the publishing
house transforming the historian's view into 'fact'.

        Work made with students is rarely given this type of
permanence. Despite the world of critical thought within which such
work has its origins, there is a lack of critical commentary and
documentation. Writing about performance made with students can
seem like a suspect task. And so student-performance becomes mute.
As an assessable component of students' work, *At Last Sight* itself was
not 'marked', although all of the Year Three students were. As I have

stated earlier I am not at liberty to publish their grades here, but I can attest to a department-wide recognition of the students' achievements. By this I mean that the marks awarded for performances within *At Last Sight* were high. This may seem somewhat surprising when one considers the assessment criteria for 'Performance' that were in operation at their institution of choice and at that time. I make these comments in order to stress here some of the difficulties of assessing certain types of performance according to guidelines which are written in an agenda-specific way.

For example, 'First Class' performance work is expected to be demonstrative of excellence which is evidenced through 'expressive control of voice', 'role or roles fully realised and maintained', 'sustained concentration throughout' and an ability to 'seize and maintain focus throughout'. None of these elements were present in the performances relating to *At Last Sight*, whereas the criteria for the lowest 'Pass' mark, which I include here in their entirety, are those which were directed into the work

> Pedestrian and lacking in confidence. Although real effort is made there is a failure to demonstrate style or focus. May be uncomfortable to watch and communicate insecurity. Does not give appropriate support to fellow performers. Mistakes may be made and acknowledged. Lacking in expressivity and awareness. May inadvertently upstage. Slow in response and uncertain.

What the expectations of 'First Class' and 'Pass' work reveals is itself an articulation of a received wisdom which does not stand up to challenge. The students involved – the human material of *At Last Sight* – are told that 'excellent' work is implicitly role-driven and focused, whilst weak work is visibly insecure and inexpressive. The criteria make too strong a contribution to the idea of absolutes. Of a right and a wrong way of making work, which not only impacts on the ways in which those students are taught but also on the views of performance they carry with them beyond graduation. There is no mention in the criteria of appropriateness; principally, I feel, because it is neither quantifiable nor fixed.

This criticism (for such it is) of the assessment procedures in place at certain institutions has nothing to do with my own predilections towards one way of working over another. My concern is not so much with issues of the marginal (whatever that is) set in opposition to the mainstream (whatever that may be), as it is with the imposing on students (and staff) of what amounts to a type of half-hidden hierarchy. By this I mean the predisposition towards certain approaches to performance, which are deemed 'more acceptable' than others, without that same agenda being made overt. It is possible to compare works that fall under one heading, perhaps 'Modernism', with others which are influenced more directly by 'Postmodernism', but these comparisons need to be made in a non-hierarchical spirit. In essence (and here this book plunges once again into those very 'isms' which the first few paragraphs of this conclusion sought to refute) I can say that *At Last Sight* was a postmodern piece. The postmodern aspects of the work were never intended as a departure from modernism *per se*, so much as an implicit denial of that faith in the power of the present and the yet-to-be which has become synonymous with modernism, *as it is generally taught*.[7] Where modernism can be seen (through that morally complex historicising lens) as an attempt to replace the nineteenth century's glorification of the past with a twentieth century optimism, postmodernism is conversely identified by an infatuation or obsession with the past. *At Last Sight*'s starting obsession with my own past – which constituted a pleading for redemption without an accompanying offering up to change – was in this way steadfastly postmodern. No solutions, no functionalism, not even any real and identifiable trace of idealism.

Artists working through modernist beliefs invented new formal languages that changed not just the way theatre looked, but the way in which spectators were encouraged to see.[8] Modernism then can be seen as no less than an attempt, through theatre and other art forms, to change the world. It was both a success and a failure. Even the most absurd and abstract of practitioner/philosophers, the futurists, dadaists and surrealists, like so many more to follow, believed that theatre had a responsibility to carry a new message. Even in the midst of mayhem there lurked an undercurrent of functionalism. A belief in the capacity of performance, art, literature and architecture to bring forth change. The aesthetic aspects of the modernists' message were carried forward successfully. And that very success may be modernism's failure … its ultimate irony. We have learned modernism by rote, and we go on to repeat that mantra as faithfully as the words of *The Lord's Prayer* spoken in chorus in a classroom assembly. Modernism failed because its spirit of optimism was lost and with it went any claim to potency. Its impotence rises to the surface in every *verfremdungseffekt* that no longer defamiliarises; in every political play which fails to persuade (and which fails even to persuade its cast). It became a Communion Mass learned by disbelievers: a ritual as empty as a ticketed trip through the Holocaust Theme Park.[9] The *zeitgeist* shifts and all that we have left are historians' words. Bound and binding.

When postmodern performance feeds off modernism it does so with less hypocrisy than modernism shows when it feeds off itself. If work is to be parasitic in nature then let that nature be exposed for what it is. It is a singularly one-sided relationship. The parasite, the maker of work, does not care what the host subject thinks or thought. It treads over the politics and philosophy of the past ... which, at any rate, can never fully match up to its own. Modernism is exposed as nostalgia, and so it succumbs to its very own *bete noir*. In displaying a pessimistic *mien* in *lieu* of hope, postmodernism seeks to provide itself with the luxury of dealing with sentimentality without at the same time seeming sentimental. It is difficult to think of a more appropriate framework to put around work that deals with love and loss. Postmodern performance thrives on our collective and individual experiences of a theatrical past, and all conventions employed are themselves only ever the hand-me-downs of work seen.

Theatre history, badly used, reduces all things to names as names-of-note. The stuff of theatre past is an intrinsic historicisation wherein careers of shifting practice are metamorphosed into systems and schools. A necessary aspect of my own analytical reflection on *At Last Sight* is the extent to which this project - which was always an amalgamation of my own previous and less coherent productions - will now become the marketplace where I shop for 'new' ideas. The point of these paragraphs then, is not to argue against the appropriation of ideas, any more than it is to argue against influence. Cross-fertilisation is an important and legitimate aspect of the ways in which performances are made and culture functions. What I *am* doing here is making explicit my recognition that a tendency exists, certainly within my own way of making work, to, as it were, cash in on history. To take ideas which once seemed radical and re-use them with no attendant re-interpretation. Which is *not* the same thing as reference.

Reference means just that: that one refers to something, that ideas of the contemporary and ideas from or of the past clash and spark and make something which is at once recognisable and fresh. That seems to be the strength of postmodernism.

And just as postmodernism has an obligation to learn from the past, to interrogate its ideas, rather than endlessly repeating them, regurgitated and reframed, so it is vital that *At Last Sight*, my own past, is not reduced, in work to come, to an alternative to new ideas. What is needed is an investigation of the varied strategies and ideas of the work and not its stylistic trickery. What is needed of work gone is not simply that it is perpetually re-questioned, but that we ask the *right* questions.

And what are these questions? They should be the questions that cannot be answered by the work alone ... questions that cannot necessarily be addressed directly or empirically, but which are elusive. They are questions such as: What is it about this particular performance that we cannot understand because we are not a part of the culture or *zeitgeist* in which it was created? What is it that we *can* understand precisely because we are not the target group ... what aspects of the work have become visible to *my* eyes? What did the performance seek to communicate to its audience and *why*? What was the relationship between intention and result? Was the performance an example of 'good' theatre of the time or 'bad'? What types of theatre were considered good or bad, or exciting or banal at that time? At *this* time? Richard Foreman has offered the apposite statement that "The spectator's question should not be, 'What does this play mean?' The question should be, 'In response to which of the world's possibilities and tensions is this play created?'"[10]

Good theatre history then should be interested in the finished product not as a point of closure or culmination, but as one stage along a continuum of process. It is because of this that theatre history has an obligation to consider the fringes of practice as well as the award-winning mainstream ... to look to work which might all too easily be regarded as insignificant. It is not enough that our published notions of marginal performance are almost exclusively limited to the marginal-made-mainstream. To Robert Wilson and The Wooster Group, to Impact Theatre Co-Operative, The People Show and Forced Entertainment ... to the formerly esoteric as the television chat show guest.

Theatre history, I would argue, needs to be something that does not see itself as being anything other than a history of ideas. Good theatre history is not actually concerned with a history of theatre at all. It is a history of ideas and therefore of culture ... two of the most precious elements to be found in Higher Education. It is not a barely changing roster of names, etched in stone, as though Twentieth Century theatre were the sole province of the famous names from Stanislavski through to LeCompte, it is the history of how we each have come to believe the things we do about theatre. If this reads like an advert for a Liberal Arts approach then so be it. As the project of *At Last Sight* took form as part of a performance project and draws to a close as a book to be read, amongst others, by performance makers it is hardly inappropriate if the philosophy that drives the language of the performance is now allowed to drive the language of the page.

If this book achieves this, then in doing so it has provided a contribution to knowledge that is fundamental to the study of Performance at this time and also at times to come. Words remain long after memories fade. This book has many aspects. It is the chronicling of a project, from inception to production; the charting of an example of performance practice as performance research; the publication of that which would otherwise remain as ephemeral as the time taken by spectators to take to their seats and then to applaud; as the analysis of a particular process of making work, including a rationale for words written as performance text and also for directional input; as a chronicle of work that has been overtly driven by the demands of a specific curriculum and which has, in its own turn, been influenced by the 'accident' of modules undertaken as a student myself, of performances made, seen and read about, of conversations and criticisms, of the inexplicable and the explained at length, of reflection and supervision, of revision and immediacy.

Tracing the Footprints constitutes an attempt at defining a position on the nature of research-driven practice. This is one of the struggles of university theatre in our time: to have practice afforded the status of research. This book functions in part then as a mechanism through which a personal example of this struggle is being reported.

Issues of status do not just affect research as practice: the status of the researcher is also an element (if one has a proven and established track record in research then 'similar' outcomes from 'dissimilar' forms may be more readily accepted). The position adopted by the researcher is equally important, making the publication of 'knowledge' *via* practice a complex outcome to determine. At London's Brunel University, for example, the situation regarding practice-based research was articulated thus in an open e-mail to the SCUDD Mailbase

142 Arrival and Departure

'Practice-based' ... refers to things like the EdD and EngD where a
substantial element of the doctorate is about professional practice -
almost denoting work-based activities .... this is not to be confused
with what we mean by the words 'practice based'. Practice, in the
widest sense of performance/artefact, and the theorising around it,
which we permit for our PhD at Brunel ... does present a challenge to
the definition of research and to the idea of credit which the QAA is
applying at doctoral level.

The QAA want to defend the PhD as research based, but will quite
explicitly allow this award where the artefact or other form of work
is accompanied by a 'written explanation that is examined'. It is only
when the artefact or performance is the sole outcome that the PhD is
not available. There is no indication ... of word count in relation to
this 'written explanation'. There has to be a rationale in place of
course, but the weighting of performance to written explanation is
something that is determined by each individual PhD.[11]

As part of an ongoing debate as to the possibilities for
practice to be credited as research *per se*, the communication from
Brunel is interesting. Whilst it offers succinct advice and a large
amount of creative freedom to a PhD student researching under its
own institutional auspices it also highlights the problem for artists
working within academic structures. For the purposes of QAA,
practice is afforded a type of validity *only* when it is subsequently
'explained' in written text. For researching practitioners this is
something of a handicap, inasmuch, at least, as one needs to
demonstrate an ownership of the 'product' which is of both creative
and intellectual worth. For the purposes of PhD this seems appropriate
... the thoughts contained within the submission need to be capable of
a dissemination which is coherent and permanent. But for practice
engaged in with undergraduates the situation remains vexed.

Processes undertaken in the creation of public performance
are unlikely to be written down in anything like a systematic fashion.
Indeed, the process of *making* almost augurs against *writing*. And I
speak from the experiences gained during the process of creating *At
Last Sight*. The making and writing *are* compatible and mutually
enriching, but the activity of making work in and with a group can, at
its most telling times, be so intense as to eat into the time put aside to
write. The pressure to present is always in the present, and the
pressure to publish follows. Writing has a life of its own and the gap

between that which is being made and the words that explain it can be wider than the researcher would care to admit.

What I have been afforded through the process of making this work has been a position of experience that may be of some benefit to other researchers within the field of performance. The words to come are offered as an encapsulation of that experience, rather than as an 'explanation' of *At Last Sight*. What follows then is an attempt at outlining the area of practice as research, both as it has applied to my own experience and as it appears as a wider issue for colleagues elsewhere. In this way, the micro of *At Last Sight* feeds into the macro of practice as research. It does so through the case study of an otherwise culturally invisible work. If there are times when the language of this chapter seems to move too readily towards generalisations and the dread of 'universal truths', it does so from a need to widen the scope of what has been an otherwise tightly focused study.

We know that a debate concerning the accreditation as research for performance has raged in recent years. Out of this debate, a feeling has emerged that the event of performance should, in certain situations, be afforded the validity of research. What it is that defines one 'situation' from another is the key area of debate. What, for example, makes one piece of work 'research-driven' and another not so? In fulfilling its obligation to address that question, this chapter will function as both conclusion and introduction: tidying up the slippage of my own processes and offering a point of departure for others.

The differences between Theatre *study* and Theatre *training* still exists. They are many, but we might say that chief among them is that the former looks at *why* decisions are made, whilst the latter concentrates on *how* those decisions are carried out in performance. It is a crude but nonetheless useful distinction, with some considerable bearing on the ways in which notions of practice as research have been regarded. Where practical work, or performed output, is prioritised, theory may find little room; where theoretical study is the aim, practice may be regarded as no more than a 'playing'. A small number of Drama departments at British universities are moving away from the assessment of practice, and, whilst this movement is regarded by some as a response to questions of quality assurance rather than as a positional shift which is supported by a persuasive philosophy, its significance should not be overlooked. What this is saying to students on its courses in Drama is that practice in and of itself is not commensurate with the presentation for assessment of thinking that is deep and analytical.

This looks likely to achieve two things: it will widen further still the gulf between scholars and practitioners, which the *industry* of commercial theatre is already predisposed towards.[12] And it will reduce the belief in the potency of performance as its own expressive language which is in need of no further explanation.

I shall deal with these issues in order. It is a fact of life, rather than a rumour, that students graduating from accredited Drama Schools in Britain, who are also graduates of academic Drama programmes at universities, are advised by many of their Drama School tutors and agents not to mention their academic histories to casting agencies and directors.[13] The logic of this advice is clear. Directors are looking for practitioners: they want doers, not thinkers. The British tradition of 'intellectual' directors and 'instinctive' actors is clear for all to see. Directors are also scholars, whereas actors are not. The exceptions to this rule do little to affect the overall picture. It is rare to find a mainstream director of influence who is not also a graduate. [14] Notwithstanding their much greater number, it is rare to find a mainstream actor who is a graduate (or who broadcasts this history). The difference is no less pronounced in British cinema and television. Whilst the American system does not provide an exact parallel, inasmuch as a college or university education is more commonplace than in Britain, the American film actor and director, Sean Penn, has likened directors to hammers and actors to nails.[15] It is a violent image, but one which is nevertheless apt within a profession (an industry) that sees the ideal performer as somebody both 'beautiful' and 'stupid'.

To stop students from 'doing' practice as a part of their assessable academic programme is to perpetuate the myth that separates out instinct and analysis. This is not to argue for students' performances to demonstrate no more than a technical accomplishment, so that a juggler keeping three objects in the air is seen as weaker than s/he who juggles with four. Technical accomplishment in terms of the craft of performance is much more the stuff of drama schools than of university departments. What performances within academic departments can and should provide are opportunities for students and staff to engage in research through practice. This remains the principle distinction between the types of 'training' offered to students, and it is precisely why universities have provided professional 'experimental' or 'alternative' theatre companies with so many of their core members.[16]

This brings us to the second danger. The mainstream has operated on something of a policy of exclusion with regard to Drama graduates, but this exclusion is in no way one-sided. Students who have spent three years engaged in critical thinking about and *through* theatre are probably more inclined to gravitate towards a professional practice that is concerned with change above reiteration. Indeed, hindsight allows us to see that the rise in 'fringe' companies in Britain owes as much to the upsurge in and availability of Drama as an academic programme of study as it does to the students' uprising in the Paris of 1968, an uprising which history has written as being of seminal influence. The majority of Drama graduates do not seek employment as professional practitioners: these paragraphs are not intended to argue a case for the employability or otherwise of Drama graduates *per se*. But former students on degree programmes (primarily Drama programmes) do form the mainstay of non-mainstream companies. Accurate figures are impossible to obtain. Companies come and go, sometimes lasting for the duration of only one short tour; personnel can change rapidly; and many company members are not also members of the actors' union, Equity. Proof, such as it can be said to exist at all, is offered only by the evidence of one's own experience. Anybody who has regular social contact with non-mainstream companies will know that they are predominantly Drama graduates, and also that very few will have opted for an additional postgraduate year at an accredited Drama school.

Taking away the opportunity for non-Drama school students to engage in the practice of performance, which is recognised as commensurate with the practice of writing essays, is a doomed idea.[17] What it might gain in accountability, in that an essay is a tangible and permanent record which can be assessed according to recognised criteria, it must lose in terms of the faith those students might have otherwise gained in the potential of performance to speak for itself.

In addition to the internal differences between institutional and individual approaches within the Higher Education sector, all academic Drama staff are aware of the difficulties of having practical work credited as research-significant by colleagues from other departments. Senior management are traditionally cautious in terms of sanctioning an adequate hourage for production work, whilst the term 'publication' is still seen to refer to publications in print rather than performance.[18] The predominantly audience-friendly product of university 'drama societies' only adds to this difficulty. When unsupervised students are seen to mount a full-scale play entirely from their leisure time (and when that play is also 'successful' in terms of its feel-good popularity and box office receipts) then timetabled productions can appear esoteric and self-indulgent.

Theatre professionals may harbour feelings of suspicion towards scholars, with their intellectualising of that which the profession regards as alchemical. 'Those who can do; those who can't teach' is an adage that continues to carry weight in our culture.[19] The vocabulary of academic critique is so markedly distinct from the vocabulary of the professionals' rehearsal room as to leave little room for constructive cross over. Where the vocabulary is antithetical, communication is lost before it is able to take root. This is true despite the fact of once-marginal companies like *Theatre de Complicite* and *The National Theatre of Brent* becoming part of the fabric of mainstream performance. Notwithstanding these transformations, it is still the case that *thinking* or *talking* about theatre is held in less regard than *making* it, and making a *public* form to suit a *private* agenda is seen as an equally dubious endeavour.[20]

In this climate, one has to ask what the role of scholarship might be. Is it self-serving, inasmuch as it speaks of a desire on the part of academics to engage in practice without any of the pressures of commercial success which would ordinarily accompany production-work? Is it of long-term benefit in that its influences will come to fruition in future performances? If the study of theatre is regarded with distrust by the theatre profession itself, is the exercise fundamentally flawed? If theatre scholarship serves no more than the interests of the scholar (tenure, readerships, professorships etc.) is it automatically invalidated? It may be the case that much of that which appears as theatre scholarship is merely self-promotion in disguise. If I am to be honest about my work on and around *At Last Sight*, I have to recognise the fact that I have been driven as much by a desire to concentrate attention on a given project as to make that project worthy of the attention of others. This may mean that my sustained enthusiasm for the project has been misplaced. That my time would be more appropriately spent in the analysis of the performance of more weighty others, rather than labouring within the assumption that I am capable of creating a comparable theatre product of my own.[21]

To suggest this, however, is to deny my own status as both maker and scholar; as the creator of that which I am simultaneously holding up to the light of analysis and explanation. What does it mean to create? To write that I have created *At Last Sight*, albeit as one part of a team, is to imply that I have an answer to this question. This brings with it an attendant obligation.

Art is usually something made by an artist. The artist creates. The word 'create' stems from *creare*, meaning to generate or provide offspring. The word 'procreate' reminds us of this. The Spanish use the term *criatura* to refer to a child. The type of making employed by an artist is then the type we call creating. Art is made deliberately by artists. Artists can create art even when they have no real sense of what that art will be.[22] What follows is that the (prospective) artist needs to find the means through which an as yet unknown activity, event or object will find expression. When we say that an artist is creative, we are saying that s/he has produced something that is different from that which has gone before. Art is distinct from written analysis in this key regard. If I am offering a performance as research-in-practice, then the form of that performance will be likely to subvert expectations and extend conventions, whereas, by contrast, an essay, a thesis or a dissertation will probably conform to conventions. We link creativity to change, so that it is always in some way experimental.

The artist is always also a critic. Not necessarily in the way that I am offering critical information here on *At Last Sight*, but inasmuch as an artist inevitably functions in two simultaneous ways. S/he is the imaginative producer of art (in my case, the event of *At Last Sight*) and s/he is also a critic, observing the work as it proceeds. In this way, the activity of self-criticism is always spectatorial. The artist's critical faculties are prompted by personal experience to the extent where it is difficult to envisage an artist creating, by choice, something which lies beyond the parameters of her or his own 'taste'.

With *At Last Sight*, I have been working creatively in terms that related to a central theme, which was in turn favoured by my other identity, that of the critic. It has been apparent throughout this process that whatever I thought, as well as whatever performance decisions I made, have been constantly taken apart and reconfigured in the light of developing attitudes. There is an appropriateness to this. For just as I had set myself the challenge that *At Last Sight* should not misconstrue my personal mode of thinking (about theatre, about teaching, about my own life) then I have also been forcing upon myself an unusual alertness to precisely what it is that I think.

The published writings of theatre makers are often found to be contradictory, evasive and elliptical. Even for those of us whose making exists within an education framework, what we do and what we say often function at a tangent to one another. We have a concern with events, with moving bodies through time and space, which does not always dovetail comfortably with the theoretical notions we might discuss as part of our formal teaching. As researching practitioners, we have a duty to address these contradictions, which is why this book is written in the way that it is ... one that is similar to the logic that the work of *At Last Sight* embodied.

There is a way in which the maker of work is also an onlooker, a beholder and reader of the work made. As such, the maker (the 'I' of the artist) suffers - and suffers no less than any member of the art event's audience - from the problem of defining just what it is that has been thought and made. A mixture of conjecture, anecdote and metaphor are the likely companions of a working process which is concerned with the ambiguities of performance and the clarity of words written.

Recent exercises in the assessment of research within universities have been useful in many ways ... not least in that they have created in their wake discussion as to the primary object of research. The Higher Education Funding Council for England offers the following definition

> 'Research' for the purpose of the RAE is to be understood as original investigation undertaken in order to gain knowledge and understanding. It includes ... the invention and generation of ideas, images, performances and artefacts including design, where these lead to new or substantially improved insights.[23]

The document goes on to define scholarship as "the creation, development and maintenance of the intellectual infrastructure of subjects and disciplines, in forms such as dictionaries, scholarly editions, catalogues and contributions to major research databases.[24]

We can say then that, like other forms of research, research by means of performance has the aim of making a contribution to knowledge, and that this will usually be achieved by suggesting new perspectives on the known. Contributions to knowledge will rarely be manifest in expansive leaps of consciousness. Contributions to knowledge are complicated phenomena within the study of live performance. Research outcomes are open to challenge through the unreliability of evaluative processes as applied to performance. Where multi-interpretation is prioritised over a monologistic 'meaning' this is doubly difficult. If a commonality of understanding is being denied at source, then the utilisation of the tools of a standard scientific enquiry are simply not adequate. In fact, we may find the answer closer to home than we might imagine. The ways in which we can assess the 'findings' of research through performance are not dissimilar to the ways in which we can assess practical work submitted by our own students.

It is to these issues of assessment that this book now moves. In doing so, two purposes are served. In the first instance, I am able to offer a position on assessment as it applies to students who may be participating *for assessment* in the practical research projects of members of staff. And here the experiences of my own graduating students of last year, having been assessed for their work on *At Last Sight*, are uppermost in my mind. In the second instance, the suggestions can provide parallels between the ways in which we assess the work of students and the ways in which we wish our own research projects to be assessed.

There has been a long-standing difficulty in assessing the live product of students and the introduction of Drama and Theatre as academic disciplines has met with considerable resistance. This resistance has stemmed from a position which deals in universal standards of 'truth'; viewed from such a perspective, where findings are presented as quantitative results, outcomes (practical performances, workshop participation, this research) can never be fully or comfortably accepted. To respond to this with the writing up of generic criteria to cover a diverse range of practices is to engage in an unmanageable and misleading conflation.

Assessment procedures in the study of performance, as in other areas of the curriculum, must be capable of revealing progress ... or a lack of it. Procedures need to be capable of offering objective criteria for what counts as achievement. In performance terms, it is frequently the case that the criteria for achievement are implicit, rather than being formulated explicitly. For example, as a lecturer running a module in Devised Theatre, I need to have an implicit (although not exclusive) notion of what it is that counts as devising. Documentation which makes this implicit understanding explicit needs to do so with an awareness of the prejudices of one's own position. Many of us who teach Performance in the university sector are reluctant to make explicit the criteria on which we inevitably depend. We feel, perhaps, that to state an objective criterion is to generalise in a way that would inhibit our students' opportunities for individual creativity, or to tie us into one mode of practice at the expense of others. In practice, however, the fact that we are all engaged in assessment as a natural consequence of our professional lives means that we do need to be possessed of an ability to articulate a rationale for grades awarded. Certainly, when we are increasingly offering our own work for assessment as research, the obligation to couch a vocabulary of assessment in a way which provokes rather than prescribes is of paramount importance.

The following points can be made: In order for an academic judgement to be regarded as 'objective' it does not also need to be 'true'. We are prepared to accept scientific judgements as objective even though there might be fundamental conflicts of opinion - or 'findings' - within the scientific community. We can go further than this and state that it is actually the indefinite possibility of differences and changes of opinion which gives objectivity its status. What is meant by this is that it is a feature of theory that it is, in principle, falsifiable, and *not* that it will be held as true for all time. Changes of perspective wrought by new research inevitably change the character of that which we are still able to term as an observation or outcome. Artists work within conceptual notions, and usually within one paradigm ... or at least one paradigm at a time; spectators and/or other 'readers' of the work will not necessarily be functioning within that same paradigmatic frame. The perceiver may regard the work in a different way to that which the creator intends. As professional assessors, we need to be able to recognise the conceptual framework within which the work is created and *offered*, and this requires sensitivity to a number of different approaches.

This is not about denying our prejudices so much as recognising and controlling them.

It says nothing whatsoever against the possibility of objective assessment of performance that there have been and still are changes of opinion and approach. Quite the opposite. We can see that such variety, alongside assessment criteria which embraces diversity is vital for the advance of practice as research. In work submitted there is an unlimited opportunity for individual differences of imaginative and creative approach. The assessment of this work has to be justified by reference to what is objectively there. To what the work is, rather than to what the specific assessors might prefer it to be. And this needs to be carried out with a recognition that advances come from new insights and conceptions. The fact that different types of work can emerge from the same stimulus is the nature of our subject. To assume that 'objectivity' means 'similarity' is to reduce creativity to the crass.

Facts rely on theories. A fact is only given any sense by an underlying conception, or theory. Facts may be objectively established, but this is inevitably done in the light of a particular theoretical approach. As theories are always open to modification, so are facts. The situation of no permanent absolutes does not mean that we cannot regard ephemeral theoretical positions as objectively arrived at phenomena. We can assess the articulation of a position (in whatever forms that articulation might take) without having any personal belief or investment in that position.

It is incorrect to assume that there can be no objectivity where judgement is based on interpretation. To believe this is to equate objective assessment with quantifiability. I can be objectively convinced that somebody is delighted, irate or in love without necessarily being able to reach such a conclusion by procedures of quantification. *All* judgement is interpretative as a matter of course and no quantification can exist without interpretation. Scientists interpret data in their field, just as we do in ours. Interpretation and judgement, not quantification, are the methods of assessment in performance-related subjects such as Theatre or Drama. What matters most to the creator is that this interpretation and judgement are informed.

The distinctive feature of performance is that feelings can be, and generally are, expressed *via* artistic means. That is to say that emotional content is a characteristic of performance. The presence of an emotional content does not imply that the work cannot be objectively assessed. Judgements about the emotional resonance of a performance are just as open to rational justification by reference to objective criteria. The feelings expressed and evoked by a particular performance, *At Last Sight*, for example, are assessable by reference(s) to objective features of the work. There can be no workable separation of understanding and feeling, of knowledge and experience. In order to be able to *respond* to the work a spectator does not need to have understood it. In order to *judge* the work (academically) an assessor does. Performance involves a negotiation of emotionally complex structures: we need to be able to be carried along by the work, but not to the degree that we are not also able to recognise and respond critically to the arrangement and ordering of those structures. In short, we need to be both responsive and receptive,

What underlies our resistance to stating objective assessment criteria is a fear that it would stifle creativity. In fact, the opposite is true. That is to say that unless the student has a sense of what counts as achievement, there can be no notion of personal development. If there are no declared criteria, the notion of development becomes meaningless. Thus, it is the lack of objective criteria which is, in fact, restrictive. Nevertheless, it is frighteningly easy to impose narrow criteria on students' work to the exclusion of other equally valid possibilities. Assessment needs to provide room for difference, and this can only be achieved when the assessors are as open-minded as is possible.

In order to be capable of creating a performance which is appropriate at a particular level of submission, an ability to work through processes is required. This is a skill in itself. A technique. To concentrate on the acquisition of technical skills, however: juggling, stilt-walking, verse-speaking, tumbling etc. is to run the risk of applauding a display of technical competence, rather than the work of an artist who has something to say. Too rigid an emphasis on the learning of technical skills is likely to have the consequence of destroying creative potential; of imbuing skills with the status of an end-product rather than as choices which may or may not be taken in the pursuit of a given means. A performance should not be assessed according to its degree of success in the instantiation of skills, so much as to the ways in which such skills as are employed contribute to the effectiveness of the particular performance.

The skills we need to encourage, and I speak here of practice as research at all levels, are the skills of discrimination and discourse. *At Last Sight* was illustrative of discriminatory skills at a level appropriate to my own position. And the participating students' reflective essays reveal an impressive ability to discriminate, and also, by definition, an ability to express that discrimination through discourse.

Discriminatory skills open up a subtle and complex range of possibilities of performative expression and appraisal. Discourse skills consist of a means whereby discrimination is given voice. It consists of a knowing how to use the vocabulary of a particular art form. Learning the use of working vocabularies provides a means of communicating clearly with others about one's areas of interest. This is not about using language to obscure, to create a closed world where only the initiated can enter, although that may well be a consequence. Facility in language, again, whether that language be the language of a performance, an essay, a *viva voce* or this book, is critical for the development and dissemination of conceptual repositionings.

Skills of discourse allow us to identify the research project to be undertaken and to locate that project within a broader field; to accumulate relevant information; to analyse the results of the project and to disseminate any conclusions. A willingness and ability to engage in and promote discourse is perhaps the most important distinction between academically driven practice and practice which might be regarded as existing for its own sake. Tracing the footprints that lead to the work is so central to the principle of performance study that it almost goes without saying that it is the scholar's greatest asset. It is also a process which involves an increased workload. Whereas the maker of work where the performed product is the sole outcome 'only' needs to be concerned with dissemination *via* performance, the researching practitioner's dissemination will almost always include an attendant written explanation.

Research through performance is at once similar to and distinct from other forms of experimental research. As in any approach, we can say that in instigating the research, any number of practices through which the investigation can develop are employed. Because practice as research - when that research involves an analysis of somebody else's practice - is not the material of this book, what it is that distinguishes research *via* performance is that the research is based upon the researcher's own location *within* the work to be studied.

This involves and engages an essentially heuristic position. The position makes it vital for the researcher to be self-reflective and to move carefully through those areas where an objective terminology is offered as the articulation of subjective beliefs. When the distance between the researcher and the researched is dissolved to such a degree, the results are imbued, at best, with a unique and intimate perspective; at worst, those same results are so contaminated by the researcher's intention *in the act of making* that they disseminate little more than the researcher's own private agenda.

The dangers in assuming that one's own position should be regarded as universally applicable are clear to see. Notwithstanding the belief in objective criteria offered in previous paragraphs of this conclusion, we do need to proceed with caution. Objectivity is not a term which we can have any faith in if it is assigned on an almost *ad hoc* basis to each and every researcher's *nuance*. The findings of personally complicated research need to be analysed for what they are, according to the critical faculties of s/he who is analysing the work. Research through performance is providing scholars and practitioners with remarkable opportunities to have their voices heard and to extend the shelf-life of work which would otherwise suffer the inevitable end of all ephemeral product; but this does not automatically mean that what we hear is important.

In searching for cures for cancer scientists discover a formula for anti-depressants; in research towards anti-depression, scientists find a strategy for dealing with drug-dependency. The examples of scientists discovering something of value, which was not what they were looking for are legion. Performance research is no different. With *At Last Sight*, the findings do not create an accurate match up with the intentions. There are accidents. The group size shifts. People fall in love. Autobiography and a search for truth make way for group collaboration and presented lies. It is the nature of *all* performance research that the environment is never fully controlled. There is no sterility. There are no opportunities, ever, for repeating an experiment, simply because the human material of that experiment is never the same material twice. In this regard we can say that performance is a generative process. Findings in practice as research threaten to fix as permanent what is in reality only ever a fleeting perspective on an equally fleeting event.

An engagement in practice as research necessitates a familiarity with the ways in which the project in question was organised. A heightened understanding of the importance of the researcher's own positionality is equally vital, alongside an acknowledgement of the limitations and privilege of that perspective. Researchers need to be able to have sufficient control over the vocabulary of their chosen field in order to articulate their findings to a reasonably informed third party, and also to be able to defend their research verbally.

Research through one's own practice requires a concentration. A focusing of the attention in a specific way, so that one is as aware as possible of all of the implications and possible developments of a performance project. This runs parallel to an awareness that performance research (and in this it is no different to performance itself) has no givens. No absolutes. None other than the fact that every maker of performance has something which is demanding of expression. Every maker of performance is of her or his time, and is so impelled to create within the spirit of that time. Exceptions to this can only result in a type of 'museum-art', and even this is marked more strongly by the age in which it was made than by any age it might be seeking to emulate.

We can see this in photographic evidence of re-staged historical plays, where even in the frozen moment, the physical *attitudes* of the performers (not to mention hair styles) will give us a close approximation of the decade at least in which the work was re-staged. Notions of reality do not stay fixed. Images of psychic chicanery from the turn of the century read to us now as so obviously fake and staged as to be laughable, and yet we know that they were, *at the time*, regarded by many as being 'real' manifestations of the recently dead. Faked paintings, indiscernible from the original at the time of their appearance at auction houses, emerge, over time, as obvious copies, as though time is exposing the space between versions. We make art of our own time then, even when we are actively intent on recreating the past, and this is one of the identifying features of creativity.

The word 'conclusion' seems not quite appropriate for the words of this chapter. It is as though I am seeking to bring the book to a point of arrival, when in fact that point feels much more strongly like departure ... an opening up of possibilities. A braver writer than I would grasp the nettle here and abandon the term completely.

Just as *At Last Sight* was concerned with a resistance to closure, so its documentation is equally disinclined to state its case. As though to do so would stand as a betrayal to interpretative license. Issues of essentialism, of ownership, of frames of performance, of process and articulation, of borrowing and bending theoretical positionings at will and by default have been constant in each and every aspect of the work ... whether I was always aware of it or not. It is only now, with a pause, that I am able to gain perspective on the breathlessness of the book. A chain of doing, writing, talking, writing, doing that has taken this project from the relative clarity of first intentions to the confusion (a more appropriate chapter heading than 'Conclusion') at its end.

What is most important is not what I have learned or think I know so much as what it is that the reader takes away. This is neither apology nor evasion. It is the premise on which the project was started and it remains that premise now as that same project draws to a close.

These words mean that I am faced with feelings similar to those at the end of rehearsals for *At Last Sight*. When adjustments cease, the maker is effectively saying that the work is ready. It is now to be given away. It becomes the property of the reader, and the safety of the desk - like the safety of the rehearsal room – is sacrificed to public perusal. This is not about fear. It is not about the fear of response, of criticism, of disapproval. It has much more, I think, to do with the pleasure of making ... and this has really been the thrust of everything connected with this book. The pleasure of making. And, as with *At Last Sight*, that which has been made has been constructed in the knowledge that it would inevitably pass from my hands into the hands of others.

Notes

[1] In many ways the *assemblage* of which I speak is part of a recognisable shift within performance work as part of undergraduate study, albeit not at every institution. University departments carve their own agendas and new members of staff and students bring new ideas. The journal *Studies in Theatre Production*, available through SCUDD, provides examples of the types of work engaged in at a number of institutions. The practical work undertaken at places such as Liverpool John Moores University and Bretton Hall, with their emphasis on theatre as a story interestingly told, is different in kind as well as intent to work at Manchester Metropolitan University and Nottingham Trent University, where dramatised narrative is less likely to be a focus for students' engagement.

[2] See Berger, J *Ways of Seeing*. BBC/Penguin Books, London, 1977.

[3] Eugenio Barba discusses the organic transference of performance techniques and traditions in *The Paper Canoe*, (Barba) Routledge, London and New York, 1995.

[4] Edgar, A and Sedgwick, P. *Keynotes in Cultural Theory*. Routledge, London and New York, 1999. p.2.

[5] Phelan, P. *Unmarked: The Politics of Performance*. Routledge, London and New York, 1993. pp.148 -9.

[6] Willet, J. *The Theatre of Bertolt Brecht*. Methuen, London, 1959 and Esslin, M. *Brecht: A Choice of Evils*. Heinemann, London, 1959 are standard academic texts on the work of Brecht.

[7] My 'evidence' here is based on fifteen years of lecturing, with experience at a number of institutions, both in further and higher education, with considerable experience of seeing student work at festivals, and from discussions with colleagues and students.

[8] There are many published and available works which describe the development of modernism in theatre.

[9] The Holocaust Memorial Museum in Washington DC, U.S.A provides a 'theme park' approach to the acts of genocide perpetrated in the Second World War. Visitors are allocated identity cards, which approximate as closely as possible to 'real life' victims of the Holocaust. Some victims lived and some died. The museum visitor inserts the card into various terminals located at computer stations along the museum's route and is provided with updates of their 'character's' progress. Video footage plays as part of the 'experience'.

[10] Foreman, R *Art +Performance: Richard Foreman* Gerald Rabkin (ed). The Johns Hopkins University Press, Baltimore and London, 1999. p. 18.

[11] Edwards, B. *QAA + PhD*. Electronic correspondence to SCUDD Mailbase. 14th April 1999.

[12] When Kenneth Rea writes that 'The standard of acting in university or polytechnic productions is likely to be lower than that of the average drama school.' (Rae, K. *A Better Direction.* Calouste Gulbenkian Foundation, London, 1989. p. 111 he is arguing from a mainstream perspective that seeks to reinforce rather than challenge the status quo.

[13] My evidence here is anecdotal, but consistent.

[14] 'While the older director tends to be Oxbridge, male and ex-public school, among the younger generation there is a higher presence of women directors, less Oxbridge dominance, but a greater degree of university education. Thus, eight out of ten directors under thirty are graduates.' (Rea, 1989. p. 24.) '39% of theatre directors have come from independent schools, which is extremely high, considering that the overall national figure for independent school education is only 7%.' p. 25

[15] See Mathur, P. 'Method and Madness' in *Blitz*, October 1988, No. 70. pp. 44-50

[16] Again, the evidence for this is anecdotal, and also of one's own eyes. Small and middle scale touring theatre companies, dealing with non-mainstream practice, feature fewer drama school graduates than graduates of arts-related disciplines at universities. Talking with company members reveals this to be the case, as does following the careers of former students. Not all of the companies in question are members of the ITC (Independent Theatre Council), issuing Equity contracts to employees, and the itinerant nature of the work makes data unreliable. In this instance, the best evidence is of experience.

[17] '(University) Drama departments often encourage their students to create their own opportunities, and indeed this has given rise to theatre groups that have stayed together on a professional basis.' (Rae, 1989. p.114)

[18] The document *RAE 2001* published on the internet at http://www.hiss.ac.uk/education/hefc/rae/2001/2.html

[19] This is in many ways a British phenomenon. Teaching performance skills, as part of a traditional student/teacher relationship, is highly respected in many parts of the world: in mainland Europe, in Asia and also in America, where actors such as Al Pacino regard time spent teaching at the Actors' Studio in New York as valuable.

[20] Under the heading 'Quality Control', Rea (1989) draws on the opinions of two people, Les Blair and Peter Gill. Blair is credited with 'Who is going to teach these courses? Please don't let it be the academics' (p.100), whilst Gill says 'I don't think (university) drama departments, as they are organized at present, are of any use because they reflect the prejudices rather than the enthusiasms of the teachers' (p.101). No contradictory views are offered in this section.

[21] In some ways, the early decision to concentrate attention on my own practice was based on a pragmatic approach. As a full-time lecturer with a relatively heavy teaching load, my commitments would make it difficult to

spend enough time with a professional company to make an accurate assessment of their making processes. This, combined with the fact that I am obliged to make at least one piece of work each year with undergraduates, had some bearing on my decision.

This is not to suggest that the chief reason was not to observe the creative process from both inside and out, so much as it is a recognition that some aspects of decision-making are driven less philosophically than others.

[22] Henry Miller writes 'I know nothing in advance ... I have faith in the man who is writing' (in Ghiselin, 1952. p. 180). Miller's views are consistent with many artists working across a range of fields. It is interesting to note that even when the artist *does* know how the artwork is likely to proceed (as was the case with Francis Bacon, if Joule is to be believed) the idea of instinctive progression is adopted as an aid to even greater artistic credibility.

[23] *Research Assessment Exercise in 2001 (RAE 2001).* Published on the Internet at http://www.hiss.ac.uk/education/hefc/rae/2001/2.html. p.4

[24] *ibid*

Postscript:
Claims and Disclaimers

'Every practical procedure ... presupposes a theoretical perspective of some kind'.[1] With the practice of performance, theories - some of the theories of postmodernism, for example - are part of the conceptual apparatus of making work. This is not the same thing as saying that theories provide fixed referents. In the context of the documentation undertaken, and also with the performance that was *At Last Sight*, the theoretical perspectives ranged from multifaceted interpretations of the maker/writer's own intentions to methods that offered apparently coherent narratives of empirical evidence. In this way, something of the spirit of selective eclecticism that fuelled the process of creating *At Last Sight* also informed the methodology of documentation.

Whilst the approach to making *At Last Sight* was consistently made subject to theorisation, the theorisation was not always consistent. A number of positionings were adopted and discarded at will. The processes of making and of making-reading were synonymous with 'the human condition of trying to construct a viable and meaningful existence' when those meanings were being undermined by their own internal contradictions, and this demanded a relationship with theory.[2] What art-theory is about, according to Lyotard, is encapsulated in the question: 'Why does something happen rather than nothing?'[3] It is for this reason that the approaches to theory in this book were used in the ways that they were: as evidence of what happened rather than of nothing happening at all, and of why things happened in the ways that they did.

When Susan Melrose argues for a reappraisal of 'theory' within performance, she remarks that 'theory may, indeed, be counter-productive in the context of effective performance-making.'[4] My conclusion based on research with *At Last Sight* leads to both a reiteration and a rebuttal of these claims. Theory is not *something other*, something *applied*, either before or after the event of performance. What we think is what we do, and the investigation has been a charting of this process of thought as deed and deed as thought.

Tracing the Footprints has been an experimental action, the outcome of which could not have been foreseen as the work was commenced. (In Jeanette Winterson's 1991 preface to *Oranges are not the only fruit* she asks the question 'Is *Oranges* an autobiographical novel?' Her answer of 'No not at all and yes of course' is equally true of this work.)[5] The book acquired its own determination, within which the writer's intentions were only one factor among many. Of equal significance to the reader may have been those elements that remained (and remain) unknown to the writer. In this way the reader has been more capable of determining the meaning of this book than have I. We should, however, remember Zygmunt Bauman's assertion that the reader 'understands as much as his knowledge allows him…. If the author sends his signals from an island whose interior he has not and could not explore in full, the reader is a passenger who walks the deck of a sailing ship he does not navigate. The meaning is the instant of their encounter.'[6]

Tracing the Footprints has been concerned with fieldwork. Fieldwork varies, as a practice, according to the degree in which the observer controls the situation s/he is investigating and the extent to which s/he participates in that situation and interacts with the subjects under investigation. Because the fieldwork in question was a construction and rehearsal process carried out with undergraduates in the final year of their degree programme, my participation and interaction, as tutor, director and observer was both complex and full. The ways in which the relationship between observer and observed developed over the period of a full academic year formed a narrative that went undetected during the period of writing, but which has emerged, in subsequent readings, as a central feature.

There is a distinction between the 'I' of the knower and the 'Me' of the known, and we can say that the self contained in this book has consisted of both parts. Similarly, *Tracing the Footprints* had a preoccupation with ideas of 'truth' at the same time as it dealt in lies (that this is a curious admission with which to conclude a contract between the reader and the read is not in doubt). This amounted to an invidious-seeming essentialism. Whilst much of the *language* of this book dealt in uncertainties much of the addressed revealed a search for something 'true', so that my public self embraced postmodern terminology at the same time as my inner self sought (and not always consciously) to imbue feelings with authority. If there is any evidence of catharsis in either the book or *At Last Sight*, at least for the maker, then that catharsis was achieved in the pursuit of something 'true'. Why this truth was sought at all in art, rather than elsewhere, where one might argue that it matters more, has been dealt with in the body of the work.

If we accept that the certainty of 'truth' is lost to us, which is a *theory* rather than a *fact,* then it becomes difficult to see any space beyond this for theory to occupy. Interpretation *per se* relies upon arriving at a distinction between what is offered as the surface of a text and what is thought to exist beneath it ... interpretation is in this sense the making of a distinction between surface and depth. If all that we are able to say is that something *happened*, or did not (to take Baudrillard's assertions that the Gulf War never really took place) then there is little left for theory to do.[7] If the degree zero of postmodernism is left unchallenged, if truth is to remain as a disenfranchised concept, then the idea of academic honesty is equally bankrupt, for we cannot believe in one type of 'honesty' in a world where no truth can be said to exist.

This contradiction is a part of making performance. The printed word has a permanence (and a status) that is denied to the ephemerality of performance. However, the existence of live performance in the *now* imbues it with a different relationship with truth. The work seen may be illusory, but the *seeing of it*, in this space and at this time, is rarely, if ever, in doubt. Readers of words written are not usually witnesses to the process of writing. Words, no matter how truthfully they may read, are constructed in the elsewhere, whereas performances, no matter how other they may seem, are constructed in the here and now. Where, on the surface, this book has charted a wrestling with the contradictions between truth and lies that contradiction has been between performance and print.

Whatever it was that I was working through *at the time of making*, I was also always aware of myself as a thinker. In this way the existence of the 'I' that was aware created a duality: partly known and partly knower, partly observed and partly observer. We can relate this to Zupanic's statement that

The fact that somebody else views me as an object of his outer intuition does not yet permit me to draw any conclusions about my identity. Such an inference would be possible only if I were able to put *myself* in the very place from which I am being observed, if *I* were able to view myself *at the same time* as object of inner and outer intuition – if *I* were able to *see myself the way the other sees me*.[8]

This book has shown that the act of making performance, no less than the documenting of one's own creative processes, demanded the inner and outer intuition that Zupanic's comments deny.

Notwithstanding the temptation to make post-performance adjustments to this book, it has remained a narrative written in its own present. Because the present *is* live performance this method of documentation has been consistent in kind with its subject. As performances shift, fold in on themselves, find new forms and strategies, so the processes of documentation need to develop and keep pace. The documentation that has been this book has comprised part of that development.

Identifying the methodological approaches appropriate to an area of investigation is a major element of the process of research. The documentation of performance has no singular defining methodology, and different writers will document in different ways. A distinction between research and documentation *per se*, however, between scholarship and *reportage*, is that in research the methodologies need to be identified and articulated. This distinction continues inasmuch as researchers need also to separate methodology from method. For the purposes of *Tracing the Footprints*, I am taking 'methodology' to refer to the theoretical framework which informs analysis and 'method' to refer to the procedure(s) of gathering information for the study. In this way, method is the 'how' of the research and methodology the 'why'. Richard Beardsworth urges caution, however, in terms of a too-readily arrived at acceptance of 'method'. He notes that Derrida is careful to avoid the term

> because it carries connotations of a procedural form of judgement. A thinker with a method has already decided *how* to proceed, is unable to give him or herself up to the matter of thought in hand, is a functionary of the criteria which structure his or her conceptual gestures.[9]

Notwithstanding Beardsworth's reminder of Derrida's *caveat*, we can say that the method is the 'how' of the research and methodology the 'why'.

The process of making *At Last Sight* has been charted in a way which is identifiable as a method, and yet that same method has been approached in a way that seeks to resist the type of closure that Beardsworth identifies as Derrida's fear.

Whilst this book has adhered to its own particular method, what is of equal significance are the methodologies that the writing has revealed. This creates an open relationship between words written and words read, inasmuch as 'methodology' is something the reader, no less than the writer, will bring to the page.

A weakness with much documentation of performance is that it tends to concentrate on the phenomenon of performance rather than what it was that led to the work being produced. This *leading up* is vital to our understanding of how performances are made. Without it we are left with the idea of performance as something magical, as alchemy. The documentation entered into here is as closely concerned with the processes leading up to performances as to descriptions of that work as 'finished product'. Pavis warns us that 'No performance description is ever without subjective elements that influence the fundamental understanding of the work'.[10] Accordingly, this documentation is subjective and partial. It would be futile to pursue an objective and complete documentation, since on the one hand every decision to include is also a loss, and on the other the activity of observing brings with it its own impositions. The issue of documentation has two elements: *what* to document and *how* to carry out the documentation. These elements are choices, and choice cannot be separated from subjectivity. I chose to write about *this* material, at *this* time and in *this* way. What marks this book apart from much that has gone before is that the writers' subjectivity is rarely concealed behind a screen of objective terminology. The subjectivity is open and discussed. The reader, like the writer, has to remember that the documents encountered here were created out of particular approaches. The writing does not articulate what it *was* so much as *how* it was seen and how I *choose* to make that seeing seen.

Were I to concentrate more fully on *At Last Sight* as an example of theatre performance I would be imposing my own reading on that which was made to be given away. *At Last Sight* as a performance text belonged to particular times, places and people. Performers, director, crew and spectators remember it happening, and each of these memories determines what it was that took place. My documentation of the processes leading to *At Last Sight*, and also out of it, is my own. Any one of the performers would write differently about different stages, but this partiality, like all others, is unavoidable. To offer something under the guise of a 'full account' would necessitate the impossibility of everybody involved writing about everything that happened before, during and after we met ... and in what font? The partiality of process, however, is less severe than with product. The product was created to be interpreted by hundreds of strangers. The process was for nine performers and myself.

That said, this documentation is not a surrogate for performance. Neither is it a surrogate for process. The documentation *is* the documentation. It is from the selectivity of the process that its reliability and scholarly relevance comes. It identifies documentary as fiction; albeit a fiction that seeks to seduce its readers into belief.

Theories are not self-contained. They bleed into each other. This does not mean that we cannot apply a particular analytical framework to any type of performance event. This is not about transforming research into calcification. That the adoption of a mode of analysis enables the researcher to utilise certain investigative procedures does not mean that the investigation-outcome is either assumed or predetermined.

The researcher's intervention has been made manifest in the personal pronoun. This is an acknowledgement that the 'I' has an overt function. We need to remember Barthes' warning, however, that the 'I which approaches the text is already itself a plurality of other texts, of codes which are infinite or more precisely, lost.'[11] This applies to the researcher's 'I' no less than to the 'I' of a subsequent reader. The sense we send is the sense we make. This sense is flawed and incomplete, but only inasmuch as it is born of partiality.

Scholarship will always reveal more about the student than the studied. Approached thus, the choices we make as to what we omit are as significant as the ways that we deal with what remains, and partiality is accepted as an act of revelation. When Geraldine Harris writes of Rose English's *The Double Wedding* (1991) she explains that 'the theoretical terrain in which this piece appears to be placed, in and of itself, suggests that in the final analysis this is a show which cannot be interpreted, only described.'[12] This is a negation of the fact that all description is interpretative. What it is that Harris chooses to describe is the result of an interpretative act, not *vice versa*. To suggest otherwise is to argue for a type of factual reporting that we know is impossible, and, ultimately, undesirable. What makes Harris' reading of English as interesting as it is is the perspective she brings. The place that we view from is as central to our findings as the subject on which we fix our gaze.

The words of *At Last Sight* function as both substitutes and prompts for physical activity. This amounts to text as verbal deictic reference.[13] Because *At Last Sight* conveys a number of messages about actions, which subsequently do or do not take place, we can say that verbal deixis is its dominant code, both as a written and performance text. The text was written for narration as much as for any conventional notions of representative acting. The ways in which the narrators describe events will affect the spectator's understanding of the narrators' motives, which will have some bearing on the 'trust' felt and the level of 'truth' attributed to that which is narrated. If the spectator trusts the narrators then s/he will be inclined to believe the descriptions presented, even (or especially) when the narrator is both speaker and doer. With the role of narrator in *At Last Sight* these aspects of 'trust' are subject to a continuous shift. As a link between the overt fiction of performance and the assumed fact of an outside world, the narrators' function is problematised by their own failure to locate themselves for any length of time within one world or the other. This signals a deliberate collapsing of confidence in the distinction. Inside and outside performance is no greater a distinction than inside and outside any place at all. Conventions may be different, but that does not mean that one place is 'real' and the other 'false'. The performance of *At Last Sight* is as much a part of the 'real world' as a trip to a supermarket or an hour spent in a library.

Essentialism is often associated with biological determinism, with the attribution of particular traits as being unchangingly human. In this way, essentialism could be regarded as a denial of cultural shifts in the ways that different people function. Approached from this perspective it is difficult to regard essentialism as anything other than *naïve*. We know that differences in gender, race, health, wealth, education and class, for example, have ramifications on the ways in which we live. However, this is not the way I am using essentialism here. For the purposes of this book essentialism has been used to refer to certain phenomena, which, whilst they might be no more than cultural impositions, are so deep-rooted as to be *regarded* as essential to the way we live our lives. I include in this our need to distinguish between 'truth' and 'fiction' ... a distinction that is critically impossible to uphold. Nevertheless, in the way we function as people we make constant decisions as to the truth-status of events. As a father, I believe in the love of and for my children as something unchangeably 'real', even in the same moments that I read, write or talk about truth as a Nietzschean illusion.

In performance terms, we do not always know whether a particular work makes any claim for truth. In these circumstances it is difficult, and perhaps even inappropriate, to arrive at a judgement as to 'truthfulness'. Because performance *per se* has the complex relationship with 'truth' that it has, any assessment has to be arrived at through consideration of context. In certain contexts, for example, actions or words might be regarded as ironic ... in other contexts the same phenomena might be regarded as truthful.[14] In its broadest sense, contextualisation is provided through features of the work that are suggestive of intent. Certain forms of address claim to deal in truth, and their reliability can be measured against this intention. These forms can be assessed according to their self-imposed terms. A news report, for example, sells itself as a truthful reading. So does a scientific report or a thesis. The writings that make up this book are expected to function as 'truthful statements'. Similarly, programme notes to a performance would be expected to conform to our cultural expectations of reliability.

Any work that makes a claim for truthfulness is compromised at source by the inevitability of its mediation. The truth in performance, no less than in performance writing, cannot be regarded as either absent or present ... the differences between production and reception make any such claim redundant. We might argue that the here-and-nowness of performance makes it more 'truthful' than the there-and-thenness of writing; however, performance is no less subject to mediation than is written text. Any apparent immediacy is illusory. The moment is loaded, and only partly by the performance maker. To say that activities take place in the same context in which they are read is to disregard the fact that the frame around performance is always also a contextualising framework within the spectator.

This takes us some way towards an understanding of truth's adulterated transference - as an omnipresent act of spectatorial deconstruction – it also throws into doubt the possibility of truth having any currency for the performer. If truth has no possibility of 'successful transmission', then its value as currency is reduced; equally, we have to question the extent to which a performance maker has an adequate understanding of how and why performative choices have been made. What we think is the truth may not be so. This book has operated within a fluid arena, a place of shifting relationships between investigations and omissions, between claims for truth and untruthful claims. The doubly-autobiographical nature of *At Last Sight* and this book has resulted in a number of truth-claims, many of which have been created with as honest an intent as has been possible. It has been possible for the reader to identify me as the writer, in a way that makes the authorial

'I' my own. It has not been as possible for the spectator of *At Last Sight* to make those same assumptions.

The performance project was instigated out of an interest in confessional art, and yet it is this book that has developed into a confession, at the same time as it became increasingly apparent that *At Last Sight* had little or nothing confessional to say. *At Last Sight* was an identifiably autobiographical work, even within the context of *all* work being autobiographical, but it was not confessional. I am drawing on Derrida here in his distinction between autobiography and confession. For Derrida confession is connected to the idea that truth is concealed until its moment of confessional articulation.[15] Confession denies the possibility of anything other than a truth-claim: its whole *raison d'être* is a claim for truth. This has been the case with the book, but not the performance. Part of this is to do with authorship ... the words written are mine, the sentence and paragraph lengths are chosen by me, even the choice of font is mine. As J. M. Coetzee says of his own work

> This is a question about telling the truth rather than a question about autobiography. Because in a larger sense all writing is autobiography: everything that you write, Including criticism and fiction, writes you as you write it.[16]

While the words I choose remain my own - at least prior to the act of being read - the performance of *At Last Sight* was mediated, long before it reached a public audience, by the concerns, attitudes and individual nuances of the performers. Like Derrida, Coetzee tells us that confessional writing is identified "on the basis of an underlying motive to tell an essential truth about the self."[17] The writing of this book has been governed by a need to write what it is that I do not yet know, and to do so as part of the same activity of writing as a claim for truth. The essential truth of the book is also then the essential truth of my self. That which *Tracing the Footprints* has confessed has been my own need to confess. The confession has made the book a witness to my own witnessing of the process of making *At Last Sight*, and this act of witness could only be achieved *via* the setting down and the giving away. The documentation of *At Last Sight* has not amounted to a truthful documentation so much as to an act of confession. The publication of the document is necessary then in more ways than the obvious one of disseminating the findings of a particular experience. It is necessary because confession cannot be separated from language and because language can be defined as an attempt to shape an experience into a comprehensible form.

Derrida has it that a "true act of giving (only) ever occurs ... without any consciousness of the possible response of the other."[18] I can make no similar claims for this book, and yet it remains an act (a 'true act'?) of giving. That which began as the documentation of a process has developed into the documentation of a methodology of documentation. Immersed in all of this, in every page, every line and every word, has been the documentation of the self who documents. Rather than pulling the focus away from an analysis of performance-making this has resulted in a deepening belief that who we are is what we make. Making a deliberate choice to write ourselves into the ways we write about the work we see is not 'more honest' than choosing otherwise, but at least the dishonesties are borrowed less freely from others.

This book makes no claims for documentary truth. It provides no more than a fleeting glimpse of the ways in which a performance was made, and the ways in which that making has been subsequently described. Its value lies not so much in any idea of objective authority as in its recognition of bias.

If this form of documentation reveals as much about the student as the studied, then this is a consequence rather than a denial of the autobiography of spectatorship. The seeing self is not distinct from the self who then makes seen. Such could never occur. This book is a record of a particular process of seeing and of making seen: a work created through a claim for truth that draws to a close with a disclaimer.

> There is no such thing as an objective, innocent, primary document. The document ... is the result, above all, of an assemblage, whether conscious or unconscious, of the history, the time and the society which have produced it, and also of the ensuing periods through which it has continued to be used, even if perhaps in silence.... The document is a monument.... In the end, there is no documentary truth. Every document is a lie.[19]

As it was with the act of *At Last Sight*, so it is with the words that have sought to discuss it. They end not with closure or emphasis, so much as with a fading away ... a running out of space.

171

Notes

Barry, P, 1995. p. 35
[2] Smith, D *Zygmunt Bauman, Prophet of Postmodernity*. Polity Press, Cambridge, 1999. pp. 137-138
[3] Blistene, B "A Conversation with Jean-Francois Lyotard," *Flash Art: Two Decades of History, XX! Years, pp. 129-130*
[4] Melrose, S. 'Restaging'Theory' in the Postgraduate Performance Studies Workshop' in *New Theatre Quarterly* Volume XV Part 1 (NTQ 57) February, 1999. pp. 39- 44
[5] Winterson, J *Oranges are not the only fruit*. 1991
[6] Bauman, Z *Hermeneutics and Social Science: approaches to understanding*. Hutchinson, London, 1978 p. 229`
[7] For an elaboration of Baudrillard's thoughts, see Norris, C *Uncritical Theory: Postmodernism, Intellectuals and The Gulf War*. Lawrence & Wishart, 1992.
[8] Zupanic, A. *Ethics of the Real: Kant, Lacan*. Verso, London & New York, 2000. p. 70
[9] Beardsworth, R. *Derrida and the Political*. Routledge, London, 1996. p.4
[10] Pavis, P. 'Notes Toward a Semiotic Analysis' in *The Drama Review*. Vol. 23, No. 4 (T84), December, 1979. p. 95
[11] Barthes, R. *S/Z*, trans. Richard Miller, Hill & Wang, New York, 1974. p. 10
[12] Harris, G. *Staging Femininities*. Manchester University Press, 1999. p. 23
[13] Matejka, L & I. Titunik. 'The Hierarchy of Dramatic Devices' in *Semiotic Art*. Vintage Books, New York, 1983. p37
[14] A phenomenologist would argue here that this sentence is unsupportable, inasmuch as a different context denies the possibility of 'the same phenomena' taking place. Indeed, no performative phenomena could ever exist within the same, repeated context, precisely because contexts shift no less than anything else. What happens at one moment can be repeated, but never absolutely and never to the same effect.
[15] Derrida, J. *Acts of Literature*. Derek Attridge (ed.) Routledge, London & New York, 1992, p.34
[16] Coetzee, J.M *Doubling the Point: Essays and Interviews*. David Attwell (ed.) Harvard University Press, Cambridge, USA, 1992. p.17
[17] *ibid* p.252
[18] Derrida, J *Given Time*. Peggy Kamuf University of Chicago Press, Chicago, 1991. p.11
[19] De Marinis, Marco. 'A Faithful Betrayal of Performance: Notes on the Use of Video in Theatre' in *New Theatre Quarterly*. Vol. 1 No. 4, November, 1985. p. 383

John Freeman

John Freeman was editor of *Performance Practice* between 1994 and 2000, and is now associate editor of *Body, Space and Technology*. He has written recent articles for *Studies in Theatre and Performance, Total Theatre, Consciousness, Literature & the Arts, Journal of Dramatic Theory & Criticism, Research in Post-Compulsory Education, Higher Education Review,* and *The Guardian.* His original performance works *Pentimento, Ephemera, Love Lessons, At Last Sight* and *Cabin Fever* have been presented to wide international acclaim. Through his links with IATU and ELIA he has undertaken residencies in Helsinki, Casablanca, New York, and Belgrade.

John's background as a performer includes Insomniac's *Clare de Luz* and the world premiere of Edward Bond's *Jackets*, alongside touring with a range of companies. In addition to engaging in ongoing performance compositions, he is currently the lyricist for the Madrid-based band 'Magic Toast'.

John followed his MA dissertation *Myth, Ritual and the Urban Sensibility* with research towards PhD in the Department of Performing Arts at Brunel University. That research is developed here into *Tracing the Footprints.*

John Freeman is Senior Lecturer in Performance Studies at De Montfort University, UK.

Index

Note: Some entries that appear throughout the book, such as *At Last Sight* and the names of the performers, alongside references to postmodernism, reflection, heuristics and the making/documenting processes undertaken, are not listed in the Index.